CW00494873

THE WILD LIFE

www.**rbooks**.co.uk

THE WILD LIFE

A Year of Living on Wild Food

John Lewis-Stempel

Doubleday

LONDON · TORONTO · SYDNEY · AUCKLAND · JOHANNESBURG

TRANSWORLD PUBLISHERS
61–63 Uxbridge Road, London W5 5SA
A Random House Group Company
www.rbooks.co.uk

First published in Great Britain
in 2009 by Doubleday
an imprint of Transworld Publishers

Copyright © John Lewis-Stempel 2009
Map © Neil Gower 2009

John Lewis-Stempel has asserted his right under the Copyright, Designs
and Patents Act 1988 to be identified as the author of this work.

This book is a work of non-fiction based on the life, experiences and recollections
of the author. The author has stated to the publishers that, except in such minor
respects not affecting the substantial accuracy of the work, the contents of this
book are true.

A CIP catalogue record for this book
is available from the British Library.

ISBN 9780385613903

This book is sold subject to the condition that it shall not,
by way of trade or otherwise, be lent, resold, hired out,
or otherwise circulated without the publisher's prior
consent in any form of binding or cover other than that
in which it is published and without a similar condition,
including this condition, being imposed on the
subsequent purchaser.

The lines of poetry on page 8 are extracted from *The Earliest English Poems*,
edited and translated by Michael Alexander, 1992. Copyright © 1992 Michael
Alexander. Reprinted by permission of Penguin UK.

Every effort has been made to obtain the necessary permissions with reference to
copyright material, both illustrative and quoted. We apologize for any omissions
in this respect and will be pleased to make the appropriate acknowledgements in
any future edition.

Addresses for Random House Group Ltd companies outside the UK
can be found at: www.randomhouse.co.uk
The Random House Group Ltd Reg. No. 954009

The Random House Group Limited supports The Forest Stewardship Council
(FSC), the leading international forest-certification organization. All our titles that
are printed on Greenpeace-approved FSC-certified paper carry the FSC logo.
Our paper procurement policy can be found at
www.rbooks.co.uk/environment

Typeset in 10/16pt Versaille by
Falcon Oast Graphic Art Ltd.
Printed and bound in Great Britain by
Clays Ltd, Bungay, Suffolk

2 4 6 8 10 9 7 5 3 1

Mixed Sources
Product group from well-managed
forests and other controlled sources
www.fsc.org   Cert no. TT-COC-2139
© 1996 Forest Stewardship Council
FSC

For Penny, Tristram and Freda. Naturally.

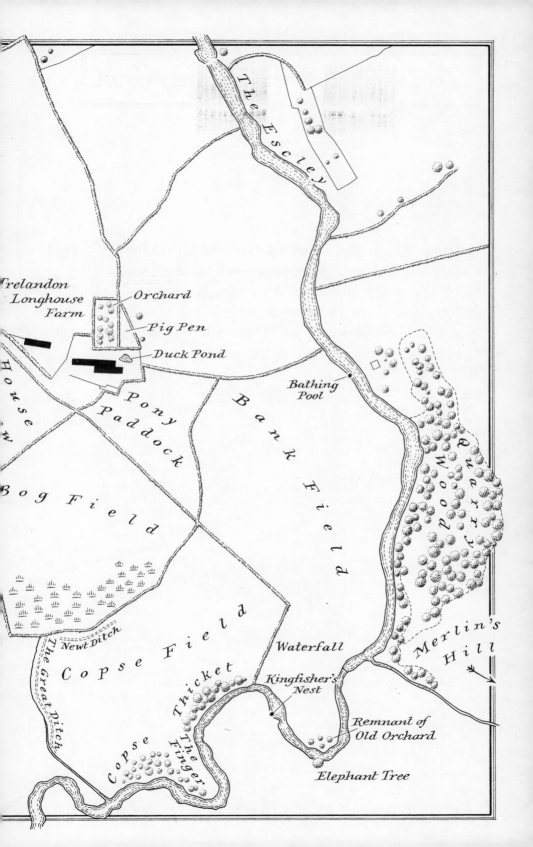

The Escley

Trelandon
Longhouse
Farm

Orchard

Pig Pen

Duck Pond

House
...w

Pony
Paddock

Bog Field

Bank Field

Bathing
Pool

Quarry Wood

Newt Ditch

Copse Field

The Great Ditch

Copse Thicket

The Finger

Waterfall

Kingfisher's
Nest

Merlin's
Hill

Remnant of
Old Orchard

Elephant Tree

This is the story of a year living off the land in the last valley in England. To protect the guilty, I have changed some names.

The reader should also be aware that some wild plants and fungi can cause allergic and adverse reactions in susceptible people; consequently an authoritative field guide should be consulted before consumption of the foods mentioned.

OCTOBER CLAMPS THE VALLEY. In the hedge bottom, mouldering oak and hazel leaves produce a burnt-incense spice so thick it suffocates. My trigger finger is pinewood-pale with cold; to get looseness back into it I flex it frenetically. All the while I scan the field before me. Nothing.

A blackbird erupts like a car alarm. For a moment I think I've been spotted but in the twilight the culprit, a dog fox, lopes across the field's narrow promontory into the Escley brook and away into the copse.

The valley returns to its mausoleum silence.

I'm here in hope, no more than that. Two days ago I saw them, by chance, when they came out of the wooded old quarry across the Escley but there is no certainty they will visit again.

I wait on into the gloom. I'm about to give up when they come, sailing in over my head, as quiet as spirits.

Scolopax rusticola. Woodcock. Three of them. If I was a sportsman I'd shoot them in flight, maybe even try a celebrated 'right and left'. But I'm not a sportsman, I'm someone who is hungry, someone who is hiding in a drainage ditch up to his chest hoping for a sure-fire kill. I allow the woodcock to land – a mistake, as it turns out. Momentarily they probe with their needle bills – and one disappears. Then another. Amid the gathering dark, the drifted leaves and the tufted grass the woodcocks' marbled camouflage works to Darwinian perfection. Only the movement of the third bird allows me to see it. I slip the safety catch off and mount the Baikal 12-bore shotgun to my shoulder. And fire.

Thirty yards to my front, the woodcock performs a crippled cartwheel. The other two woodcock, flushed out by the echoing gunshot, fast-beat it away in the ether.

I'm as glad to be able to rise from my dank hide as I am with my kill. Hobbling with pins and needles I gather up the broken bird.

There are few creatures more plainly beautiful than a woodcock. I dislike killing them. But then I don't truly like killing. American Indians used to ask an animal's permission to take its life. I do it all the time.

I slip a collar of pink baler twine around the woodcock's neck and, bird hanging from the gun-free hand, trudge up the sodden dark fields to the farmhouse, lying long and low out of the weather. Away to the west, across the valley, a last smear of daylight silhouettes the looming wall of the Black Mountains, the absolute edge of England. As I walk I ponder, with unceremonious saliva swilling into my mouth, tonight's meal. Woodcock with blackberry sauce? Woodcock with crab-apple sauce? Whatever, it will make a God-thankful change from rabbit, dish of the day – and night – for the last week.

When I open the door to the kitchen, light explodes out into the cow byre we use as a mudroom. So do dogs, four of them, headed by Edith, my year-old black Labrador. She sniffs, quivering, at the dangling woodcock. Somewhere in her head is the archaic understanding that, in some way, the bundle of feathers should mean something to her. That latent knowledge is what I must work on if I am to train her to become a hunter's best friend, a dog that flushes and retrieves game; the pity is that I have

never trained a gundog before. 'Don't worry, Edith, we'll get there one day,' I say, as much to reassure me as her, and tickle her in the suprasternal notch under her chin.

Only the dogs are home. Penny

and the children are not back yet. I lay the woodcock on the wooden table and lean on the Aga, surveying the kitchen. It looks like a Dickensian chemist's shop, overflowing with jars containing strange pickled shapes and bubbling demijohns and earth-filled boxes with protruding mangled roots. But the kitchen's concoctions and specimens are not for the arts of the apothecary; they are the wild foods I eat. My studying of the kitchen is not idle; I'm looking for inspiration, the accompaniments to the woodcock. It has to be the blackberry sauce, violently purple and fresh-made. Roasted burdock roots and steamed sorrel too.

I'm also procrastinating; de-feathering woodcock is tedious and fiddly. Reaching along to the worktop I pour myself a delaying, fortifying glass of elderberry wine. Some pleasure before the pain of plucking. However, I cannot linger for too long because I need to pluck the woodcock while it is still warm, since this is easier than pulling at feathers set firm by rigor mortis. Besides, I am gut-achingly hungry.

At the table, I pull off the woodcock's chestnut feathers into a carrier bag, before undertaking the cadaveric preparation peculiar to the bird; after the woodcock is beheaded the gizzard is drawn out through the neck. The entrails are left inside. Pimply and plebeian-puny, the naked body of the woodcock will dry quickly in the Aga's roasting oven, so I smother it with mallard fat, and stick a shield of crab-apple slices over it, to act like the heat-retardant tiles on a space shuttle.

When the woodcock and burdock chips are committed to the Aga, I sit sifting the green sorrel leaves, snipping off stalks and rejecting those thickened by age. Outside in the night a fox yips, close by. The dogs on the yard give a desultory bark, but they are more interested in the kitchen's warmth and the wafting aroma of the cooking woodcock. They scratch at the door and I let them in. I, though, cannot resist going out into the bat-black night for a moment. Now that the fox has sloped off and the dogs slipped in, there is not a sound in the valley, save for the whispering of the Escley in the deep of the valley bottom. Around and above me, as I stand alone on the yard, stretches an infinite, perfect dark, sullied in its purity only by one orange farm light over on the mountain a mile away. This is night as nature intended it; vast and awe-inspiring. And yet as soothing and peaceful as velvet.

The smell of the woodcock drifts out to lure me inside.

Before going into the house, I take a glance back, to the east beyond Merlin's Hill, to where we came from. It is a glance back into the land of dawn, back to a time when life promised a different future. We came to this place, Trelandon Longhouse Farm, pitched on a fold of land above the Escley brook in the shadow of the Black Mountains, to rear cattle, sheep and pigs, not to live off its wild animals and plants. Not for me to become a latter-day hunter-gatherer.

BEGINNINGS

A FEBRUARY DAY, two years ago. A mist ceiling hangs just above the roof of the Land Rover. Penny, my wife, is holding the sale details for Trelandon in her hand, with a convenient map on the back. In the event the property is easy to find: a sign, *Trelandon*, hangs off a telegraph pole on the lane.

'The last time I saw a sign like that was in a spaghetti western,' says Penny.

The rough concrete track down to the farm is coursing with water.

The farm is for sale in two lots. Lot One, Great Trelandon, a gaunt Victorian stone farmhouse, is already sold to a Ms Janet Rees and a Mr Gerry Musson. We drive on down to Trelandon Longhouse Farm.

In the estate agent's particulars Lot Two is 'The original semi-derelict stone-built farmhouse and attached stone and timber barn in the traditional longhouse manner and believed to date from the eighteenth century'. Pulling into the yard, we can see that at least half of the estate agent's description is a fallacy. For a moment we sit incredulous in the Land Rover. The farmhouse is not semi- but wholly derelict and there is not one attached barn but at least two. Since most of the buildings have fallen in and have winter-naked elder trees growing out of them, it is impossible to tell precisely what *is* in front of us.

The estate agent might have struggled to describe Trelandon Longhouse Farm accurately but a poet once did. Into my head

spring the words of the Saxon bard who had seen the remains
of Roman Bath:

> Well wrought this wall:
> Wierds broke it.
> The stronghold burst . . .
> Snapped rooftrees, towers fallen,
> the work of the Giants, the stonesmiths,
> mouldereth.

Solemnly we get out of the Land Rover and walk across the
yard. Somewhere above us in the shrouding white a buzzard
keens.

'Hang on,' says Penny, looking at the photograph in the
particulars, which shows an altogether more upright structure,
'where is this taken from? The back presumably.' For a moment
we brighten and I follow her through the remains of the barn
doors in the centre of the wasted building, and into an overgrown
garden, dripping with mist. The buzzard keens again. There is no
other sound. The mist closes in. We might be the last people on
Earth.

Sure enough, if viewed from the right distance and a particularly narrow angle, the building looks remarkably solid. We
head back inside, to look at the western, standing end. An oak
frame, complete with wattle-and-daub insets, partitions the
former living quarters of the farmer from those of his animals. I'm
entranced by the wattle-and-daub. Touching it cautiously with my
fingers, I say, 'I'm not an archaeologist but there is no way that
this is from the eighteenth century.'

Penny cannot hear me; she has disappeared through the door
in the partition. 'Wow,' she shouts, 'come and look at this, this is
incredible.' I follow her voice through the door. There is just

enough light from the two small windows on each side to see that this room, the original sitting room-cum-kitchen, is largely intact, save for the ceiling which, between the blackened oak beams, is open to the roof. Across the flagstone floor there is a fire recess with a bread oven built into it.

But it is not the 'original features' that stun: it is the scale. I walk in and have to duck instantly to avoid banging my head on the beams. I'm five foot eleven and the beams begin somewhere near my chin. (Later I measure from floor to beam bottom: it's five feet seven inches.)

The room was made for medieval peasants. Or hobbits.

Whoever they were, in this one room and the two rooms above lived a farmer and his family. There is something terrifying about the hard, bare simplicity of the room, which is a statement in stone about the harshness of the life the farmer would have led on this exposed hill on the upland edge of western England before Wales.

The room is so damp and depressing that I have to go outside, for the mist is refreshing and uplifting in comparison. We don't even bother to look at the forty acres of land that come with the farm.

The drive home does not take long. We live only six miles away, although it might as well be sixty. The Golden Valley where we live is as good as its name suggests; it is a place of yellow grain fields and parkland, a place that, although peaceful, has the definite feeling of being connected to civilization. The nameless valley we have just been to, near the village of Longtown, is a far-away place of small family hill farms, whose mountain peak of the Black Hill (or the Cat's Back if you're local) is the highest point in southern England, and whose primary school at Michaelchurch Escley is officially the second most remote school in the country.

We know this lost valley a little, from meals at the Bull's Head pub in Craswall, from buying sheep for our farm from a breeder on the mountain, from the Christmas craft fair where my wife sells the felt bags and slippers she makes. We know, then, why we would like to move here. This quiet, unspoilt valley is the literal and the metaphorical last of England.

The valley has something else that entrances everybody who strays here: a view on to the long, magnificent brooding wall of the Black Mountains.

They say you can't live on views. We think you can. We aim to buy a bigger, more picturesque farm than our current small-holding and do self-catering holiday accommodation, supplying the punters with our own organic, rare-breed bacon, beef, chicken and eggs. This captive audience should also be enticed to buy Penny's exquisite felt work.

'Has it actually got views?' says Penny as we thrum along home, squinting at the passport-sized photographs on the estate agent's brochure of a brook and a long-range, wrong-end-of-telescope shot of a grey lump. 'It felt claustrophobic to me, because of the slope it's on.

'Not for us, darling,' she adds, folding the particulars into the Land Rover's dashboard pocket.

A week later we are back at Trelandon. After all, the farm does have forty acres. We have been looking for a property in the valley for a year, and this is only the second we have found with land under £1 million. (We discounted the first because the divorced vendor left one book behind, carefully positioned on a coffee table in the middle of a bare room: *50 True Murder Stories*; I don't do feng shui, the ancient Chinese art of sofa arrangement, but that *was* a bad vibe.)

Arriving on the yard at the farm this time, we don't stare yokel-like at the decrepit house, we stare slack-jawed in the other direction. The air is crisp and clear, and a 180-degree vista of the wall of the Black Mountains is perfectly framed by a round hill of chequer-board meadows to the left (which we later discover to be called Merlin's Hill) and the slope of hillette on which Trelandon resides.

'That is amazing,' says Penny.

'That is the best view in England,' I say.

This time we do tramp across and assess the land, which straggles in a series of hedged fields from the lane to the Escley brook in the shape of Italy sticking her boot into the Mediterranean. All the fields are permanent pasture; there is a small copse beside the brook. 'The land, surprisingly, is classified as disadvantaged,' states the estate agent's brochure, surely with its tongue in its cheek, or at least its fingers crossed. A flattish field at the top has a good sward, rich in clover, and is presumably the hayfield; the remainder are rough grass on a heavy cold clay, with no proper drainage, and the water oozes up around our feet as we walk. So wet is one field that it is half-bog, complete with marsh grass, while a six-acre meadow at the bottom, which has a looping bend of Escley brook in it, has been ravaged by wireworm and has a thicket squatting in it at least twenty feet broad on its water side. This isn't the wild-flower-rich sward our sheep and cattle are used to; instead great beds of nettles and thistles acne the fields.

But we don't care. We have seen the view of the mountains. We have also stood on the bank of the Escley brook, which forms the eastern boundary of the land, watching it quietly pool on the flat sandstone then spill over rocks to glide beneath the overhanging trees, the wan February sun catching it in a flash.

'Brook' is a misnomer, for here the Escley is twenty feet across. A river maybe.

We can envisage our children, Tris and Freda, paddling and swimming in the Escley. There are some things we cannot see. Standing on the bank of the Escley, in the bowl of a private valley looking up to the Black Mountains a mile away, we cannot see a single house save for Trelandon Longhouse.

I can't remember which of us said it now, but one of us beat the other to it by a pip.

'We have got to have this,' one of us said.

Somehow, by selling our smallholding in the Golden Valley and borrowing money from a commercial lender (standard mortgage companies dislike land and development; the two together are a no-no), we not only find the money to buy Trelandon, we do so before we can be gazumped by somebody 'from off'. Because that is the great fear of locals: that some marauding chatterati, enticed into the area by the Hay-on-Wye literary festival, have just sold their terrace in Camden for a million and have the cash to outbid. Fortunately for us, the property is for sale with a small local agency which doesn't top Google searches for 'Herefordshire+property+land' and the vendors, to whom we have written directly, have a shred of sympathy for us because we want to farm and because we are local; or at least I am 'Hereford born and bred' – my wife I had to drag here by her long raven hair from London.

We move to Trelandon Longhouse on 6 June, our own personal D-Day; we have nothing to live in save a tent. There is cold running water from a standpipe on the yard, but that finishes the list of creature comforts. There is no phone, no electricity. I cook our first meal on a barbecue, which glows red hot because of the oxygenating wind. Ah, the wind. It doesn't stop blowing that day, or for days to come. The Longtown wind is a phenomenon. Our neighbour along the track at Great Trelandon, Janet, pops in to say hello. And to complain about the wind. 'A few weeks back,' she says, 'it damn near blew me over.' This I find as staggering as Janet must have done, for she is what her retired farmer father cheerfully calls 'a big girl'. Janet and her partner Gerry are also local. More local than us, apparently; I find out that Janet complains that 'John's from Herefordshire but he's not real Herefordshire.' Absurdly, when this judgement is passed along to me I want to protest. I want to point out that, if I walked up Merlin's Hill and stood on tippytoes, I could see the hamlet of Marlas where my mother's family was farming three hundred years ago; I want to state that both my parents were born in Herefordshire, as were theirs, as were theirs, as were theirs, and that, oh sure, I moved away at eighteen but I came back. But if I'm honest, I know what she means: I don't have an h-dropping local accent and speak instead in a detached RP rumble. I also have a night job that is very definitely the sort of occupation that in-comers have: I write books. Besides, trying to play more local than thou has definite shades of the sitcom village Royston Vasey in *The League of Gentlemen* about it.

Camping can be fun on holiday; as a way of life it has nothing to recommend it, even when we purchase a calor-gas camping stove: the constant flapping of the nylon, the ceaseless damp which penetrates our clothing, the lack of proper lighting . . . We would like a second-hand caravan but all of them for a radius of fifty miles have been bought by a fruit farm near Leominster to accommodate Polish workers. Eventually we find a two-berth caravan to buy in Blaenavon, which I tow to Trelandon with the jeep, parking it beside the only bit of the linear wasteland of the longhouse which is whole and safe: a thirties brick cow byre. Across the yard is a concrete piggery built in 1962. We know the year exactly because the farmer who did it, Mr Jones, inscribed his initials and the date in the wet concrete wall: 'LJ 1962'. The space between the cow byre and the piggery is as protected as Trelandon Longhouse gets from the north wind which harrows up and down the narrow fold of the Escley.

For the children, who are ten and seven, this camping and caravanning existence is a permanent Enid Blyton adventure; the adults in our family, however, like real loos, as opposed to a hole in the ground with canvas propped around it and sky for a roof, and find washing – and washing in hot water in particular – really rather pleasant. I smell rank because I'm shearing our sheep, and their taint becomes locked into my skin. A hosing down with cold water and body shampoo on the yard fails to break through the greasy sheep's lanolin which covers my arms and legs and I go to speech day at Tristram's school with an odour that causes the coiffured woman next to me to move along two places in the humid marquee.

Still, as Penny and I say to each other, 'It's an experience, isn't it.' At least the farming is going well. In addition to the forty acres at Trelandon, we have retained the rental of thirty acres of land over in the Golden Valley. Seventy acres is about fifty less than we need, but we feel we are on our way. In the fairy-tale luminescence of Midsummer's Eve we lie in the caravan with the windows open and listen to the lullaby hush of the Escley five hundred yards away at the bottom of the bank. 'It's magical here,' whispers Penny to me, over the two children sleeping squeezed between us.

We wake from our midsummer dream because the elephant on the farm wakes. We have tried to ignore the dilapidated, fifty-five-yard-long building but we have a £150,000 loan for its renovation. The loan is for a year only. That year begins on 1 July. One local builder swears he wants the job, does one day's work before declaring that 'the levels are too difficult' and disappears into the thin mountain air. Penny tracks down another builder who, taking pity on a family living in a caravan, agrees to rearrange his schedule and do the renovation for us.

Bob Higgs, naturally, is known to all as Bob the Builder, a joke he acknowledges with the toy Bob sitting in the front window of his builder's regulation-issue white Ford Transit. Can Bob fix it? Yes, he can. Unfortunately, it becomes apparent that Bob can only fix it slowly. Bob is a craftsman. Everywhere Bob goes, a cloud of 'he does lovely stonework, Bob does' trails behind him. We don't need an artisan, we need a jobber. We also need an army of people.

Lovely guy, though, Bob, as is his son Martin, who was once on the books of Cheltenham Town FC until glandular fever intervened. 'Shame, that, eh?' says Bob at regular intervals, to silent face-straining by Mart. Bob and Mart are joined by Mike. Mike is not a builder. Mike is an ex-heating engineer and Mart's friend. Mike is learning on the job.

There's a noir novel by the fifties American pulp writer Jim Thompson which starts to the effect, 'The day began well so I should have known it would end badly.' Long ago I adopted this as my personal motto, but for some fathomless reason I forgot to apply it to the renovation of the house.

For two months the work went swimmingly, as Bob, Mart and Mike toiled like ancient forest miners digging underpinnings for the old sitting room, before erecting breeze-block walls at the other end on the footprint of the lower barn and the two lambing courts attached to it. With the flowering of the Michaelmas daisies in the overgrown garden at the back of the house came the first buds of disaster. 'I think I'll do the stonework on the chimney breast,' said Bob one day. Knowing little of Bob and nothing about building, we said, 'Good idea, Bob.' And so Bob spent days lovingly repointing the interior chimney breast until it was just so. 'Lovely stonework, Bob,' we said.

'Lovely stonework,' says David Morris, the supervising architect appointed by the bank, a few days later. Put plainly, David Morris's role is to make sure that the bank is getting value for the considerable amount of money it is bunging our way. The rule of thumb is that X (amount of work done in a month) plus Y (amount of materials used in said month) increases the value of the property by Z. If all is well, the bank pays X+Y.

Thin and blond, David Morris, standing in the gloom of the sitting room, holding a sheaf of time sheets and invoices, looks bewilderingly like Edward the Confessor. 'But,' he says, looking up at the lovely stonework, 'what else have they done?' Penny and

I shuffle our feet while I make noises about a lot of unseen work, such as the moving of materials to more effective locations. Clearly unconvinced, David Morris signs off the work anyway. House prices are shooting up so gloriously that the lender's largesse is more than protected by the worth of the asset. Before climbing into his BMW Z3 coupé, David Morris feels obliged to warn us, 'They're working too slowly. And stonework is cosmetic at this stage.'

'What do we do about that?' I ask. 'Get new builders?'

'You don't want to swap horses in mid-race. You need to get Bob working more effectively.'

This is easier said than done, especially when Desmond Buckley the carpenter comes on site. We've already tried out one carpenter, Simon Roberts, whom I took an unreasonable dislike to simply because he carried an artist's satchel on his shoulder. Bob didn't like him much either. The feeling was mutual. When Bob and Simon started fisticuffs on the yard, Simon had to go.

Bob was none too pleased to find that Desmond Buckley was the only replacement carpenter Penny could find from trawling the Yellow Pages. 'I worked with him once and he thought he was the bloody boss,' said Bob, before going back to some stonework.

A triffid of trouble had just pushed through the earth. Within two days I was declaring to Penny that Desmond had to go. I had wanted him to chamfer a beam. He refused to work above his head: 'All that stretching up and the dust, it'd be a fucking nightmare.'

Penny was less certain about my hair-trigger firing policy. 'If we don't have a carpenter now, all the building work will stop.'

So Desmond stayed, and even expanded his team. A pony-tailed hippie, Dick, became Desmond's lieutenant. Their one ordinary ranker was Kurt. Florid-faced Kurt was Desmond's nephew. He was also a pig farmer's son with no experience of carpentry whatsoever.

More hands did not make lighter or faster work. They did treble the wage bill.

Within a week Desmond had genuinely convinced himself that we had hired him as project manager. By his sheer hyperactive omnipresence, he convinced everyone else. Returning home one afternoon, I noticed that one gable end had been finished in lead sheeting. Tracking Bob by the trail of wet mortar, I ask, 'Bob, why on earth have you done the gable end in lead sheeting?'

'Desmond told me to,' he says, before returning to his stonework.

Tracking Desmond to the roof by the manic laughter, I ask him, 'Desmond, why the hell did you tell Bob to do the gable end in lead?'

'I thought it'd look nice,' replies Desmond, clearly affronted by my temerity in questioning his decision.

'The fucking planning permission states clearly that it should be done in weather-boarding! As do the fucking plans,' I shout.

'Phh! Planning permission. I mean, you don't want to worry about that . . .' says Desmond, sulking off to his mates. I descend the scaffolding ladder, choleric. Bob comes over to see what all the noise is about. I explain. Bob says, shaking his head, 'I don't know how Desmond's wife puts up with him.'

As it turned out, she didn't. The next week she left him.

Desmond starts bringing his Alsatian dog on site. We ask him not to, because it snarls at our dogs, Hatty, a geriatric golden Labrador, and Sniffy, Freda's miniature Jack Russell with the perfect heart-shaped patch. 'Bodger wouldn't hurt a fly,' says Desmond with smiling certainty.

One March day, Bob, Mart and Mike are in their van having lunch. Sniffy, as is his habit, joins them, sitting alongside on the grass, chewing on a rabbit. Bodger lopes over, savages Sniffy and takes the rabbit. So serious is the savaging that it costs a thousand pounds in veterinary bills to have Sniffy put back together. I bring the matter up with Desmond a few days later. 'Couldn't have been Bodger,' says Desmond, 'he wouldn't hurt a fly. Must have been another dog which looked like Bodger . . .'

Eventually we agree that the blameless Bodger will remain at all times locked in Desmond's van.

I suggest to Penny once again that Desmond is dismissed. She replies, 'We won't get another carpenter and the building work will stop.'

'It's going so slowly it has almost stopped.'

'If the building work stops, David Morris will not OK any more payments.'

And that's the rub. If the work stops, so does the money. There is another, bitter truth, which we have not dared tell anyone, which is that we are having our own cash-flow problems. I am barely working, so overtaken am I by the building work and the deprivation of living in a caravan on a hillside. Hell, I am barely sleeping.

It is at this point, in late March, that I get frostbite. Having spent a bleak afternoon in rain and wind assisting two ewes in their lambing, I forgo changing out of my wellingtons and force myself to spend eight hours in front of the computer, in the unheated 'office caravan', the broken-down two-berth shell we've just bought which was deemed too bad for casual fruit pickers. The next day I'm dimly aware of a numbness in my toes. A week later my right little toe has turned black and my foot is too swollen to put on my shoe. Penny tells me to go to the doctor; I tell her the problem will pass. By pure, unadulterated coincidence I read in *The Times* – not my normal newspaper – about someone who contracted blood poisoning via a foot wound. The symptoms described match mine to an alarming degree, including the shuddering agony. My GP, Annette Wissler in Ewyas Harold, prescribes the statutory antibiotics. An hour after I return home, Annette Wissler – God bless her – telephones and says,

'On reflection, I think I should refer you to the county hospital.'

The next day, the consultant, a Mr Tippin, takes one look at my foot, makes a silent 'O' with his mouth and says levelly, 'We need to find you a bed.'

'Are you sure?' I ask.

'Well, put it this way,' he replies, 'if we don't get to work on it straight away bits of your foot are going to start dropping off.' As far as Mr Tippin can determine, the tiny speck of suppurating frostbite allowed some hideous organism – common enough on a livestock farm – to enter my bloodstream. He sketches a dotted line on my foot. 'In fact, if the infection spreads past here, we'll have to amputate.'

My response to this is an external jollity, the pathetic hallmark of the English middle classes in adversity: 'Oh well, could save on shoes,' I say.

Fortunately, pumping me with antibiotics every four hours from a syringe the size of a bicycle pump prevents the need for amputation. After four days of treatment the danger is over, but I have to be kept in 'for observation'. This, as Penny is quick to point out, is a rather cushy berth; all meals provided, nothing to do except read, listen to Radio 3 and watch films on Sky TV. 'I want to be looked after,' says Penny, visiting one afternoon. 'I want a turn in a warm hospital bed.'

Truth to tell, I am far from anxious to return to the travails of the building work, but after a week the hospital ejects me. In my absence, nothing has improved. Everything is still in freefall. David Morris is still signing off the money but is also sending the bank cautionary notes about building progress. Or, more accurately, its lack.

Bodger, who should be in Desmond's van, has taken up residence with the carpenters on the scaffolding. A bodger and three fiddlers on the roof then, I mutter sourly.

Mart is asking every day, 'Do you wish you'd never taken this on?' He then helpfully points out that you could fit eight houses like his inside ours. I know his house, a spick and spanking new, draught-free applianced semi on the edge of Ross. Lucky Mart. 'Nice spot, though, this,' adds Mart.

And that is what everyone says, from the DHL delivery guy to the structural engineer summoned in an emergency to calculate the size of the RSJs for the upstairs when it becomes clear that the old oak beams won't take a modern weight load of bed, ensuite and wardrobe. Everyone also prefaces their observation on the beauty of the surroundings with a wry, eyebrow-lifted look at the house and the words: 'Have you been watching *Grand Designs*?' No, we gaily explain, we don't have a TV. We have been deranged enough to do this without external influence.

Have you been watching *Grand Designs*?

Nice spot though.

Have you been watching *Grand Designs*?

Nice spot though.

Have you been watching *Grand Designs*?

Nice spot though.

H-h-h-e-e-e-l-l-l-p-p-p!

By July I cannot take any more. I've begun fantasies of suicide, where I dive, assuming a perfect crucifixion shape, into the Escley. I am aware of the hint of pathetic martyrdom, but the dogging depression is true enough. So is the lassitude which engulfs me. A visit by Jimmy the scrap metal merchant provides the catalyst for a rare moment of energy and decision. Six months before, I'd arranged with Jimmy that he could buy the sheets of corrugated iron from the barn roofs. He's come to collect. Jimmy stands on the yard shaking his head. 'Bloody hell, I thought you'd have the lot finished by now.' Most of the corrugated iron is still up on the roofs.

I call in two estate agents and get them to give market estimates. They both independently value the property at £600,000 in its current pathetic, one-third-finished state. 'We can get out,' I say to Penny, 'and we wouldn't have lost anything.'

For reasons I can never quite pin down, even now, we don't get out. Probably we were too enervated and it was easier to let things go on. Besides, it *is* a nice spot.

Crunch time comes at the end of July when the architect's ill-drawn plans invalidate the planning permission and the lender, unable to see any correlation between the money advanced and the building work done, refuses to release more money. We go and cry on the shoulder of our friend Niall Robertson who has an embarrassment of attributes, including being a property developer. 'By hook or by crook, and probably the latter,' says Niall with a distinct smile behind his beard, 'we'll sort it.'

We do. Niall 'bigs up' the plans by adding another ensuite. The bank loves this so much that it frees up another fifty thousand. Niall also redesigns the problematic upper-storey windows as cat-slide dormers and secures retrospective planning permission for them. Although the building work isn't completed within the year, enough is done to raise a mortgage to redeem the development loan. And we do have eight rooms finished: a palace compared to a caravan.

Even if we could raise more money to do more building work, we need a break from builders and carpenters. We pay them off; as the carpenters drive away up the track I realize that their expensive hand-built windows are letting in water. Do I challenge them about this? Call in the solicitor? I do neither. I don't have the energy.

Although the building work was halted, our slide towards financial oblivion continued. I'd only half-worked for two years; the farm had gone to rack and ruin. My Amex card was maxed. We were overdrawn at the bank. (Both of them.) I'd taken to writing the children IOUs, because their Halifax money boxes had more money than I did. Shopping was restricted to supermarkets that still took cheques. 'Oh sure,' I said to Penny, 'the bounce will cost twenty-five pounds but we need to eat now, don't we?' The day I knew we'd hit bottom was the day that, after trawling the house for small change, I stood behind a queue of teenage Polish fruit pickers in Sainsbury's to use the Coinstar machine. In went my gathered small change, out came a voucher for £5.51, to be cashed at the customer service desk.

Cheryl the adviser tried to avoid pitying me as she handed me the cash. But her smile betrayed her: it was too wide.

We needed money. And we needed to spend less. Our mortgage would make Brazil weep.

I'm pondering these problems in mid-September 2006 as I walk around the farm. Along the wooded bank of the Escley I reach a glade and look into the water to see a trout bullet for cover. There are field mushrooms in the grass and in the hedge of Bank Field, where it runs to a close on the Escley, grey squirrels are eating hazelnuts, haws are shining lipstick-red against the blue sky and tendrils of blackberries cascade down. A wood pigeon is coo-cooing in the quarry wood across the river. Wouldn't it be wonderful, I thought, if I could just live on what nature provided for free.

Wouldn't it?

The idea becomes an obsession. After a week or so I put it to Penny, when she is cutting carpet for the long hall. She stops scoring the white carpet with the Stanley knife to say gnomically, 'It's very you.'

'Meaning?'

'It's very you. You know: because you were a young ornithologist, because you shoot, because you hate being indoors, because you like to test yourself – and you do. It's only because I threatened to divorce you that you didn't go off to be a war correspondent.' She goes back to incising the reluctant fabric. 'You'll never get the kids to do it though, and I don't have your cast-iron stomach. Also, I'm a vegetarian. There aren't enough vegetables out there for me. But for you – for you it might be good.'

'I'll think about it some more,' I say.

I do. A primitive hunter-gatherer needed a hundred acres to support a family. Surely I could support myself on forty acres? I also begin to prise apart why I want to do this thing, because it isn't wholly about money. There's something else. Something to do with the fact that I am so exhausted that every fibre of my being feels like a tooth root exposed to air. Could I bind myself back together by binding myself to the earth? And this red earth, this newly acquired forty acres on the edge of England, in particular?

The notion of living off the wild is knocked home by a visit to Rules restaurant in London, where we go to celebrate Tris's stupendous achievement in winning a scholarship to the senior school.

Way back in the shoulder-padded, Perrier-drinking 1990s, when I freelanced for a trendy Covent Garden magazine, I was on rare occasions taken to lunch by the literary editor, whose lunchtime compass was set unwaveringly on a line to a subterranean bistro that served nouvelle cuisine. The scantiness of the food – a one-note riff on cold roulade with a slice of exotic fruit – the dreadfulness of the wine (non-European Pinot Grigio, always), the difficulty of making the sort of witty intellectual conversation that would entice more work, together with the forbidding presence of Lynn Barber (who, in memory at least, was permanently holding court in the smoke-swirling darkness) made these occasions dismal to the nth degree. They were made worse by the fact that the journey from the office to the bistro took us past Rules restaurant in Maiden Lane, through the windows of which I could glimpse plush red banquettes, great bottles of claret, and hearty types enjoying hearty food. Rules came to represent, in my mind's eye, the voluptuous, carnivorous comfortable life I wanted, as opposed to the insipid, Filofax-wielding, PC existence

I was leading. Although I never actually passed through Rules' doors, I must have banged on obsessively about the place for a decade because when Tris was asked, 'Where do you want to go for a celebratory meal?' he replied, 'Rules.'

Fortunately, Tris's desire for a slap-up meal in London's oldest restaurant (it was founded by Thomas Rule in 1798) coincided with unexpectedly good, and rather appropriate, royalties from the American edition of an anthology on fatherhood I had edited. Rules in the flesh was as good as Rules in my dreams. The décor of Rules is what Betjeman described as the 'gradual accumulation' of centuries. Every wall is plastered thick with portraits, paintings, busts, stuffed animals and soft lamplight, while the floor is a swirling gold-on-red carpet. The white table linen flaps heavily against the thigh, the waiters and waitresses tread lightly by. The whole place has a sensuous, pleasantly guilty air. Small wonder that Edward VII entertained Lillie Langtry there.

Then there is the food. Rules doesn't just do English hearty, it specializes in red-blooded game. Sitting there in the fug of claret-enhanced luxury and family happiness, filled up on wild mushroom soup starter and mallard mains, I read the Rules notice which states that most of their game is sourced from their own Lartington Estate in the High Pennines, 'England's Last Wilderness'.

'Er,' I say to Penny, 'surely *our* valley is England's last wilderness.' Some sort of parish-pump patriotism then kicks in, because the next thing I say is, 'It is the most remote place in England after all, isn't it?' Soon I am making an equation in my head, which goes: living in a remote area + living off the game and plants on our own land = Rules.

By the end of the meal I am casting the Rules visit as a kind of karmic ordainment of my desire to go wild in the country.

'You know my idea of living off the land?' I announce to the table with due solemnity. 'I'm going to do it. Just for a year.'

Tris and Freda raise their eyebrows. 'Yeah, right, Dad,' they chorus in uncanny unison.

Penny pauses for a moment, then looks me in the eye and says, 'It *is* very you.'

Why do I have the feeling that she understands why I need to do this better than I do?

'You can't use the freezer, though,' she adds.

'Why not?'

'Well, the food is not seasonal, or anything like, if you freeze it. It's not natural. Pickling would be natural because it uses a natural process. You can't say that for refrigeration.'

'True.'

Walking back to the Bonington Hotel in Bloomsbury, there is a Land Rover Series III stranded on the bright orange pavement, door open, while its owner rushes a suitcase on to the front seat. In the back window of the Land Rover is a sticker for the British Association for Shooting and Conservation, an image of a pheasant's head. On this sign alone I decide to begin my year of living on wild food on 1 October, the beginning of the pheasant season.

AUTUMN

ONE SWALLOW MAY not make a summer but the leaving of the house martins surely means summer's end. At first light I see a last straggling house martin making its way south through the net curtain of mist in the valley. Our house martins departed a week ago, the swallows, which built their mud nests inside the derelict outhouse, the week before. The swifts are long gone. Nature is on the move, groups of finches and buntings chitting-chatting as they fly overhead, their flight paths mirroring a passenger jet above them in the white.

Aside from the tinnitus of high aircraft, birdsong is all there is to hear. A raven croaks absent-mindedly down by the riverside fir in which it nests. I can hear blackbirds, jackdaws, song thrushes too, but not the one bird I want to hear most. All summer long an old cock pheasant has been taunting me with his *cok-cok* cry. Now, on 1 October, he is fair game. Edith, my black Labrador dog, pads along on my left side. Except that she is not quite my dog: since her teenage pregnancy in the spring Edith has been her own dog, more concerned about her puppies than serving me. The whole laborious process of getting her to be a gundog must start over again. As we march down to the copse, past the burning autumnal hedges of the paddock and Bog Field, I take some comfort in her exuberant, licky-licky personality since, as the old adage has it, dull people have dull dogs. I must be very entertaining to have such an interesting dog.

As we reach Copse Field the mist suddenly parts and the sun catches the dewdrops on the long tufts of grass and, for a second, before the mist closes in again, I am standing in a shining field of diamonds. This wondrous sight is almost compensation for the fact that neither feather nor scale of the pheasant is to be found, although we search every wooded cranny. Perhaps the pheasant, by some fantastic internal calendar, has realized that the shooting season has begun and vamoosed. More probably a lucky fox has beaten me to him. Whatever, the old cock pheasant, with his distinctive collarless neck, never makes another appearance on the farm. All the pheasants that I see over the next months are much younger birds. Some may be his children, though most are wanderers from shoots in other valleys. Hand-reared, these pheasants are so tame that they stand still to be shot.

Which is exactly what happens in the afternoon, when the mist has gone away and the sun is hot enough for shirt sleeves and bluebottles. I'm on the yard, looking down to the bottom fields for the dogs, when a pale hen pheasant slow-glides over my head into House Meadow, lands, and walks softly into the hedge in my plain view. A shotgun is standard for pheasant-killing but, as I have the Weihrauch .22 air rifle in my hand and the bird is plainly not afeared of humans, I chance on getting up close enough to shoot her in the head. No stalking is actually required. I walk along the hedge, where she is slinking back and forth; she sees me and crouches down, I feed the gun barrel through the darkened tangle of hawthorn trunks until the barrel end is by her yellow eye and then I pull the trigger. As she makes her death flaps I am suddenly aware of the intense smell of tart autumn hedge fruits on the air.

While I find no joy in killing, I know that when you're finished with twenty-first-century sentiment, a weapon in your hand and dead meat at your feet feels right. An atavistic male function has been fulfilled: the caveman has slain a mammoth for the tribe. And this I know too: killing wild game has a purifying honesty about it, because one does not hand over the responsibility of death to an

anonymous worker in an abattoir. With a gun in the hand all the
ethical aspects of meat-eating are there in one intimate, stark
moment and cannot be blinked away.

*Blue Peter*ishly I have survived the day thus far on a foodstuff
I picked earlier. Since I always, superstitiously, follow the old
country convention of never picking blackberries after
Michaelmas (29 September), because you'll find the cast-down
Lucifer in the bramble bushes, I have dishes and bowls, bags and
boxes of blackberries stashed in a disused linen cupboard in the
hall. Some blackberries I have boiled into a cordial and bottled,
some I have eaten raw and some I have turned into bramble jelly,
using my mother's cast-iron jam cauldron, which surely started
life as a prop for the witches in *Macbeth*. In the making of the
bramble jelly I have substituted honey for sugar; we no longer
have wild honey bees living in the wall of the barn, so I have
bought in a supply. I have allowed myself one other provision from
off-site. Salt.

My stomach is aching too much for sophisticated preparation
of the pheasant; I chop off the legs and wings with secateurs, gut
the bird with the feathers on, then make a small incision below the
crop, slide in my fingers and pull the skin off over the shoulders
and back end to expose the flesh with its yellow straps of fat. Then
cut off the neck. The bird is roasted, crammed with wild crab
apples from trees in the straggling hedge bordering the Grove
farm; in truth, it is too early for the crab apples and I only put them
in to prevent the bird from drying out in the oven. Served with
bramble jelly and hairy bittercress collected in a bunch from the
drainage ditch dug into the red sandstone marl of Copse Field, I
remember why pheasant was once restricted to the aristocracy. It
is a dish fit for a lord. Albeit a tiny dish. In the bottom of the roasting pan the pheasant's carcase, sitting in the shallow pool of its
own fat, looks pathetic. With the manners and appetite of Obelix I
eat most of the bird in one sitting.

To stave off hunger in the evening I pick at the pheasant's carcase and eat scores more blackberries.

Later, cleaning the gun before going to bed, I find that I have shot the pheasant at such point-blank range that a spot of blood and a tiny, downy feather have stuck to the barrel's mouth.

⸺

One larder of food is closer to hand even than the pheasant in House Meadow. At the far end of the farmyard is a briar patch, home to a warren of rabbits. The older rabbits are more circumspect – you don't get to be an elderly rabbit without being circumspect – but the young and unwary rabbits have an engaging habit of playing tag on the concrete yard. Or sitting atop the neighbouring pile of discarded builder's sand to lick their paws in the shrouds of morning mist. Such as a rabbit is now doing.

The evolutionary mistake of the rabbit is that when it hears a worrisome noise it stills or raises itself on its haunches for a better look around, displaying its pale breast for a shootist to aim at. Nature must have a sly sense of humour to give a bunny a target for a chest.

There are few times when, sitting at the open kitchen window at the beginning or the end of the day, I fail to bag a rabbit with the Weihrauch .22 air rifle. The German Weihrauch may not have the cachet of a British Webley, but it's reliable and it's the legal maximum power. It will punch a hole through marine three-ply wood.

I hiss loudly. The rabbit stops its ablutions. Its pale chest appears in the telescopic sights of the Weihrauch. Thud goes the rifle. The rabbit does a little jig-of-death into the air. *Vorsprung durch Technik*.

There are three other warrens on the farm, the biggest, with thirty burrows, dug into the drainage ditch which borders the Grove. Up to a point, the rabbit population, like the weed population, if chopped down comes back hard to keep the

 numbers as they were. A doe rabbit can have as many as eight litters in a year. Winter only slows, does not stop, the laporine production process.

I intend, though, to be careful in my rabbit pruning, taking a mix of ages, easing off the trigger when I sense they are being preyed upon hard by the buzzard, the fox, the stoat, the owl and all the other creatures who look down on them. It's not a holocaust of rabbits I want. It's a sustainable future. The warrens need to be there next year. And the year after.

Our rabbits might have a sustainable future. I'm not sure that they will sustain me more than a little, since they have to be the least nutritious of animals. Why, one wonders, did the Romans ever farm them? 'Rabbit starvation', the Athapascan Indians of the Great Bear Lake region called the phenomenon of eating plenty of rabbit but starving anyway. Rabbit is too lean for much human good and the sole reason it is talked about with enthusiasm by octogenarians is that it was plentiful during Hitler's war (there were about 100 million rabbits in Britain then) and cheap. If not free.

There's more to be said for the taste of rabbit, which is light and chickeny. One can't go far wrong in roasting it with a little salt rubbed into the skin, as I do this morning, though if I am honest rabbit for breakfast is not immediately appealing.

Like the rabbit, ground elder was introduced into Britain by the Romans, who used it as a pot herb. The medieval English found it appealing as a vegetable, but ground elder fell from favour because, paradoxically, it grew too well: given half a chance, and it needed less, it would annexe the entire garden. As far back as the sixteenth century John Gerard was complaining that 'once taken roote it will hardly be gotten out again, spoiling and getting every yeere more ground'. From the garden it was but a short burrow for ground elder's hegemonic rhizomes to reach the wayside and other shady places. These include the hedge around the orchard by the house, where it infests the floor almost the entire year round. I pick a large handful of its pale green leaves to try as an accompaniment to rabbit. Perhaps, I reason, the two Roman arrivals will complement each other in the kitchen? They do not. The burst-on-the-tongue menthol taste of the ground elder, when steamed like spinach, is too strong for my rabbit roasted.

For Keats, October was 'the season of mists and mellow fruitfulness'. I'm not sure how he so wrongly conjoined mist and mellowness. The fruits of autumn, especially the rosehips, crab apples and sloes on our two miles of hedges, need blue skies and frost to finish and sweeten them. Outside the kitchen window the world is suffocated by a pillow of fog. I would murder for a cup of tea or coffee. My intention had been to make an ersatz coffee from acorns in the tried-and-tested manner of German civilians in the Second World War, but nature has not obliged me; although we have three mighty thousand-year oaks clinging to the bank of the Escley, they have not fruited one single acorn between them. Failing that, there was the health shop favourite of rosehip tea. But the rosehips are not ready.

In desperation I thumb through Richard Mabey's classic *Food for Free*. And my eyes alight on dandelions.

> Dandelion, yellow as gold, what do you do all day?
> 'I wait and I wait in the long green grass
> Till the children come to play.'

Or a forager digs me up. Dandelion roots can be roasted and ground into a coffee. Which is what prompts me to spend a wet afternoon in House Meadow with a spade. With this I dig up thirty dandelions, some of which have taproots a foot long, but it takes me the best part of the light hours to do, searching through the overgrown grass, littered thick with fallen leaves. There is still all the brouhaha of roasting and grinding to come. Foraging, I am beginning to understand, will occupy all my waking hours.

Dandelion coffee
Collect a goodly supply of dandelion roots (look for older plants, with bigger rosettes of leaves), calculating that 8 pints/4.5l roots will produce 16 pints/l coffee. Dandelion roots are at their fullest and most nutritious in the autumn and early winter. Wash, then pat dry the roots, before cutting into 2in/5cm lengths. Place the cut roots on a baking tray in the centre of the oven and roast at 400°F/200°C/Gas Mark 6 for about two hours, turning once or twice to ensure even cooking. Leave the oven door slightly ajar to let the moisture out. Allow to cool, then grind in a grinder. Generally speaking, dandelion coffee matches ground coffee in strength, though not in caffeine because it has none. The taste is nicely nutty if bitter. Add honey to sweeten.

God must have heard my lament about mist, for day after day of blue sky follows, the perfect tonal background for the luscious red of the hanging hawthorn haws.

At the end of such a day, when the cold is beginning to ache my face and I'm picking haws from a wind-stooped bush in the garden, three mallard come whistling up the valley and flutter down to land on the river. Johnny, I say to myself, get your gun.

Within minutes I've loaded the Baikal shotgun with lead-free cartridges and am heading down the bank, past the cows, the frost beginning to settle on their backs. Either the mallard dislike their night-time feeding spot or something spooks them because they are whirring up into the sky before I'm halfway to the brook. Two of them wheel away east but one, panicking, breaks west and, to join the correct flight path, circles towards me. The sun has gone down behind the whale-backs of the Black Mountains, leaving a fluorescent band of light against which the mallard is silhouetted. I miss with one barrel but, because the duck is performing a turn, it carries on flying at the same aerial radius from me. The second shot crumples it and it plunges to earth.

Some creatures are easier to kill than others. Mallards I find hard to shoot, and I do know why: it's the remembrance of the childhood pleasure that came from going to the duck pond in Hereford, Mother's Pride bread in its red-and-white waxy bag, and the excitement as a bird seized (when I was brave) a bit of bread proffered on my hand. One of life's greatest pleasures is one of life's simplest and earliest: feeding quacking ducks with your parents.

So, as I search through the reedy grass in Bog Field for the fallen duck, I almost hope that, despite the evidence to the contrary, I missed it. But I did not, for I find it lying in a frosting white fold, its green head and neck grotesquely bent under its chest. A male in his fine plumage, the drab months of the 'eclipse', when he looked indistinguishable from his mate, a month past.

When roast, the duck provides me with a quarter cup of fat, a resource I desperately need for cooking and preserving, for rabbit produces none and the pheasant only a spoonful.

Hawthorn jelly

Adapted from Jason Hill's Wild Foods of Britain, *1944*
Pick and de-stalk the hawthorn fruit (haws). Add a handful of
crab apples and simmer till soft in a preserving pan, with
½ pint/300ml water to 1lb/450g fruit. This will take slightly
more than half an hour. Mash and strain the liquid through a
jelly bag, adding clear honey at the rate of 8oz/225g to every
pint/600ml of water. Stir in the honey until dissolved and then
boil. Pour into a mould.

The resulting rust-red jelly closely resembles avocado to taste. As Hill says, 'the yield of the juice is small, but the fruit is plentiful'. The old wives' saw 'Many haws, many snaws' founders on the fact that haws are plentiful *every* year. Haws can be gathered as late as December if they have been unaccountably overlooked by migrating members of the thrush family, who love them.

Even before I enter the kitchen I can feel the tension. Ducking in through the old cow-byre door I see Penny standing at the Aga cutting up potatoes into a saucepan. The steam is rising into the vapid half-light of the low-energy bulbs overhead.

She looks pointedly at the two wood pigeon dangling from between my fingers, shot as they travelled along their same-old, same-old flight path from the oaks on the track to the ash in Home Meadow. 'Do you know, I just don't think I can stand any more animals being dissected in my kitchen.'

I'm about to argue with her proprietorial view of our kitchen, but instead I whine like a small schoolboy. 'Look, I've been out for hours, I'm cold and knackered and it's too dark and windy to do them outside, OK?'

'I just don't want the mess.'

'I won't make a mess.'

'You always do . . .'

'Like when?'

'Like yesterday, when I found the rabbit fur under the table after your supposed cleaning up.' Penny points the Sabatier kitchen knife at me like Kitchener pointed his finger at the nation.

'I suppose,' I say in a jokey, beaten retreat to cordiality, 'that this is a pre-Bobbit moment?'

'Call me Lorraine.'

'So where should I go?'

She points at the five-foot-high hobbit hatch I've just bent through.

I want to object that the cow byre is full of furniture save for the corner by the yard door which Penny has bagged for her felt-making and is as draughty as a wind tunnel but what the fuck. I silently put the Baikal away in the gun cabinet, stick my butcher's knife in my coat pocket, grab the chopping board and stoop back through the old oaken doorway and down the three steps into the cow byre.

A brick extension to the bottom of the main building, the cow byre is lit by a single dangling light bulb, the only use of which is to throw expressionist shadows of our piled furniture on to the walls. The byre to my ire – I've started crap rhymes in my head, always proof of tiredness – is so rammed full with furniture that I'll have to clear a space before I can begin butchery. Worse, the wind is whistling under the concrete roof sheets, through the yard door and in through the broken windows. A rabbit I shot earlier in the day hangs from an iron girder and swings in synchronization with the light bulb.

Edith, lying on sacks of fleece at the bottom of the steps, questions me with a brown eye.

Yes, actually, Edith, I do have an idea. Tossing the pigeons on to a bookshelf I start moving boxes out of the top stall, until the stall and the trough at its head are bare down to the concrete. Telling Edith to guard the pigeons from our three other dogs I go off with my pocket torch to the lean-to. When I return ten minutes later Edith is where I left her, as still as if her portrait was being painted. So are the pigeons. She allows herself a wag of her tail, but is more interested in what I'm dragging, scuffing behind me: a large board of Kingspan, hardened insulation foam between silvered paper.

I hate DIY. Ergo I'm the proud master of the quick fix. With a tenon saw I cut the sheet of Kingspan in half, then punch a hole in the corners with a hammer and a six-inch nail, then tie with the inevitable baler twine one section of Kingspan to the metal bars on one side of the stall. And then tie the other section to the other side of the stall.

In less than five minutes I've got a cosy place to sit. I hook the old inspection lamp over the girder above, plug it in and lo! there is light too. The trough makes a good place to toss feathers. Three buckets of disinfectant slopped over the stall and it's even sanitary.

I sit in my bare stall on a chair and start plucking at the first wood pigeon. Tug, tug, tug . . . even a small bird can make one's finger ends ache. I've known grown women cry from the pain of plucking. Much is made of hanging game, invariably by people who never have to dress it, who never have to pull out dead-set feathers. Certainly, some game needs to be hung for a few days, to allow lactic acid to tenderize the flesh, but pigeons and rabbits are perfectly edible without stringing up.

I forgo feathering the neck and instead brutally decapitate the pimply cadaver on the board with the heavy butcher's knife. Then I amputate the legs and wings. And then I snick across under the breastplate, stick my fingers inside and pull out the innards into a bucket.

After the second bird I decide I might as well, while I'm in my fucking plucking place, do the rabbit too.

This is the bit the artfully posed, glossy photographs in Hugh Fearnley-Whittingstall's books leave out. With the heavy carving knife I chop off the rabbit's paws and head, then with a small sharp kitchen knife slit open the rabbit from neck to arse. Pulling with my fingers from the slit outwards, I yank off the rabbit's fur coat to leave its pale marbled body naked. With a sideways slit across the stomach the rabbit's string-sausage guts tumble over the floor. Finally, I prod my fingers into the narrow chest cage to tug out the lights, heart and liver.

There's more blood up my right arm than Macbeth's after he's murdered Duncan.

I also know that all the seas incarnadine, plus a truckload of Crabtree & Evelyn soap, won't get rid of the earthy, iron smell of pigeon and rabbit blood. The door to the kitchen opens, and Penny comes down the steps with an armful of washing. 'There is no way,' she says walking past me, 'that you are going to touch me with any part of your arm from the fingertips to the shoulder for the next week.'

I can only assume that Mrs Neanderthal was not quite so particular as Ms Modern Homo Sapiens. Sheep farmers' wives, though, famously do not allow their husbands near them at lambing time, since a man's hand inside a ewe all day is an entirely effective contraceptive thought. As Wyn down at White Hall Farm says every February, 'You'll not find many kids born to farmers in the autumn.'

In the mudroom I turn on the shower and hose down my hands and arms, before scrubbing them with a loofah. Then a nail brush, till the skin reddens. A nail file gouges out the congealed blood from under my fingernails, and the shower basin swirls with red like the shower scene in *Psycho*.

But no, every time I hold my right arm to my nose I can still smell haemoglobin and shit.

———

Just before seven in the morning the sun is rising over Merlin's Hill, the rays catching the heather on the Black Mountains, which redden in a modest English version of Ayers Rock. The pearl-button moon is pinned in the sky and the ghost of frost haunts the still, dark ground. A farm dog barks far off. Three ducks, too small to be mallard, come in from the south, looking oddly like ornaments on the wall of a suburban sitting room. They are mandarins, a protected species, so the shotgun stays propped in its slipcase against the tree and I commence picking the last chandeliers of purple elderberries hanging off the hedges. It is not only

I who have been summoned. Four magpies are pecking at the elder behind the pigsty before my arrival shoos them on. I pick without gloves, and the popping of the small purple alveoli stains my fingers. As dye, elderberry juice is so effective that Roman women used it on their tresses. For the English, the magic of elderberries has lain in their ability to ward off witches and illness. The scientific evidence for the former proposition is in short supply, but not for the latter, since elderberries have high levels of vitamin A (600 IU per 100mg) and vitamin C (36mg per 100mg). Eaten raw, elderberries are reminiscent of dulled blackcurrants and gloriously thirst-quenching. They are said to be direly diuretic in this state, although I have not noted any ill effects when taking them in moderation. Anyway, my intention is to dilute and adulterate them into elderberry cordial, English nature's own health tonic.

Blackbirds, in particular, find elderberries irresistible. In the first week of October, our blackbirds, their numbers boosted by winter incomers, stripped more than thirty elder trees scattered around the farm, leaving the umbrels suspended like so many discarded models of the airways of the human lung.

Elderberry cordial
A recipe which is simplicity itself:

8oz/225g honey
1 pint/600ml water
25 elderberry heads

Strip the berries off the stalks with a fork and put into a saucepan. Add water, bring to the boil, then add honey. Stir continuously until all the honey has dissolved. Then turn down the heat and simmer for ten minutes. Cover with a tea towel and leave overnight. Strain and bottle.

The cordial will keep for three months in a cold dark place, but can be consumed immediately. A tot of elderberry cordial is the ideal livener on an autumn or winter morning.

Of course, a longer-term method of storage is to turn the elderberries into wine. This I do too. (The necessary proportions are 4lb/1.8kg elderberries stripped from their stalks, 8 pints/4.5l water, and 2lb/900g honey; the price of good elderberry wine is eternal vigilance in removing any trace of bitter stalk from the fruits. There should be enough wild yeast on the berry skins for natural fermentation to occur in a warm place. And, as with all recipes that substitute honey for sugar, the amount of honey required is approximate because of its myriad variations of strength and taste.) Elderberry wine takes a minimum of six months to mature, but is better at twelve. Serendipitously, the calendar has then gone full circle and it can be drunk with game, which plays well with its heavy fruitiness. Not so long ago, elderberry wine was a commercial proposition, with the elderberries grown in proper orchards, like apples.

My method of learning how to train a gundog is exactly the same as Manuel's method of learning English in *Fawlty Towers*. I learn from book. A few months ago, whiling away five minutes by browsing the Sue Ryder charity shop in Ross-on-Wye, Penny found a copy of *Gundog Training* by Keith Erlandson, published in 1976. 'It's a bit dog-eared,' said Penny, who has the habit of un-intentional puns, 'but it looks quite useful.' Erlandson's *Gundog Training*, it turns out, is that rare thing, an instructional manual which is a good read. I soon come to swear by it, though I do add a bit of modern dog psychology; as with the schooling of humans, the education of dogs has moved from cane to carrot (or more precisely small squares of mature cheese). The other ingredient I add to the Erlandson-Mod mix comes from watching a female farmer on a Pembrokeshire hill give a sheepdog training class. 'If you want to command dogs,' she shouted in a voice that would have made an RSM wince, 'try bloody looking like someone who can give orders. Stand up STRAIGHT!' Her pupils, who were shuffling holidaymakers filling in a windy day by visiting a pet farm, looked as though they wished they could leave, but daren't.

Her advice, though, was true enough; dogs read body posture. If you want to dominate your dog – and you do, because you are pack leader – you have to assume a commanding look. So, with my shoulders back, I spend two quarter-hours a day with Edith re-doing the basics: walking to heel, dropping and recall, the latter two to voice, hand and whistle commands. For a whistle I use the Acme Thunderer, beloved of football referees, which does little for local tranquillity but does mean that Edith has no excuse for not hearing me.

Me seeing Edith is a different matter. With a lesson squeezed in at the dark end of an autumn day, training a black dog has its exasperating moments. This evening is a case in point. Edith tends to heel too far away from my leg (the left one: a gundog always walks to heel on the opposite side to the arm carrying the gun), a habit I am correcting by putting cheese in my left hand and walking parallel to the long stock fence down the side of the track. Trapped by the fence (Erlandson's tip) and baited by food (a Bruce Fogle tip), Edith is sticking a tight half-inch from my leg. Except when she stops to crap, and I carry on into the night without her.

Back in the house, Edith flat out in front of the fire, I tot up her good versus bad points, as a preliminary to the next phase of training: the retrieve. For a dog who has no breeding and who was an accident, Edith has, I think, the makings of a reasonable retriever. She likes to carry (OK, our socks at the moment, but it's early days) and she passed the crucial Erlandson test: when sitting does the dog look to the handler or look around? Edith looks to me, for 90 per cent of the time. She is also steady to the gun; I know because I got ahead of Erlandson and prematurely tried Edith's steadiness under fire by loosing off an ancient Chinese .177 air rifle over her head. This made a noise some decibels above Thor slapping his hands together. She didn't blink, although I dropped the gun because I thought it had exploded on me.

On the negative side, if I am too affectionate to Edith – and it's difficult not to be affectionate to a dog with such soulful brown eyes – she loses her composure completely and wants to play. For hours. She also chases rabbits and will not desist. My fault, I should have intervened earlier, but a problem still.

I'm about to read Erlandson on 'Retrieving and steadiness to the dummy' when Tris comes in and says, 'Can I finish . . .' At which Edith jumps up, wags her tail so hard that her body contorts into a shuddering series of S-shapes and charges out into the hall for playtime.

'Whoops,' says Tris. That is the other problem with Edith. Her release word, the word that ends her instruction, is 'Finish'. My fault again. I should have chosen something no one is ever likely to say, such as Chumbawamba. As it is, we cannot use the F-word around Edith.

There are, I am discovering, actual advantages to living on an ex-building site. Some wild plants positively love the waste land. The summer produced a fine, straight crop of garlic mustard (Jack-by-the-hedge) on the red earth dumped from the sitting-room excavation and now, in mid-October, the grassed area where Bob parked his van is pimpled white with shaggy ink caps. On days of lethargy and continuous rain, these mushrooms, a ten-yard walk from the house, are true convenience food.

Up close, the shaggy ink caps bear a resemblance to Apollo rockets, or at least they do until they unfurl phantasmagorically into black umbrellas. By then they are decaying and useless. The boon of the shaggy ink cap is not its taste – it has none – but its slimy, sensuous consistency, which is utterly unlike the coarse greens that pass for my vegetables nowadays. So fragile is the shaggy ink cap, sadly, that it does not dry or preserve well. You see it, you eat it.

Some people peel off the scales on the cap that give the mushroom its alternative name of lawyer's wig. I do not bother. All it needs is a dash under the cold tap, a pat dry, and frying for five minutes in duck fat and a crushed wild garlic clove. A surprise awaits the first-time cook of the shaggy ink cap: for a mushroom that is so showily big, sometimes measuring almost a foot tall, it reduces insanely in the cooking.

By the end of October, the shaggy ink caps in the grass parking area are no more. The shortness of their season here is a peculiarity due to Trelandon's height above sea level. In more hospitable places in Britain the shaggy ink cap can be found for half the year or more; the Great War forager T. Cameron found them growing as late as January in Buckinghamshire. These shaggy ink caps, recorded Cameron in *The Wild Foods of Great Britain*, made an excellent adjunct to chicken, although the meal was somewhat spoilt by the cook hovering in expectation of his demise from eating 'such terrible poison'. Cameron, who thought frying mushrooms (unless they were strongly flavoured types, such as vegetable beefsteak) a crime, was adamant that the best method of cooking shaggy ink caps was to lay them in a heavy saucepan with a knob of butter, a pinch of salt and a dusting of pepper, and just enough milk to cover the bottom of the pan and prevent them from catching.

Even with the shaggy ink caps over, the parking area remains a useful wild larder. Plantain and dandelions are there in profusion, much to the disgust of my parents when they visit. 'John,' my father says, 'can't you do something about these weeds?'

'That,' I say, pointing at the parking area, 'is my garden.'

The powder-blue skies hold for another week. Make hay while the sun shines is the farmer's maxim; pick hedgerow berries when Jack Frost visits is the forager's. Picking from a soaking wet hedge dampens the spirits as well as the clothes. Besides, rosehips and sloes need Jack Frost to make their skins permeable.

Up here in the hills, we still have frosts which turn the ground to iron and the water in the cow trough to plate glass, two inches thick. I like frost. I like the knowledge that it is cleansing the ground; I like the feeling of exhilaration it engenders.

So I don't have to prod myself too hard to get out in the morning to gather rosehips, the scarlet fruit of the dog rose.

When Rupert Brooke penned his nostalgic couplet

> Unkempt about those hedges blows
> An English unofficial rose

he must have had something like Trelandon's hedges in mind. After three years of benevolent abandonment they ramble with dog roses, some tangling ten feet into the sky.

According to legend, the root of the dog rose can cure rabies. The more prosaic explanation for the shrub's name is that it was originally 'dag rose', in honour of its sharp thorns, a dag being a dagger.

In childhood, I picked the elongated hips for the hairy seeds close-packed inside, which made a rustic itching powder. Now it's the high vitamin C content in the hip that I want. The rosehip has twenty times the vitamin C level of an orange, a quality which prompted the Ministry of Health in wartime Britain, when there was a dearth of imported citrus fruit, to organize the collection of rosehips. By 1943 around 450 tons of rosehips were gathered annually.

After half an hour of picking rosehips, it is my fervent opinion that the wartime collectors, if any of them are still going, deserve a medal. The hips either are unwilling to come off or burst in a sticky mess. The protective rings of thorns are turning my right hand into a mass of weals. One thorn has penetrated the end of my little finger, leaving a blob of blood that won't clot. I try wearing leather gardening gloves, but these prove unwieldy. My jumper constantly becomes tangled in the barbs; if I take it off the barbs penetrate my shirt. It's too hot in the sun to wear a Barbour coat. For this pain and effort, about half a pound of hips lie in the base of the carrier bag. My heart sinks. By my estimate I need, at the very least, 20lb/9kg of hips. Forty hours of picking.

On this day I manage six hours, and the sky over the Black Mountains has turned to a dying mash of Turneresque grey and mauve by the time I tramp up the bank to the house with my carrier bags. A flock of fieldfares, gobbling hawthorn haws, mocks me.

I do at least have enough hips to make syrup.

Rosehip syrup

In the kitchen I try out the instructions for rosehip syrup in the Ministry of Food's leaflet 'Hedgerow Harvest', 1943, reasoning that it has been tested by thousands.

The recipe requires 2lb/900g hips. For sugar I substituted 12oz/335g honey. I reproduce it in its entirety.

'Have ready 3 pints [1.7l] boiling water, mince the hips in a coarse mincer, drop immediately into the boiling water or if possible mince the hips directly into the boiling water and again bring to the boil. Stop heating and place aside for 15 minutes. Pour into a flannel or linen crash jelly bag

and allow to drip until the bulk of the liquid has come through. Return the residue to the saucepan, add 1½ pints [900ml] boiling water, stir and allow to stand for 10 minutes. Pour back into the jelly bag and allow to drip. To make sure all the sharp hairs are removed, put back the first half-cupful of liquid and allow to drip through again. Put the mixed juice into a clean saucepan and boil down until the juice measures about 1½ pints [900ml], then add 1½lb [650g] of sugar and boil for a further 5 minutes. Put into hot sterile bottles and seal at once. If corks are used these should have been boiled for ½ hour just previously, and after insertion coated with melted paraffin wax. It is advisable to use small bottles as the syrup will not keep for more than a week or two once the bottle is opened. Store in a dark cupboard.'

Rosehip syrup looks like tomato soup. It has a taste reminiscent of sour apple chews.

While the syrup is hubbling and bubbling in the cauldron, I take another pound of hips and painstakingly split them with my thumbnail and scoop out the hirsute fawn-coloured seeds, of which each hip contains about twenty-five. It is a sticky and literally irritating task for lacerated fingers. Eventually the hips are de-seeded and I put the split skins in the oven on 110°C, with the door open, overnight. These will be ground coarsely to make rosehip tea.

—

Driving the children to school next morning I catch sight of my hands, scratched and festering, on the steering wheel. They look like the hands of a killer in a fifties film noir.

John Lewis-Stempel in *The Night of the Hunter*.

As soon as I get home I slap on Germolene, in which I have an almost religious faith, inherited from my grandmother. Even the pink ointment, however, cannot stop my right hand from swelling stiff. If I move my index finger the cuts on it crack and leak pus. Clearly, there will be no rosehip picking today. Equally clearly, my plan for a sustained period of rosehip picking is a non-starter, which worries me, since the universal forager's wisdom is that rosehips are useless after the end of October.

My anxiety proves to be foundation-less. I pick a half-pound of hips almost every day until the winter solstice, most of them as luminescent and firm as their October fellows. Encouraged by the observation of the Stuart herbalist John Gerard that '[rosehips] maketh the most pleasant . . . tartes, and such like', these hips are turned into an invented rosehip pudding of de-seeded rosehips boiled with honey, simmered and reduced down into a mush, then cooled. Rolled out and reheated, the mush makes a handy fruit chew which can be cut into strips.

In Sweden sweet rosehip soup is popular.

Rosehip soup or Nyponsoppa

In the standard Swedish recipe, Nyponsoppa is thickened with potato flour (or cornstarch) and sprinkled with almonds. Here is a more wild and free version. Serves 6.

1 pint/600ml rosehips
2oz/60g finely ground hazelnuts
2oz/60g liquid honey
5 pints/2.8l water

Rinse the rosehips and put them in a heavy-bottomed saucepan and bring to the boil. Simmer, stirring occasionally, until the hips are soft. Strain through a jelly bag or similar, add the honey and all but a heaped teaspoon of the ground hazelnuts. Bring to the boil again, stirring all the way. Serve with the saved hazelnut powder sprinkled on top.

According to the nutritionist Walter L. Voegtlin, author of *The Stone Age Diet*, the human stomach is made for meat. Fruit, vegetables and nuts should be mere accessories in the diet of *Homo sapiens*, whose teeth, jaw and stomach are near identical in function and structure to the carnivorous dog's. The codicil to Voegtlin's *Weltanschauung* is that the human stomach benefits most from wild meat, since game is generally more nutritious than its domestic counterpart. Game has had more exercise (resulting in better muscle tone and lower rates of saturated fats) and a more varied and natural diet (resulting in higher levels of minerals and vitamins). A comparison is illuminating: a domestic chicken typically provides 443kj/100g energy, 20.1g/100g protein, and 0.2mg/100g iron; the respective figures for a pheasant are 505kj/100g energy, 27.1g/100g protein and 1.0mg/100g iron. Meanwhile, the cholesterol levels in chicken flesh are significantly higher than those in pheasant meat, 3030mg/100g compared to 2710mg/100g. Game is good for you. Game has a better life and death than its farmed counterpart. In Britain at least, game means the conservation of whole swathes of countryside, including the chemical-free, somewhat overgrown and ramshackle fields, hedges, thickets and riverbank of Trelandon Longhouse Farm. And so I shoot animals for food.

If Voegtlin's carnivorous view has its merits, the flaw in modern man adopting the eating habits of prehistoric times is that Neanderthals must have had stomachs of cast iron, like dogs and pigs. (No details required or given.) Another problem with following the caveman diet today is that the human brain of the Western man and woman, after 3,000 years of the farming of carbohydrates, is utterly addicted to soft starchy food. The more refined the food, the better we like it. Thus I dream at night and dream in the day of McDonald's burger buns with sesame seeds on top,

Scott's 'porage' with treacle, custard creams with strong china tea, Bath Olivers with cheddar cheese, and Farley's Rusks, these last of course being the ultimate in comfort food and once the national dish of British babies.

If I am honest, there are other psychological clouds to foraging. The whimsicality of nature makes me feel like a box kite on the end of a fraying cotton string: one chill blast and I'll tumble down from grace. There can be no planning – 'I know, I'll do shooting on Tuesday' – because Tuesday may be driving rain and gales. There can be no certainty because the weather might rot the sloes waiting to be gathered or frost kill the apple blossom, or some botanical condition might cause the acorns not to fruit this year (as has just happened). Disease could kill the game; two years ago our rabbits contracted myxomatosis, causing them to lumber around with bleeding eyes. It might happen again. Who knows?

I haven't even begun to open the mental box of loneliness yet. True, I quite like my own company; as a child I remember my father saying to me, 'You're one of life's lone wolves,' which as it turned out was an unintended but useful encomium for a would-be forager. I do love the solitude of the fold along the Escley where we live. But day after day passes when, from the time Penny and the children leave in the morning until they come home in the evening, I do not see a living soul. Three hundred and sixty-five days of solitude.

Am I whingeing? Perhaps. I shouldn't. I'm spending most of my days under a big sky, in pure crisp air, in an English paradise, picking along shimmering Klimt-gold autumn hedges from which flocks of migrating fieldfares and redwings, gorged on haws, explode in silver flashes before me. Or beating through the fields, kicking fallen oak leaves in steps of childhood, after pheasants and rabbits. I have not suffered the expected debilitating hunger, although I freely admit this is because I am using rabbit as filler. My eating habits might be unorthodox, rabbit-heavy (at least one every two days), but so far I have not dropped dead of scurvy, courtesy of a steady supply of sorrel, hairy bittercress, plantain, Good King Henry, and a dwindling harvest of nettles now stunted by frost. A moment or two of light-headedness – which I assume is caused by low blood sugar – has been cured by taking a spoonful of honey.

At dinner Penny tells me, 'You need a plan.' She and the children are tucking into Waitrose salmon, mashed potato and broccoli. I eat another rabbit, this one stewed with chanterelle mushrooms and ramsons, the harsh-tasting wild garlic, dug up from our third-of-an-acre copse on the bank of the Escley. Steamed nettles are the accompanying vegetable.

'My plan is to live off wild food.'

'That's not a plan. That's an aspiration. You need to sit down and work out how much carbohydrate you need per day . . .'

'Whoa. That makes me panic. If I start thinking rationally, scientifically, about living off wild food I freeze up. I believe I should just listen to the cravings in my head.'

'Did you say "ravings"?'

'Ho, ho, ho.'

'It might help to follow some recipes.'

'Do you know what the problem with supposed wild food recipes is? Half of their ingredients come from a delicatessen. I mean when was the last time you saw gnocchi growing wild. I'm mostly having to make up recipes as I go along. And this,' I say, pointing at the rabbit chunks, 'is pretty good.'

'You could try older recipes though. Something medieval, for instance.'

I acknowledge that this is a good idea, at which Penny disappears out of the dining room and comes back with a carrier bag, which she hands to me. 'A present for you.'

The plastic bag is full of green sputniks. Sweet chestnuts. I'm about to protest that they are in contravention of my 'on-site only' policy when she says, 'Don't look a gift bag in the mouth. I gathered them from outside Clodock church, for goodness' sake.' Clodock is a mile and a half down the valley. Practically on the doorstep, then.

—

By going to Hereford reference library to research old recipes I miss the surprise visit by two Americans, on the 'trip of a lifetime' to England. They're Henry Landon Sr and Henry Landon Jr, who have called in to see the ancestral homestead, from which their family departed to America in the mid-1700s. Stupidly I've never mused on the house's name before: 'Trelandon', meaning house of the Landons, 'Tre' being the Welsh for house. Penny doesn't wish to disappoint them and therefore doesn't point out that their family might have come from another Trelandon, two miles down the valley.

The valley wasn't truly incorporated into England until 1534, when Henry VIII merrily set the boundary between England and Wales along the top of the Black Mountains. In a masterpiece of touristic ahistoricism, this demarcation line is now the Offa's Dyke Footpath, although the eponymous Anglo-Saxon king did not manage to push the boundary of English settlement beyond the Dore valley six miles to the east. From the time of the Romans to the time of the Norman Conquest, the Longtown valley was the heart of a Welsh 'commote' called Ewyas (probably meaning 'sheep district'). The Conqueror, in order to secure Ewyas, sent in one of his hardcase soldiers, Walter de Lacy, whose family built the perfect round stone keep (still standing) in the village and bequeathed the area a new nomenclature, Ewyas Lacy. Marcher lords like Walter de Lacy were petty kings, in whose territory it was said 'the king's writ did not run'. Neither always did the de Lacys': to subdue the wild west land of Ewyas Lacy, where raids and rustling by the Welsh were endemic, the Norman overlords were obliged to construct, as well as the castle at Longtown, four other motte-and-baileys in the southern bottom of the valley, at Pont-Hendre, Rowlestone, Walterstone and Llanvihangel. By the thirteenth century the Norman overlords had effectively brought the valley within the political orbit of England, though culturally the valley retained a strong Welsh identity for centuries after. The valley was the last to be incorporated into England. It's the last of England now. Standing in the dying sun of an October afternoon, looking down the valley towards Clodock church, past the draughtsboard of small meadows on Merlin's Hill and the great wall of the Black Mountains, I cannot hear one human sound.

This is not uncommon at Trelandon. Such gyres of silence occur throughout the day, and when the human interruption comes it is generally a far-off tractor on the lane or a transatlantic aircraft up in the dome of the sky, whispers in a cathedral. If anything, the landscape is quieter now than it was a century ago, when the fields would have been constantly trafficked with farm labourers on their chores. Mechanization has reduced the sheep and cattle farms in the valley to one man, his dog, his ATV and his tractors.

A landscape needs a soundscape. The sound of silence suits Trelandon well. Me too.

Actually, the landscape is never wholly silent, for I can always hear the Escley, in summer when it runs low and creeping, in winter when it rages like the continuous crashing of sea surf, and in all the many intermediate stages. The Escley is the soundtrack of my life.

On a night when a full moon rises over Merlin's Hill into a sky of racing clouds, on a night for foxes and the French Resistance, I am still picking hazelnuts, torch in my left hand, a bucket by my feet. I have been gathering hazelnuts on and off for a fortnight. On and off is the only way I can do it, because picking hazelnuts is a literal pain in the neck, for one has to keep looking up.

By my rough computation we have 200 hazel trees and bushes on the farm, from which I have garnered a scant 33lb/15kg of nuts. The hazelnut is one of nature's most favoured fodders. Squirrels like it, woodpeckers like it, nuthatches like it, jays like it, wood pigeons like it, wood mice like it. I like it, but am the least dextrous in the queue of competitors this last week of October, when the nuts have long turned from thin green to golden ripe. My dearth of hazelnuts, however, is not caused only by the prior plundering of beasts and birds. It has been a dry year for dry tree fruits.

There is no sensible reason for me to be out at eleven at night, shining a torch up into the leaves and incipient catkins, gathering hazelnuts. Whatever is left on these few last trees will remain till first light, when I will have to come back anyway with the shepherd's crook to pull down the high branches, an exercise impossible to combine with torch-holding. I am picking solely to be doing *something* to satisfy a squirrel-like urge to store up for the oncoming winter.

The hazelnut is an ancient food, known to hunter-gatherers of the Mesolithic era. The nut's name comes from the Anglo-Saxon 'haesel' meaning a hat, in reference to the frilly cap in which the fruit sits. Common throughout the isles, the hazel is not always as wild as one might suppose. On this bend of the Escley the rustling hazels are so regularly placed that they must have been planted intentionally; they have certainly been pollarded in the past, with the result that their profusions of shiny stems stand soldier-straight in the moonlight. Hazel makes ideal bean poles, and thinner hazel stems can be woven into fencing and into wattle for house-building. Hazel leaves were once used to feed cattle and can be eaten by humans.

Much the most nutritious part of the hazel, though, is the nut, which packs ½oz/15g of protein per 3½oz/100g. Which is more than a hen's egg.

The hazelnut may be a wonder food, but it is not its nutritional qualities that make it my breakfast staple, it is its taste. I crave its milky sweetness. Even the jaw-ache that comes from eating raw hazelnuts in quantity cannot keep me from them on cheerless autumn mornings, when I grind them into a rough approximation of muesli by adding honey and chopped dried rosehips.

Hazelnuts are more amenable to the jaw when roasted, when they become starchy, like semolina. Roasted hazelnuts can also be pressed for oil. The process is laborious and the amount of pale amber oil that can be obtained from a pound of nuts is to be measured in parts of a teaspoon.

Hazelnut oil is precious. Outside of duck fat, it is the only cooking oil I can obtain from the land. I need that oil, because I have not shot a duck for over a week.

———

A typical autumn day in the life of a twenty-first-century hunter-gatherer. Up at 6am, before the light crawls over Merlin's Hill, because the early bird gets the worm. Birds need to eat first thing in the morning, to adjust their body weight after slumber. Thus the early-rising shootist gets the bird that gets the worm. A hot drink of dandelion coffee (or rosehip tea, or a hot fruit cordial), plus a muesli of ground hazelnuts and honey, out shooting with Edith for an hour or two, always in my Barbour slick with water-repellent wax, always with a Boy Scout 'Be prepared' pocketful of little blue freezer bags to collect unexpected morsels, such as fairy ring mushrooms. The remainder of the morning is given over to picking. Lunch. In the afternoon, picking, picking, picking until 3.30pm, then out shooting with Edith until last light. Food preparation and preservation – plucking, bottling, stripping, boiling, skinning, de-pipping, toiling, toiling in the kitchen – until dinner at

7.30pm. Dinner. Food preparation continued until 9pm. Or, if I've failed to bag anything for the pot, shooting coneys with a lamp. I used to think that farming was hard work, but in farming you get to sit in the warmth of the tractor cab, trundling up and down listening to the radio, drinking coffee from a thermos.

Where is the balm of sleep? Anxiety prevents me from sleeping more than five hours a night. I can hear the clock ticking, even when it is removed out of the bedroom and far down the house. The terrible tightening vice of autumn darkness means that each day I have less time to hunt and to gather. And each tick of the clock means that winter, with its dearth of plants, is closer still. Do I have enough pre-serves laid down? Enough hogweed roots? Will they go mouldy? What happens if I fail to shoot something for days in a row? What if I'm ill? Without refrigeration one eats more seasonally, that is cer-tain, but also eats more hand to mouth. There is no back-up, no security of mind, no lovely thought that, as it pisses down or the snow piles up to the lintel, 'It doesn't matter, the freezer is full.'

I know, of course, that if famine befell the land I could bail out and drive to Waitrose. But that is not the point.

Tick goes the clock as it inexorably counts down to winter. Tick. Tick. Tick.

On this soft, moist late October morning I can see, even from the house windows, that the pony field has come up white with mush-rooms. They should be picked while still dewy but my back aches from gathering hazelnuts, and picking mushrooms is the second-to-last thing I want to do, beaten only by going nut-gathering again.

But it's pick them or lose them. Poppy the pony is already up and eating and she'll trample the mushrooms. Or crap on them.

So it is that I'm out with my trug by 7am, bleary and aching; dandelion coffee doesn't kick-start the system like Brazilian beans.

There are puffballs galore. In only a quarter of an hour I've filled the trug, borrowed Poppy's feed bucket and filled that too. As fast as I twist and pluck mushrooms I spot others unpicked. A mushroom bonanza. The great mushroom rush. There are more mushrooms than I can pick. Aside from the puffballs, there are fairy rings of some yellow mushroom I can't identify, and troupes of magic mushrooms, psilocybin. It's hippie heaven on earth. Gandalf's Mushroom Garden.

I trot back to the yard, grab an old sugar-beet sack lying on the floor of the cow byre and go down to the copse. There are mushrooms there too. Lying on the copse's edge is a pashmina of exquisite golden chanterelle, the mushroom which people once thought could bring the dead back to life. In the evening, for once I don't have to do my own cooking. While I'm slicing mushrooms to dry in the airing cupboard, Penny takes a bucket of the jumbled fungi to make a tureen of wild mushroom soup. She also kites the idea of harvesting the magic mushrooms and flogging them around the pubs in Hereford. Potentially a nice little earner but probably not an entirely wise business proposition, I suggest.

———

On a night of a million stars, when the Milky Way is girdling the firmament, I'm feeding the dogs on the yard when a shooting star flashes, burning bright before dying in black nothingness. Another shooting star sparks. Entranced, I gaze into the heavens and am rewarded with the sight of a third.

October is, for reasons I do not understand, the month *sans pareil* for shooting stars. October is also the month that the bats go out and the rats come in. The small colony of bats which roosts in the old chimney at the unfinished end of the house has gone off to hibernate, most likely in the hollow oak down by the river.

Meanwhile, the rats have come in off the fields, where they tend to colonize old rabbit burrows for their dachas, and taken up winter quarters in the cow byre. While I'm on the yard admiring the heavens, I hear a rat scuttle across from the byre to the pig pen. The dogs hear it too and roar off into the black. I know their chase is unsuccessful because they do not bring back a prize. Fetching a torch I poke around the outside of the concrete pig pen, where the beam illuminates shiny black pellets of rat faeces under a propped-up wheelbarrow: the rats' harbourage. That night, I know we have a rat problem. Lying in bed I hear one gnawing on the oak door between the cow byre and the kitchen.

Rats bring out my inner redneck. There is no grey or doubt in my philosophy on rats. I don't do humane trapping – I mean, where would you relocate the rats to? Who would want them? Would you? – I do mass death. Country rats are healthier than their city counterparts, yet they still spread diseases lethal to man and domestic pets alike.

Since I can't sleep I decide to go for the nuclear option. Taking out an 11lb/5kg bucket of Tomcat rat poison I place scoops of the bright blue pellets in the dispensers – which look like lengths of drainpipe: rats can go in, pets and poultry cannot – and place three dispensers around the pigsty. Plucking up my courage, because I am frankly scared of rats, I bang loudly on the inside cow-byre door to scare off the rat-a-chewy and then place two dispensers inside, on the steps.

The horror. The horror. When I check the poison bait next morning, it has all gone. All 5½lb/2.5kg of it. There must be dozens of rats out there in the dark, swarming around. For more nights I feed the rats, until the poison is untouched and the rats are all dead. Thankfully most of the rats die in a burrow they have mined under the pig pen, which I seal up. The rest I have to find where they have dropped, dead of suffocation caused by internal haemorrhaging. These, doused in diesel, I burn on a pyre.

A CALENDAR OF WILD FOOD AT TRELANDON

October

*Dandelion, elderberries, haws, hazelnuts, sloes,
shaggy ink cap mushrooms, woodcock, sorrel,
nettles, sloes, rabbit, ground elder, rosehips, honey,
puffballs, Jew's ear, chanterelle, crab apple, hairy
bittercress, goose grass, mallard, pigeon, hogweed,
corn salad, ground ivy, plantain, sow thistle*

WINTER

E VEN IN WINTER a sprinkling of dandelions can be found braving it, their jagged lion's-teeth leaves (hence 'dent-de-lion') making a welcome green salad or vegetable. The youngest leaves are the least bitter, and if they are left in water for several hours, or have been blanched by a molehill, less bitter still. But it is not the leaves of the dandelion that I am primarily hunting on the wet Eve of Samhain, 1 November, the beginning of winter in the Celtic calendar. It is the dandelion's roots once again, this time as a vegetable. I am having images of them so strongly in my head that they verge on hallucinations.

The nettles in the sward are burnt black by Jack Frost. Miraculously, one dandelion, stranded in its own private microclimate, is in flower, but all the rest take strenuous finding in the unkempt grass. In the kitchen I boil them for fifteen minutes, but as the roots taste bitter I quick-boil them again in changed water, for another five minutes. Then, the bitterness goes.

⁓

The flowering dandelion in House Meadow is not the only inhabitant of a microclimate on the farm. At the bottom of the drainage ditch which runs along the southern edge of Copse Field it is still summertime. Five feet below the level of the meadow, the wide ditch bottom, running through Old Red Sandstone, has vetch and violet in flower, while sorrel, docks, thistles, ground ivy, brooklime, nettles and corn salad are all standing pert. At the top of the ditch, meanwhile, in deference to

winter the foxglove leaves have begun their winter drop to imper-
sonate the ears of lop rabbits.

⟡

The wind strips the twin oaks on the river. A vortex of browned
leaves dances across Copse Field. My memory runs back to when
the children were younger, when we used to play catching leaves
on the wind for innocent hours. In the river, now running absurdly
low, a distorted submarine shape forges upstream through the
crinkled water: a brown trout moving to its spawning ground. It is
safe from me now, for it is the close season on *Trutta trutta*. The
wind gusts so strongly that it takes my breath away as I yawl
through Copse Field, our only truly flat land. At the Finger, in a
blizzard of leaves, I pull brown Jew's ears fungi off the parched,
cracked bark of a bowed elder vibrating in the gale.

When, wind-assisted, I reach home and show Freda the Jew's
ears fungi, she says 'Yuk' because they do indeed look like human
ears. She holds one in front of her own to prove the point and
requests that I cut her two for next Halloween. Penny's worry is
nomenclature. 'Isn't the name just the tiniest bit racist?'

I slice the Jew's ears and fry them, together with ground elder
leaves, in duck fat. 'Another classic meal, then,' says Tris,
exaggeratedly peering at the cast-iron skillet on the oven hob. He
has a point. This is not a meal worthy of Rules; this is another
survival special. The Jew's ears are rubbery and insipid and the
ground elder is only minutely improved by being cooked in duck
fat. I need to spend more time experimenting in the kitchen but
where will I find this slippery stuff that is 'more time'?

⟡

When Caesar invaded Britain in 55 BC he found the Celtic inhabitants fermenting the juice of the native crab apple, *Malus
sylvestris*. The Romans titled the drink 'Sicera'. Cider.

It's almost impossible to press apples for cider without breaking into regular choruses, with sub-Wurzel voices, of 'I am a cider drinker.'

This dank November afternoon is no exception. Freda is doing the conducting. 'You've all got to join in when I say ' "Ready" . . . Ready: I am a cider drinker . . .'

We're gathered, the four of us, around the mechanical Vigo press and crusher I once bought in a flush moment. We're standing at what we call the back of the house, but which was once the front. Here, during the building work, gigantic stone slabs were turned up by the digger, including some with runnels, which I recognized as the base of a cider mill. Of the rest of the mill, there was no trace; quite possibly it was sold, like so many others, as a garden ornament. The cider made in the mill would have been from cultivated apple varieties originally imported by the Romans (who found *Malus sylvestris* too tart for their sophisticated palates) and which grew in Trelandon's two orchards, one by the house and one, more sheltered, down by the river. The cider made on the farm, as on all Herefordshire farms, wasn't just for the farmer and his kin: it was part of the workers' wages, 2 quarts/2.25l a day for a man and 1 quart/1.15l for a boy. Once, picking sloes, I found a perfectly preserved earthenware cider bottle, the sort used to carry the liquid wages, under a hedge, mislaid by someone in another age. Brown glass cider bottles, from later times, regularly tip up in the natural recesses of Trelandon; unfortunately these, the suspicion is, were not dumped by thirst-quenched labourers but by the Trelandon farmer who was driven to drink in the 1960s.

For my cider I have picked four sacks of wild crab apples from the trees in the far hedge of House Meadow. Actually, most of them I didn't pick, I shook the tree with a shepherd's crook, so that the apples fell down on to a tarpaulin stretched out across the drainage ditch below. Shaking down apple trees is something I know how to do: one of my earliest memories is of watching my grandfather, Joe Amos, in the cider orchard at the east Herefordshire farm he managed, brown 'smock' (a duster coat) gathered around his waist with baler twine, pulling on the trees with a purpose-made pole with a crook end.

The apples go straight into the spinning steel teeth of the crush, tipped in willy-nilly; only the most rotten and sluggy ones do I bother to pick out and toss into the barrow for Freda's Gloucester Old Spot pigs, Snorty and Primrose.

I've never made cider with crab apples before, which are much smaller and tarter than cultivated varieties. Crabs will some-times turn red, but not up here in hill hedges; our crabs are a thin yellowy-green and only the very topmost have any blush of summer.

As fast as Tris winds the crusher and the pulped apple falls out Penny shovels it into the barrel press, on which I wind the wheel handle to screw down the pressing plate. The surprisingly cloudy brown juice runs out into the cast-iron dish and down the runnel to be caught by Freda's bucket.

Freda takes a test sip of the juice and pronounces it 'disgusting'.

We all take a taste. She's right. It's so astringent that it paralyses the tongue.

'I'm not a cider drinker,' chirps up Tristram.

I'm not sure it's worth carrying on, but Penny points out that crab apples are the sort used in the antique English alcoholic drink lambs wool, so it must be palatable when fermented.

On we go, mashing, pressing, filling, swatting away wasps and sweating till all four sacks are done, and alchemized into 9 gallons/40l of crab-apple juice, stored in a 6.5 gallon plastic fermenting cask in the sitting room. When the fermenting cask is full I tip the surplus into demijohns, which are stopped with plastic fermenting locks. This is the apple juice I want to turn into cider vinegar, which I desperately need as a pickling agent.

I'm standing admiring the bubbling of the fermentation process three days later when Freda runs in, face flushed red and screaming, 'Dad! Dad! Come quickly, the pigs are ill . . . really, really ill.'

I rush out behind her, across the yard to the concrete pig pen, where, sure enough, Snorty and Primrose are in a bad way, walking blindly, robotically, into the wall. Primrose then falls over, her eyes rolling in their slits.

It looks like lead poisoning. I climb into the pen, search around the wall and through the straw but there's no lead anywhere.

I climb back out. I'm at a loss to explain the pigs' sickness. Freda wants me to phone Peter Jinman, the vet, and I'm about to do so when Snorty lets out a belch to be entered in the *Guinness Book of Records*. Simultaneously a jet of green diarrhoea shoots out of her backside. Even at five feet the smell of the diarrhoea is overpowering. And utterly distinctive.

'Um, Freda . . . what have you been feeding the pigs?'

'The pomace, why?'

The pomace is the dried, pressed left-over apple from the juice-making. Like the juice in my fermenting vessels, the pomace has begun to turn into alcohol. Snorty and Primrose are pissed. Bladdered. Sozzled. Drunk.

There's not much to do except let them sleep it off.

Ten weeks later I know how they feel. The cider has long been racked – separated from the sediment by siphoning – and bottled, and should mature for at least another three months but the rows of bottles are a temptation too many.

To say the crab-apple cider is sour and rough is an understatement. It is authentic scrumpy. In the local Herefordshire vernacular it is 'pig-squeal cider' – because that is the noise one involuntarily makes when drinking it.

I manage one pint, leaning against the Aga, when suddenly everything melts into a Dalí painting and I slide down the Aga's front on to the floor. Later I find that the alcohol content is at 10 per cent proof. To make the cider palatable I add half a teaspoon of honey to every bottle. Then I really am a cider drinker.

Pot-roast pheasant with cider

1 old pheasant
1 clove wild garlic, chopped
½ pint/300ml cider
pinch salt
1lb/450g crab apples

Pheasant is best hung for a week in a cool place. An old pheasant is not worth the plucking, so de-skin instead.
Wash the gutted, decapitated, de-winged and de-legged (below the knee) carcase and pat dry. Slice the apples into the base of a casserole and put the pheasant on top. Marinade in cider, salt and chopped garlic for about three hours. Cover tightly and pop into an oven for an hour and a half at 350°F/170°C/Gas Mark 4. Serve with steamed nettles and rowanberry jelly. Or crab-apple jelly, which I make twenty jars of in a kitchen that swelters in the doing. Chestnuts also make a good partner for pheasant, but not when cooked in cider.

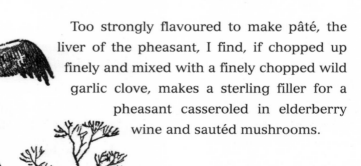

Too strongly flavoured to make pâté, the liver of the pheasant, I find, if chopped up finely and mixed with a finely chopped wild garlic clove, makes a sterling filler for a pheasant casseroled in elderberry wine and sautéd mushrooms.

Sloes, the globose fruits of the blackthorn, are the wild great-grandparents of the damson. Only the colour of the skin, blue going on black, suggests the genetic connection: the flesh of the damson is sweet; the green flesh of the sloe, when bitten into, makes the mouth instantly pucker. Nothing in the hedge hangs more temptingly than the tumescent sloe berry (except the proffered red berries of the deadly nightshade) and I can never quite believe that it is as tart as I recall. But it is, even after frost, which allegedly sweetens. All one can do with the raw sloe berry is spit it out. A berry sweetened with honey, however, can make sloe jelly or sloe wine.

Sloes are guarded by thorns up to three inches long. Such Brobdingnagian spines are, at least, easy to see, thus easy to avoid. In this first week of December, when the frost forms on the cows' red backs by four in the afternoon and darkness seeps in by 4.30, I am not bothered about picking sloes; like crab apples they can be shaken down on to a tarpaulin with a shepherd's crook. After hawthorn and hazel, blackthorn is the commonest of the hedge shrubs at Trelandon; the long hedge that eels down along-side the quarry track is nothing but blackthorn. It's been a good year for berries and two hours of beating produces a sackful of sloes.

Sloes make a wine so red that Georgian fraudsters used to pass it off as port. For me the advantage of the sloe is that the greyish bloom frequently seen on the skin is natural yeast. With some added apple skins, I get eight pints' worth of sloes ferment-ing without bought-in yeast, although the concoction needs to fight with the dogs for the fire's warmth to stay alive. After five days, I put the wine into a demijohn to continue fermenting. I take a proprietorial sip.

Even allowing for its youth, the wine is bitter and dry. My

fault, because I knowingly skimped on the honey, putting in a mere 12oz/350g. I try to make amends now by adding three large tablespoons of honey and topping up with apple juice. Only time, a year of it, will tell whether the wine is good.

Something about that sip of astringency knocks my confidence in sloe wine. The remainder of the sloes are mashed, boiled and mixed with honey to make a game sauce.

Sloe wine

3lb/1.35kg ripe sloes
8oz/225g particularly 'yeasty' sloes
1¼lb/600g clear honey
8 pints/4.5l water
skins of 5 wild apples

Put the sloes into a fermentation bucket and bang with a potato masher to break the skins. The alternative is to put them through a fruit crusher, if you have one. Meanwhile, have the water on the way to boiling. Spoon 1lb/450g of the honey into a saucepan, then pour over enough boiling water to cover. Stir the honey with a wooden spoon so it dissolves in the water. Tip the honeyed water over the mashed sloes, then add the remainder of the water. When cool add the yeasty sloes and the apple skins. Cover and leave for 5 days in a warm place, stirring at least once a day.

Strain the liquid into a demijohn and add the remaining honey with a teaspoon. Top up, if necessary, with apple juice. Fit airlock. Leave for 3 months in a warm place to enable fermentation to complete. Siphon into bottles and allow the wine to mature for a year.

By chance, as I'm labouring in the kitchen with the sloe sauce, I catch an item on Radio 4 which suggests that, as a rule of thumb, hedges can be dated by measuring a twenty-yard strip and noting the number of tree and shrub species.

On closer investigation in Hereford library, where the vault yields up a copy of *Discover Hedgerows* by David Street and Rosamond Richardson, the actual equation is more precise: age of hedge = (number of species in a 30-yard stretch × 110) + 30 years, and was devised by Dr Max Hooper in the 1960s.

Armed with Hooper's hedge-dating reckoner I set off to survey the hedges around the farm. On average the hedges turn out to be four species rich in the requisite thirty yards. The species vary a little in each section, but are some combination of dog rose, hazel, elder, alder, hawthorn, ash, willow, holly, blackthorn, oak and field maple. As one might expect, the prickly blackthorn and hawthorn predominate, being the stock-farmer of yore's best means for keeping animals in and thus likely to have been the plants with which the hedge was first laid; everything else, maybe with the exception of some oaks, is a johnny-come-lately colonizer.

By Max Hooper's device, the hedges on the farm were established some 500 years ago, a dating that chimes nicely with the estimate of the council's conservation architect regarding the house's vexed upper windows: 'Say, early 1600s.' Two hedges, though, are much older. Road Field hedge has eight species (holly, hazel, field maple, hawthorn, blackthorn, dog rose, ash and oak) every thirty yards, meaning that it is probably as old as the lane from Longtown to Michaelchurch it borders. More puzzling is the hedge which runs alongside the track down to the farm, which is consistently six species rich every thirty yards, making it two hundred years older than the farmhouse it serves.

Eventually the answer dawns. On the long grass slope from the house to the Escley valley's bottom, there is evidence of an old trackway to the river, and thence to the quarry on the other side. I had always supposed that this track was created purposely to bring stone up for the building of the house. Of course, I have the matter back to front: the house was built on the existing track to the quarry. We live on Quarry Road.

And so another circle is turned: I spent the first years of my life on another Quarry Road.

My hunch that the farm track was once a public road is easily proved. In the village shop, which has just stocked facsimile Ordnance Survey maps from 1830, I spread the Longtown sheet on the counter and there, from the Michaelchurch road to the Escley river, is the bold brown line of a road going past our house.

The oaks are rusting red, the hazels turning yellow and the ashes fading to a sick-faced green. Only the alders by the river are keeping their colour. The lane, where the hedges have not yet been cut, is a tunnel of flaming arboreta.

Who needs New England? I think as I tramp down the track, blackbirds and fieldfares tumbling out before me, their meal of haws interrupted. The game bag is empty but the heart is full is my next, pompous thought.

I would be less sanguine if there were not two rabbits swinging dead in the cow byre. As things are, I can even see the funny side of what happens next.

On going into the house I put the shotgun away in its safe. Then I happen to look out of the window: two male pheasants are in the orchard. Quickly unlocking the gunsafe, I grab the shotgun, load two cartridges of No. 6, sneak to the back door, open it and, crouching down, advance up the short slope to the orchard.

When I stand up to shoot the pheasants, I see that they are bracketed by a squirrel in the hedge and a pigeon in the pear tree. Sighting me, the pheasants run towards the stock fence at the end of the orchard. The field behind belongs to John and Claire Rooney (Janet and Gerry having moved), who rent it out to Kevin Powell the dairy farmer. His Friesians are standing there, chewing the cud. I can't shoot the pheasants for fear of hitting the cattle. Swinging the gun round, I find that both the squirrel and the pigeon have fled.

The coldest day of winter so far and the grass is frosted into blind white fronds. It's impossible to walk quietly. The grass crackles, snaps and pops like a child's breakfast. The thermometer on the yard registers −4°C. I take the long way down to the river, intending to walk along the bank towards the pool where I saw the mallard yesterday, hoping that the rush of the water over the stones will mask the sound of my approach. Holding the shotgun in two hands I stalk, stooped down, along the alder-lined bank.

I'm almost at the pool when off to the right a sparrowhawk swooshes along the top of the field hedge. Pockets of redwings burst out. The sparrowhawk ignores them and glides up into an oak, surveys truculently, a teenager stirring up trouble for the fun of it, before flapping off down the valley.

It's not only the redwings the joy-flying sparrowhawk has panicked. I can hear the mallard lifting off the water, their wings clipping the bare treetops as they break away.

No duck today. I scavenge around the copse but the Jew's ears on the elder have shrivelled to the thinness of an elastic band, and the shawl of golden chanterelles has disappeared in a perverse magic trick. In the low folds of a hazel tree I find some fallen hazelnuts, though winkling them out is exquisite agony through fingers inflamed with prickings of yesterday's rosehip-gathering. And the weeks of sloe-picking.

With festering but empty hands I walk back to the house, arriving on the yard just as the Audi estate pulls in, Penny having dropped the children off at school. Opening the Audi's door she grimaces, 'I've an injured pheasant in the car.'

It seems that Freda spotted the pheasant by the roadside on the way to school and plaintively asked if it could be picked up, 'looked after and repaired by Daddy'.

In the back footwell lies said pheasant, a cock bird, young with smooth legs, hunched on a newspaper. All the aspects of a Grimm fairy tale are beginning to accrue here. Instead of being brought to safety, the pheasant has been delivered into the hands of a ravenous wolf.

Lifting the pheasant out into the crisp bright sunshine, I can see that its wing is hanging broken and probably the upper thigh. The right side of its head is bruised, the eye almost closed. Most of all, its copper plumage burnished by the sun, I can see how painstakingly beautiful it is.

Eat the pheasant and have a full stomach, or repair it and fill my daughter's heart with joy? In truth, when my thoughts clear, I realize that there's no quandary. The gorgeous bronze bird of paradise is beyond repair. What is needed is a mercy killing. I tenderly put the pheasant down on to the concrete and leave it for a few moments to bask in the growing warmth of the winter morning. Fetching the Weihrauch, I load a pellet and put the barrel point-blank behind the pheasant's eye. There's no soul in the eye of a pheasant, an absence which makes them among the easiest of birds to kill. This one, however, has a pale, bright intelligent eye.

I suck in my cheeks and brace myself. I pull the trigger and the pheasant, despite its injuries, does a terrible flapping ballet of death. Another pellet. Fluorescent scarlet beads of blood slowly form against the royal blue of the pheasant's head, and drop on to the yard. The twitching stops.

It's too much to eat the bird, too much like a betrayal. In the yawning space of the afternoon I dig a hole and bury it, laying atop an old sandstone slab, to prevent the foxes from having what I could not.

In mid-November it snows, but not enough to keep the children off school. After driving them to Monmouth, where we are the only car with a layer of icing on the roof, I return home and walk like an excited child myself in the fields of white; by a wave of a wand in the night, the land has been turned into a mountain kingdom fit for the Snow Queen. My mind, I know, should be on baser things, like breakfast, but snow is nature's beautifier.

In Bank Field I spot a stoat, not yet in winter ermine, playing a rolling game in the snow all by itself. Hunger, eventually, gets the better of wonder, and I look for spoors. There are the dash'n'dots of rabbits and the loping footfalls of the fox and that is all. I give up hunting without really trying; I don't feel like killing, or seeing spilt blood on the snow, so I head homeward for the usual dandelion coffee and hazelnut muesli. On a whim, while eating breakfast, I google Great Trelandon, which returns a surprise. There, on pages uploaded by the local history society, are the particulars for 'An Excellent Farm Known as "Great Trelandon"' from 1920, when the farm was auctioned off by its owner, the Marquis of Abergavenny, whose family had held the lands since 1422. What was presumably a bad day for the marquis was a good one for the auctioneers, who had 165 other lots, extending to 2,670 acres, to sell on his behalf at the Angel Hotel in Abergavenny. Lot 157 is catalogued as a 'modern stone-built slate-covered house, farm buildings' and 60 acres, 3 roods, 18 perches of land. We live in the 'farm buildings'; the 'modern' house, built in 1898, belongs to John and Claire up the track. The tenant at the time of the sale is listed as Mr Williams, who paid £70 0s. 0d. rent, along with a tithe of £5 12s. 8d. and a land tax of £1 8s. 2d.

A plan of the land accompanies the particulars. Over this I pore on the warping screen of the aged Dan monitor until my eyes ache and I need to print it out. Lot 157 is coloured in grey. Almost all the surrounding farms were also under the hammer, save for the Grove to the south and a straggling smallholding, Brooklands, which separated Great Trelandon from the Wain (Lot 156, 'A Capital Farm', a description, I note, which puts it a subtle cut above Trelandon's 'Excellent'). Looking at the plan, I can see only loss. In the near ninety years since the auction the farm has been snipped at, hacked at and finally bisected. More than land has been cut; the prestigious local agricultural show, once sited on the top field, has gone to another farm. Self-sufficiency, the very soul of a small Herefordshire farm, was removed the day the river orchard was grubbed up. For there, clearly marked on the plan, is an orchard extending to 1.74 acres alongside the Escley. I have long known that the two decrepit apple trees by the river bend were remnants of an orchard, but I had not guessed it was so extensive.

Shuffling on my coat and wellingtons, I roll out into the razor-edged cold, shoulders hunched up into my neck, hands in pockets, and tack through the snow to the river. The mountain is decapitated by dense white cloud, and redwings and fieldfares, driven south by the inclemency of the weather, swarm in the sky. *Chaka-chak-chaka-chak.* Standing on the site of the orchard, the plan in my mind's eye, I can see that an isolated, wiry hawthorn bush in Bank Field was once part of a hedge that separated the orchard off. I wonder at the siting of the orchard; on the one hand, the sheltered river bottom would have prevented the blossom being blown off the trees by the Longtown wind; on the other, this river bottom is a frost hollow, which kills the self-same delicate pink flowers. But that is the story of farming on the edge: lose some, lose some. Mooching around the two lichen-splattered apple trees, on an impulse I reach into the fork of the eating apple tree, whose fruit has a sweet custard-yellow flesh. There, in the slush, I feel an apple, and reaching it down find that it is firm and almost unblemished. It is not wild fruit, but the unkempt state of the tree makes it passably feral. I know, biting into it on a winter's day, that it feels like a gift.

By the following morning, the snow has melted, causing the Escley to rise. Looking down the river as it rages past, I see a white fleece trapped against a fallen trunk, and for a moment think a sheep has fallen in. But it is not a sheep, just a length of froth, made by the churning water. Strung all down the river are similar white bundles, making up a flock of foam.

The torrent of brown rolling water exercises a near fatal attraction for Bluebell, Edith's four-month-old puppy, who slyly made herself part of the family, thus making it too painful to sell her. Bluebell is a pure expression of her genes: Labradors were originally bred to retrieve fishermen's nets from the cruel Canadian Atlantic, not partridge from rolling English country estates. And so Bluebell plunges into the churning Escley for a swim as is her wont. The shock of the cold mountain water would probably do for a human, never mind its torrential speed. Although initially bewildered by the force of the water, Bluebell goes with the flow but angles a course to the bank. My admiration for the aquatic components of her DNA and my relief at her escape are short-lived. She runs back up the field, seal-sleek with wetness, then down to the bank and relaunches herself into the water. Riding the river does not go well this time; she surfs for forty yards, before crashing into the bare-skinned corpse of a fallen elm, and then scrabbling alongside to the bank. She fails to make it to the bank; she becomes trapped in some antique barbed wire coiling into the water from a broken fence. She yelps, and I can see her starting to panic, churning the water with her front legs.

By the time I have sprinted down the field in wellingtons and scaled the wire stock fence on to the thin bank top, Bluebell's eyes are bulging white with terror as the tentacle of wire tightens. They say that before you die the whole of your life flashes before you. All I can say is that before you save a dog from peril all the stories you have ever read about dog owners dying in the attempt to rescue their pooches race through your head. You know the stories: the ones where the dog saves itself from death anyway. And now I'm about to ignominiously remove myself from the gene pool. A sheer four feet below me, Bluebell is tiring, but her eyes look up at me filled with what I imagine is hope. Mine I am sure are brimming with fear. The water is swirling. The narrow foot of bank I am standing on is greasy. All I can think to do is kneel down on the bank, hold on to the fence and lean down with my other hand and pull the barbed wire off Bluebell's back. She may be trapped but she is not still, so I cut my hand on the barbs. Shit. I lean over again, intending to grab her collar, when I realize that she is now standing in front of me, shaking herself. Somehow she has not only extricated herself from the wire but climbed a near-vertical bank.

I now have two useful pieces of advice to pass on to my children. The first is: beer followed by wine is fine, but wine followed by beer makes you feel queer (as in unwell, not homosexual). The second is: never, never, never try to rescue a dog from danger.

—

In the twilight of the sixties, when I was a very short-trousered boy, I wrote and illustrated a primary school project on plucky British polar explorers. The stiff upper lip of Scott at the South Pole touched me, but I was far more impressed, looking through the picture book from which I traced my drawings, with the tale of Sir John Franklin, RN, and his epic march through the Canadian Arctic winter in 1821.

Although bereft of supplies like Scott, Franklin and his men survived. They did so by eating *tripe de roche*. Rock lichen. I remember imitating Franklin by going into the orchard at home and scraping some green lichen scabs off the apple trees and putting them in my mouth.

The scene is repeated today, but distorted and enlarged in time's mirror. I am standing under the standard apple tree in Trelandon's orchard, breaking off great lumps of grey lichen, a flock of long-tailed tits peeping away in the hazel hedge. Biologically, lichen are dual organisms formed from a symbiotic relationship between a fungus and an algae, but so completely conjoined that they look like an entirely new being. Lichens can be divided into three basic forms: *crustose*, or crust-like; *foliose* or leaf-like; and *fruticose* or stalked, such as the lichen I am picking. All lichens are believed to be edible except for wolf moss (*Letharia vulpina*). Rock lichen, as eaten by Franklin, is considered a delicacy by the Japanese. Lichen contains carbohydrate, which is useful for survival. I am not in those dire straits. The reason that I am gathering lichen is because I am tired of thin soup, and lichen is reputed to be a thickener.

Lichen grows almost everywhere on Earth, but its favourite places are where the wind blows pure. At Trelandon, the lichen covers the bark of trees and the stones of the buildings. To offset the carbon inhalations of the children, who go to school in a town, I forever rail at them, 'Go and get some fresh air!'

Disappointingly, the lichen I gather, when boiled, shows no tendency to thicken or jell. Ah, but what an intriguing smell emanates from it, one which is heavy with the saline tang of the sea. This seems entirely appropriate, since the lichen picked from the tree looked like seaweed stranded after an ancient flood. The taste is similar to seaweed, although mustier, and I use it to flavour soups when I sicken of game.

⎯

These are the dog days of dog training. Down to the river we go, the weather as volatile as the stock market, sunburst to cloudburst almost in the same instant, Edith walking to heel. A rabbit flushes, bounds across the Finger into the copse, Edith lurches forward. I pull hard on her collar and tap her nose. 'No!' I can't fault the rabbits, who are obliging props in this business of training Edith as a gundog. Another white-bob-tailed coney runs harum scarum for home, and again Edith coils. 'No!' Another tap on the wet black nose. As I trudge uphill through Bog Field, my footsteps forming instant pools in the sodden reedy grass, a rabbit bolts off to the left along the hedge. I slip, miss Edith's collar and she pounds off. I blow thrice on the Thunderer whistle for her to come back, the peeps tearing the fabric of silence. She feigns deafness. Unfortunately, this leaves me with no alternative; I'm the alleged top dog, and have to prove it. Off I run after her, through the mud, cursing. When I catch up with her, she has her head down a burrow, her tail wagging high. I grab her by the neck and shake her, just as her mother would have done as punishment when she was a puppy. She drops her head in submission. Warily we walk back together, she on the lead.

The mantra of dog training is to end the session on a positive note. On the yard, I toss the green canvas game dummy and order her to retrieve. She collects but drops it, not at my feet but a yard short.

'OK, Edith, let's do something else.' I whistle for her to sit. She goes down like a stone. And there she stays sitting on the yard, while I go off, make a cup of tea and come back. She has not moved. 'Edith, good girl!' I feed her a piece of cheese and release her from her command with the F-word. She rolls on her back, legs kicking in the air. At sitting, if at nothing else, Edith is still world class. On one occasion I forgot to release her from a sitting command and she was still there an hour later, at the end of the hall waiting for me.

Why do dogs obey us anyway? Is it fear of punishment, or hope of reward? It might be love, actually. Freda's Jack Russell is putty in her small hot hands, and goes – of his own volition – to sleep under her bed at the same time she goes to bed. Despite being pack leader, the feeder of the gang, I meanwhile cannot do a thing with him.

—

What Nature taketh away, Nature giveth. Two days of endless rain once again swell the river into a Willy Wonka chocolate torrent which, when it abates, leaves a stranded tide of thousands of edible hazelnuts.

—

I have noticed that I have again accorded Nature a capital letter. What lies beyond the window pane is not anything as neutral or insipid as the 'environment'. The more time I spend outside, walk-ing through the fields, standing under trees, gazing up at the moon, the more certain I become that the living system around me is self-conscious, architected, immense and, ultimately, a verbally ineffable spiritual reality. One can harmonize with Nature – Pan, Creation, Spirit, Mother Earth, call it what you will – but only on its terms. Little Lewis-Stempel, Big God.

There is an ethical side effect to my concordance with Nature: since I increasingly appreciate the animals I shoot, I am not inured to their dispatch. I still don't *like* killing, which is to the good. When you like killing, when the act of taking animal life is as instrumental and uncomplicated as turning the page of a book, you have become morally coarsened. You have ceased to value Nature. You have ceased to live yourself.

How rats fit into this ethical system I do not fathom. The rats are back. So is the Exterminator with his bucket of poison.

—

At the back end of November I become ill. Outside while hunting and gathering, gathering and hunting, I have been shivering in rain for days, unable to get my body warm to the core, despite wearing thermal this and thermal that, a sweater, gilet and coat and so doing a passable impression of the Michelin man. On the dark morning of 23 November, I for once heed the advice of my archetypal wife: 'For God's sake stay in bed. You'll only get worse if you don't.' In truth, I could do no other than huddle foetal-shaped under the warm duvet, clutching a hot-water bottle, because I have not the strength to get up. My body might be fitter but it is also thinner (down in weight by a stone to a shade over twelve stone), and less able to insulate itself against the cold of the biblical rains. By my estimate I am consuming well over 2,500 calories a day, much of them from honey and fruit jelly. The hidden user of these calories is anxiety; I am fast running out of bramble jelly, elderflower cordial and crab apples. An apple a day keeps the doctor away. One apple is all I can afford.

When I arise from my sick bed I find that Tris has borrowed the Weihrauch and knocked the Hawke telescopic sight out of true. To re-zero the gun I spend hours plinking at targets like a demented Billy the Kid.

I never get bored walking around the same tract of land every day. It is like reading a newspaper: there is always something new. And it is rarely trivial: Nature doesn't do the inconsequential.

In the Finger, where Copse Field sticks a loop into the Escley, I watch a gun-blue nuthatch go about its business, now walking down the tree, now walking up, looking for insects and stray hazelnuts. (The 'hatch' in the bird's name is from the French, *hacher*, to chop.) It ignores me, and after a few minutes I ignore it and decide to check on the stock of ground ivy that creeps under the alders. A shock. Initially I can't see the ground ivy in the scrub – for its appearance has changed so dramatically after the frost.

Blotchy and white, the ground ivy's small round leaves cower where only days ago they were verdant and go-getting. I am longing for fresh greenstuff to eat. Used in small amounts in spring as part of a mixed salad, ground ivy is passable; outside that dish and that season, ground ivy is wretched and medicinal-tasting. (You will instantly know on trying it why it was once the country remedy for catarrh.) But boiled it assumes the most uplifting emerald-green hue.

I finish my morning walk, the draughts of north wind pulling at my collar, by going up to Road Field. Having plainly decided that the grass was greener on my side of the fence (which, in fairness, it was), 250 sheep have broken through from the Grove next door. The six-acre field throbs with white-faced Welsh Mountains, who barely bother to break off eating to baa at me. The crop of fine young sorrel that was clinging on unseasonably amid the green baize has been trampled and shat upon. I decide to take the philosophical approach to this news: I still have plenty of sorrel, albeit sorrel preserved in cider in Kilner jars, and anyway, too much sorrel is bad for one's liver, due to the oxalic acid in the leaves. Besides I owe Gwyn, the sheep farmer who rents the land at the Grove, a favour; last year, he was more than decent when my Hebridean ram broke into the Grove and caused some of his white ewes to have black lambs in the family.

Sorrel, a member of the dock genus, takes its name from the Old French *surele*, meaning sour, which it surely is, but in the pleasantest lemony fashion. Until the time of Henry VIII sorrel was cultivated and used, chiefly, as a green sauce for fish by grinding the leaves into a paste and adding sugar and vinegar, although little of the latter was needed because of sorrel's inherent acidity. In summer, when mowing hay, farm labourers would chew on the leaves of *Rumex acetosa* to slake their thirst, though whether this worked because of the succulence of the leaves or their saliva-producing sharpness I was never sure until now.

Standing in Road Field, letting my memory amble back to summer's haze and then picturing my biting into a sorrel leaf – ah! Even the thought of its sourness makes my mouth gush with water, so much so that I have to spit at the sheep.

A CALENDAR OF WILD FOOD AT TRELANDON

November

Nettles, dandelion, Jew's ear, pheasant, sorrel, docks,

 pigeon, rabbit, rosehips, crab apples, haws, lichen,

sow thistle, hogweed

A MISTY MORNING, the view and the valley muffled in opacity. But I have a cunning plan of Blackadderian proportion: to make a hide on the bank of the Finger with a two-way view, one on to a stretch of the Escley where the mallard like to swim and the other on to the copse, specifically a dead hazel the wood pigeon loiter on. My head is full of grand designs of woven willow and hazel, but my heart is true to my inability to produce anything arty-crafty, so I go down to the river with an armful of green garden netting, a bow saw, a shotgun and the Weihrauch air rifle slung over my shoulder. The air is heavy with the interference of moisture, which clings to the grass heads, turning them into a million mini candyflosses. When I arrive at the Finger, where a blue tit whistles a welcome from somewhere behind a veil of fog, my pitch is even better than I remembered because two stock fences come together there, with a gap between them of about four feet. The gap, now bunged up with straggling brambles instead of a gate, was to allow the extrication of sheep who had broken through to the bank but could not find their way back. With gloves and bow saw I quickly clear a four-foot-square space and drape the netting over the top and down the front and back, weighing this down with hazel brush. In what I think is a nice natural touch, I weave massive quantities of ivy into the netting. One of the other sides is screened by brambles, but how to screen the entrance now that the netting has run out? Walking up into the Finger I notice the kids' home-made wooden raft at the end, the grandly named HMS *Trelandon*, long since stranded and left to her fate. I lift it cautiously, because the No. 1 rule of the countryside is that any timber or corrugated iron that has lain somewhere for long will have a scuttling life form under it. This time there is not a rat or grass snake underneath, only a bank vole, which looks back at me with its cartoonishly too-close eyes, before running hither and thither in the grass until it finds a new place to hide. Dragging the implausibly heavy HMS *Trelandon* – I remember now: we had to stick polystyrene surfboards under it to make it float – back to my den, I find that it fits perfectly as a door, even if it does give me a hernia pulling it closed from inside.

In the den I sit lotus-like, with guns loaded and on safety, a plastic feed sack under my arse. Even in today's reduced visibility I can see thirty yards of river stretched behind me, and the edge of the copse across the grassy Finger is fifteen yards away. Little tumescent torpedoes of catkins hang down from the hazels and a handful of deluded, unseasonal buttercups infiltrate the grass. Location, location, location is the estate agent's buzz phrase; it is the sniper hunter's too. A mere hour passes before I hear, above the slap and gurgle of the Escley as it runs over the rocks on the bend, the sound of whirring wings. Ducks. Lots of ducks. They are somewhere overhead, circling. Now they land on the river. Carefully turning my body and leaning back I peep through a slit hole.

There *are* ducks. Unfortunately, they are the wrong sort. A flotilla of mandarins is paddling downstream. Originally from the Far East, the British feral population comes from birds released in Berkshire, Surrey and Buckinghamshire in the 1920s. A pair or two nest nearby, somewhere in the brookside trees which give them both shelter and the mast on which they survive the winter. The mandarin drakes, with their exotic hues, should brighten such a vaporous day, yet today the presence of these alien and protected birds only causes a welling of despondency.

Stupid with frustration, I bang on HMS *Trelandon* with the butt of the Weihrauch to scare the mandarin off. They lift with ease and manoeuvre with wondrous agility through the trees. I sit on for a while hoping for a mallard, but none comes. A rabbit, then another, ventures out of the copse into the field. Eeny meeny miny, moe. I shoot the first one. Too tired for finesse, I broadside it with the shotgun, despite this being optimistically loaded with lead-free shot for ducks.

How sick I am of eating coneys.

———

If I have misjudged one thing on my wild food odyssey it is the sheer amount of work necessary. Because once you've picked or dispatched your food you have to prepare it. Every time. The exceptions – like blackberries – can be counted on the fingers of one hand. I'm tired. And being outside every day for six weeks has taken its toll. My face is thinner and its veins have been whipped to the surface by the wind. When I look in the mirror I see the raw face of Joe Amos, my hop-farmer grandfather, who worked outside for sixty years.

So I don't have the time or the energy to maintain all our sheep. Some sheep have to go. The decision is easy because our flock of rare-breed Hebridean sheep is not the exquisite artefact it once was. Small and black with horns, Hebrideans are among the most primitive of ovines, unchanged since the Vikings farmed them a thousand years ago. They look good in parkland and feltmakers like my wife covet their fleece, which is the brown of plain chocolate.

Except that some of our Hebrideans are no longer pure of blood.

We don't only have Hebrideans. We also have Action Ram, an orphaned Suffolk × Shetland who was bottle-fed by the children years ago. Action is a pet, who can be stroked and who will eat beet nuts off your hand. He is also a wrinkled black-faced monster, who once near butted me to death (it took the arcing swing of a sledgehammer to his head to halt him). I regularly swear I'll have him castrated or turned into dog food but somehow I never do. Pride is part of it, for he once did a trick that made a sheep farmer's wife drop her jaw in amazement: he'd escaped and when I collected him I told him to jump in the back of the Audi estate (the Land Rover, being a Land Rover, having decided that even a three-day British Leyland week was too much). And he did.

He also has bollocks that draw sighs of admiration. A *Viz* cartoonist would hesitate to draw such unfeasibly large bollocks for fear of claims of exaggeration.

It's the product of Action's bollocks that trouble me now. In an epic one-night stand last year, Action managed to bulldoze a fence to reach the Hebridean ewes and impregnate every one of them. It is possible to siphon out ram semen from ewe vaginas but there are limits. Looking over the sheep now as they graze in Bank Field (our predecessors here did not waste energy on nomenclature: other field names include the Paddock and Road Field), the flock is an embarrassment of shades and sizes. The products of the ovine miscegenation must go. We'll be laughing stock for our livestock. There's also the cruelty – as I see it – in raising tender little sheep and being unable to eat them myself. In fact I no longer see the sheep as sheep, just a collection of butcher's cuts and joints on all fours.

I place an advertisement in the *Hereford Times* classifieds: 'Fifty cross-breed lambs and hoggets. Offers.'

The ad comes out on Thursday and that evening a dealer called Ian Maund phones, sounds me out and arranges to come around eleven on Sunday morning to look the sheep over. If he likes them, he'll take them there and then.

'Do you have a dog,' I ask, 'because it would save me rounding up the sheep myself with the bucket?'

'Oh aye, I've got a dog. I'll bring him all right.'

At thirty minutes past eleven on Sunday a large Nissan pick-up rattles into the yard. Behind the Nissan is a trailer with the painted legend: *Ian P. Maund. Cattle dealer and stores.*

Rangy, smiling, a fellow fortysomething, Ian Maund hops out. So do his two young sons.

I compliment Ian Maund on his shiny Ifor Williams aluminium stock trailer. 'Nice trailer, by the way. What is it, twin-deck?'

'Single-deck, but it's got interior doors . . .'

There are few things farmers like more than discussing kit. I know some who buy the 'journals', the trade magazines, just to look at the pictures. Agricultural porn.

Penny, Tris, Freda and Ian's two boys, Nat and James, sigh loudly.

'Right then, better go and look at these sheep,' says Ian, assuming a businesslike air. 'I'll get the dog.' He disappears round to the back of the pick-up and reappears with a young collie sheepdog, quivering with excitement, on a lead. 'Shall I let him go, Nat?'

'No! Don't do that, Dad, he'll run off.'

A sheepdog that runs off? Such is the first portent of the disaster that is to come.

'What's the dog's name?' I ask Nat.

'Rocky.'

Rocky, straining on his leash, leads the party down the yard into the fields below the house. The bottom three fields are interconnected, with no real fencing between them, but it is the work of only moments to interrupt the sheep and move them maa-ing to the topmost field. Sheep like going uphill; it's their natural reaction to danger. All the while Ian's looking the sheep over; I'm not expecting a fortune and Ian's not offering it. We agree a price for the lot and shake hands. All that remains is to pen the sheep.

Ian walks across to the middle of the field where Nat is standing patiently with the impatient Rocky.

Holding Rocky's head between his hands, Ian looks into Rocky's eyes. 'Now listen to me, Rocky, you're going to be a good dog and pen the sheep,' says Ian, pointing at the sheep and the corner pen fifty yards from them.

I am severely impressed by this pre-programming of Rocky.

So is Rocky. Unleashed, he rockets to the startled sheep, snaps at their heels, and starts bringing them across towards the pen.

'That's it, Rocky! Bring 'em on!'

It is at this point that Rocky decides that shepherding sheep is not half as much fun as chasing them. He darts to the middle of the tight flock, snapping and barking and jumping.

The flock explodes in all directions, like someone dropping a hand grenade in a bale of cotton.

'Rocky! Bloody get here or I'll warm your arse!' bellows Ian in a voice that echoes down the valley clear to Pandy six miles away.

Rocky, not liking Ian's attitude, decides to run up to Freda to say hello. Followed by a licky greeting to me, to Penny, to Tris, before James grabs him by the collar.

We all troop down to Copse Field, spread out in a line and drive the straggled pockets of sheep back up again. The kids are quietly enjoying themselves. Penny, Ian and I are already getting hot with the walking.

'To think,' I say to Ian, 'some lucky sods are still in bed this morning and not chasing bloody sheep.'

'Ah,' says Ian, 'poor them I say on a glorious morning like this.'

At the top of Bog Field, Rocky is once again sent off on his penning errand, with a startlingly similar result to the first time.

'Rocky, you bastard! I'll warm your arse for you . . .'

We go back down, drive the sheep up . . .

After Rocky's fourth failed attempt at penning the sheep I go and get a bucket of sheep nuts and stand, somewhat embarrassed, by the pen and shout, 'Sheep! Sheep!'

The tamest sheep come running to the lure and follow me into the pen, and I quickly close the gate. About eleven are in. After an hour I've got all the sheep in save for seven refuseniks who won't come close. It is then that Rocky finally does some penning. Nat puts him on a lead and, tugging him, runs up and down behind the sheep.

The sheep, startled by this strange conjoined animal, bolt and join their companions in the pen. I run in behind them and drag the last gate closed.

I look at my watch. We've been rounding up the sheep for three hours. Nat and Rocky walk up. Rocky looks at the sheep and barks proudly.

—

Although we sell off more livestock, we keep back twenty-five pure-bred sheep, plus ten sheep which are classified by the children as pets and faithful retainers, Freda's two pigs, and four Red Poll cows, who sail under the names of Margot, Miriam, Mirabelle and Melissa. Red Polls, which in my childhood were a common sight on British farms, are now officially a rare breed and our quartet represents about 1 per cent of the national herd. Somewhere within me burns a small candle of expectation that I will pick up farming once again, so selling them is a false economy. Besides, we have had 'the girls' for years and they are part of the landscape, wherever we have lived. I also like feeding them in winter. Red Polls, which were originally bred in East Anglia to withstand the wind ravaging off the North Sea, are as tough as the boots which could be made from their conker-coloured hides, and so we 'out winter' them. Breaking open the silage bales, with their pungent smell of pickled grass, on a raw winter's morn as the sun rises behind Merlin's Hill to catch the breath of the cows as they begin their contented munching is as good as farming gets. The worse the weather, the more I like it. Farmers will give all sorts of explanations as to why they farm – they know nothing else, they need to perpetuate a family holding, they desire to put food on people's plates – but if you scratch them deep enough you will find the truth; they actually like the struggle against the elements, they like endless hard work. Especially hill farmers: they are willing martyrs to the cause of being the last hard folk, the last individuals in Britain. A few Christmases ago, when everyone else was eating mince pies and sipping Croft's sherry in the hiatus before lunch, I bumped into a neighbour, Lindsay Lloyd, who farms at the top of Cwm Hill.

As our Land Rovers drew level on the lane, we wound down the windows and hailed each other with the season's greetings.

'Not busy eating and drinking then, Lindsay?' I asked.

Lindsay, who was then in his early seventies and working sixteen-hour days, shook his grey curls.

'You've got to check the stock, haven't you, John?' he replied. 'There's a heifer who's not too clever and I need to keep a bit of an eye on her.'

'Not too clever' is dialect for unwell. Lindsay added, 'It's nice to be out of the house, isn't it? In the fresh air.'

And that was the truth of it. Neither of us probably needed to be checking or feeding stock for the third time that morning. It was just something we wanted to do.

Winter, with its seeping cold, its miserable rain, its incessant wind, its cruel frost and its biting snow flurries – bring it on.

Some nights, just for the sheer heaven of it, I walk the fields in the dark. I never take a torch, for the whole purpose of the exercise is to enjoy the night as Nature intended it. And anyway, torches remind me of lamping for rabbits and the endless hours I spend looking along the black barrel of a gun.

Tonight the December moon is fat, silvering the fields in its light. It's cold enough this high up for the grass to be crisping with frost, and the crunch of my feet as I walk is the only sound I can hear save for the far-off yipping of a fox and the gush of the Escley. I can see, though, the silhouette of the little owl on its gatepost and it allows me to within twenty yards or so before it flaps noiselessly away.

I stand in the middle of Copse Field and play a favourite game: how few houses I can spot. There are three lights across on the mountain, John and Claire's house up the track, the pub way down the valley; on Merlin's Hill there are the lights from the Sett and Old Court; up the valley there's only the Wain Farm. That's it as far as the eye can see in every direction.

Overhead stretches the canopy of the stars. Looking up at the myriad points of light I do not doubt that God exists and I wonder suddenly if religious observation has declined in direct proportion to the growth of light pollution.

A day later I'm in Hereford reference library sheltering from the rain alongside the tramps and the heavy metal fan in a Girlschool T-shirt, when I spot a leaflet produced by the Campaign for the Protection of Rural England entitled 'Night Blight in the West Midlands'. A satellite picture shows a vast red and yellow amoeba of saturated light devouring the dark skies. I track to Longtown with my finger; it's in one of the few refuges of true black, crowded into the absolute western edge of Herefordshire.

Once again I determine to make the children value the dark, and that evening drag them out on the yard. Cloud blocks out the stars and moonlight. The children are just an arm's length away but I can only sense them, not see them.

'Look at that,' I say. 'How many lights can you see?'

'Six,' says Tris.

'I only make it five,' I reply.

'Ah, but you haven't included the light from our sitting room,' he trumps, teen smart.

'There's a car light on Merlin's Hill,' adds Freda.

We've played this game before. They, never having known city lights, take the moleskin night for granted.

But even the pedantry of unwilling children can find no more than seven human lights in the valley under the Black Mountains.

———

The time the children love the dark is when we go lamping. And I've bought a new lamp, a 5-million-candlepower torch with a glass the size of a dinner plate. Impatiently I wait the twelve hours demanded by the instruction manual for the torch to charge and then we take it out into the December dark.

It's the Motörhead of torches. Switching it on almost blasts me backwards.

'Awesome,' declares Tris as the torch's beam columns into the sky.

'Useful for spotting Jerry bombers,' I suggest.

You can certainly spot rabbits with it. When I direct the torch beam into the field in front of the house, three sets of little pink rabbit eyes blink back. The beam doesn't quite freeze the rabbits in the metaphorical manner of car headlights but the rabbits do go into slo-mo. I pass the torch to Tris and tell him to keep it on the closest rabbit, chewing away twenty yards in front.

I shoot. And miss. Freda wants a go with the torch but when she scans it around the rabbits have hopped off. She's pretty glad about this. We make a strange hunting party, as we always do. Tris and I eager to shoot, Freda tagging along in the hope that an animal will be injured and need nursing. We try the next field down, to no avail. We're simply making too much noise.

The kids have a better idea than killing rabbits. They run off into the dark and hide in the grass. I then have to turn on the torch and pick them out.

Alone in the night we play the new game of 'spotting' until it's bedtime. On the way back to the house we recite *Monty Python* lines. Most people know the Dead Parrot sketch off backwards. We, for some reason, are word perfect on the Killer Rabbit scene from *Monty Python and the Holy Grail*. 'Run away, run away, run away. That rabbit's dynamite.'

I find that I'm using the shotgun less and less, the Weihrauch air rifle more and more. With the Weihrauch the killing range is twenty yards, and then it's a head-shot if the quarry is a game bird. To get that close requires stalking. If you're stalking you've entered into the natural world as a predator. You've turned hunter.

Now I start musing on this, I realize that I have, without conscious decision, adopted more lethal methods. When taking the dog and gun I no longer follow my old habit of a clockwise walk down to the wooded riverbank, by far the most abundant killing grounds on the farm; instead I track down behind the paddock hedge. This avoids the slightest appearance on the sky-line. Usually, too, I spend some minutes in the drainage ditch, which has the depth of a trench in Flanders, to peruse Copse Field and the Finger into the Escley. If game is on, I can walk down completely hidden to within twenty-five yards of the copse, with the downhill tumble of water in the ditch drowning the noise of Edith's and my footsteps.

My senses are differently tuned now. If I'm honest I'm unnerved, frightened by this. I can see colours better, I can hear shrews in the hedge, I can smell elements instead of compounds. There's something else, something that I do not have a name for: my head strobes constantly and will sometimes, not always, detect game even though I cannot see it or hear it.

In truth, I do not know whether this quicker, sharper me is the result of the wild food diet or the prolonged habit of hunting. I do know it is real. On a Christmas holiday trip to Bristol Zoo, we chance upon an 'Animal Olympics' gadget that tests reflexes. Mine are almost as fast as a snake's.

There is a downside to becoming a natural killer. On a later winter afternoon I sit and watch the buzzard wheeling over the lower fields. Our relationship has changed. I'm no longer a passive twitcher taking pleasure. He and I are rivals. He falls on a rabbit and I'm jealous.

———

In a Martian-red morning sky I search over the wasted, wintering ground like a tramp through a bin. There is no sorrel, only some bedraggled docks and nettles. I've had cold pheasant for breakfast, with its thick tapes of custard-coloured fat, and I'll have cold pheasant for lunch and pheasant broth, from bones scraped clean, for dinner. In between I'll frantically eat hazelnuts like a squirrel.

———

In the rain I squelch and slip around the fields, Edith beside me, and find nothing to shoot at in forty desolate acres. To stand in Copse Field and look at the browned-off tussocky grass is to see a crowd of a thousand ageing footballers with combovers. I consider lurking in the hide but it has been destroyed by last night's gale. Rain cloys my face under my cap and I have to keep wiping my eyes. All we disturb is a heron on the Escley which lifts from behind the bank-side trees on wings drawn by a child. Edith and I trudge home, both of us with our tails between our legs, as the rain hammers down harder.

———

In the apple cupboard there are about a hundred crab apples left, which I decide to translate into a last batch of translucent crab-apple jelly. While the cauldrons of apples and honey boil and simmer, I fill in the time by reading Bruce Chatwin's *On the Black Hill*. Or, rereading it, to be more accurate: I first opened its pages in 1982, when it was originally published, when you could not walk into a middle-class house in Herefordshire which did not have a copy because, after all, how many times does one find a novel set in the Welsh borderland? I thought Chatwin's novel a fake then and, as I vehemently suggested to a gay Chatwin fan in the pub, believed it was only applauded because Chatwin was the golden-haired poster boy of eighties English literature. And Chatwin's book, I continued with the fortification of pint number four, was the sort of pretentious, sub-D. H. Lawrence rural novel one hoped had been killed off by *Cold Comfort Farm*. Now we lived a mile from the Black Hill which gave Chatwin his title (though his Black Hill is an elision of border locations, from Crickhowell to Longtown), I thought I should have another go at the book. A mistake. As the smarting steam of the cooking apples fills the kitchen, I cook away inside at Chatwin's vision of unremittingly miserable, brooding hill farmers, before tossing the book aside and going off to the sitting-room bookcase to find the copy of *The People of the Black Mountains* by Raymond Williams that I've borrowed from Abergavenny library.

Long ago, across the separating tide of history that was Thatcherism, Williams was a big deal in British intellectual circles, a home-grown thinker who could be mentioned in the same cheese-and-wine breath as polo-necked French *philosophes*. Professor of Drama at Cambridge, Williams was the local boy made good, being born in the tiny railway village of Pandy at the bottom of the Longtown valley. With its sidings and marshalling yard, Pandy was then an industrial incongruity in the landscape of hill farms, a red base in a blue political sea, and his upbringing there left its mark on Williams, who became a lifelong though usually unaligned Marxist.

Life, ambition, politics all took the boy out of the Black Mountains, but the Black Mountains never went out of the boy: in the last years of his life (Williams died in 1988), he turned to writing a historical novel set in the vertiginous lands around his childhood home. 'Epic' is not a sufficient description for the resultant two-volume *The People of the Black Mountains*, which arcs in time from the Old Stone Age to the Late Middle Ages (Williams died before starting a third volume, intended to bring the story up to date). Even though *The People of the Black Mountains* is what Herefordians would call 'a bit Welsh', meaning self-consciously wordy *pace* Dylan Thomas, I'm absorbed from the start by Williams's evocations of the lives of ordinary people in the valley eons ago. So engrossed that I fail to smell that the third cauldron of apples and honey is burning. After the smoke alarm goes off, the charred treacly mess has to be put in the pig bucket.

I become obsessed with Williams's book. Looking out of the house windows – which are all barless glass and 2 × 2 feet, so the effect inside is like standing amid an exhibition of landscape paintings – there is Hatterall Hill, the ancient hill-fort locus of Williams's tale, and left Merlin's Hill, which perimeters the eastward side of the action. Reading *The People of the Black Mountains* I see, for the first time really, this natural view but also, in superimposed holographic images, its human story of settlement. Inevitably, I dwell on Williams's descriptions of the lives of the valley's first hunter-gatherers, which he based on close reading of the archaeological evidence: 'It was good to know that hunting people could live off this country. Indeed, there would be more than enough, for deer and pigs were common in the oak woods.'

The deer and the wild pigs are long gone, but tiny remnants of the oak woods linger. At the bottom of our own Bank Field cling three oaks which were once part of the giant Maes-y-coed forest, which stretched from Ewyas Harold to Longtown.

And surely Williams had the stony Escley near Trelandon in mind for some of his scenes of the skirmishing and raiding endemic to this remote borderland? The echoes of the hooves of rustled cattle and the clang of Norman and Celt swords still seem to sound there above the rush of the water.

Someone forgot to tell the good people of the valley that church attendance is declining. Although we arrive at Clodock church at 6pm, half an hour before the start of the 'Carols by Candlelight' service, we – most unchristianly, I think – run to grab a cosy box pew. Built in 1740, these oak box pews are positively modern in comparison to the spindly musicians' galley of 1650, the fourth bell in the tower (cast in 1624 with the legend *FEAR GOD HONOUR*), the patches of medieval fresco on the walls, the twelfth-century stonework and the memorial stone found in the churchyard which dates from around 800. There has been Christian worship on this site under Merlin's Hill since the fifth century, when Clydawg, King of Ewyas, died. According to the medieval Book of Llandaff, Clydawg was murdered by a rival in love while out hunting. His grief-stricken friends placed his body on a cart pulled by oxen and drove it towards a ford on the Monnow, but on approaching the river the cart broke down and the oxen refused to go on. So Clydawg was buried beside the river, and the place became a site of pilgrimage, and in time a small church of the Martyrdom of Clydawg was raised there. The present church sits slap on top of the old one.

By the time the carol service begins, only standing room remains in the Norman edifice erected to the glory of St Clodock, as the English spell the saintly king's name, and when the heavy oaken door is opened to allow in latecomers those standing in the aisles have to shuffle forward, laughing, to make space. 'They'll be needing a screen outside soon,' mutters the farmer in the aisle beside me, his eyes rheumy with winter chill. Like me and others, he has felt the sartorial need for tweed, which is what passes for rustic smart. In the glow of candles and the fairy lights of the tree we belt out favourite carols, admire the singing of the choir (who do the esoteric numbers), appreciate the job-swapping of the vicar (here a preacher, there a chorister) and listen in the silent night to the readings (unless you are my children, when you occupy these inconvenient longueurs by doing animal hangman on the carol sheet) and generally get high on the feeling of community. There are people who think that *The Vicar of Dibley* is a sitcom, whereas anyone who has ever lived in a village knows that it is an uncompromising fly-on-the-wall documentary, from the bickering eccentrics to the feel-good days like these when the locals come together to sing songs of praise. Because, sitting there in the church dark, with only candles for light, we are sensing more than human fellowship. If we are careful we can hear the ethereal hum of the workings of the Universe.

When the service is over, we debouch from church, pausing only to shake hands with the Reverend Frank Rodgers, into the dark night. Over the unseen hump of the Black Mountains and a mile directly west is another ancient, tiny church of Celtic origin, St David's at Llanthony, where we were married and the children christened.

—

The Winter Solstice, 21 December, the shortest day of the year. An insipid mist hangs in the air, making the day blurred, indistinct, as though caught in a Victorian photo. The world is dead. A farmer, lost somewhere on Merlin's Hill, knocks in posts in an attempted resurrection. Freda wants to ride her pony the mile down the lane to Hope's, the village shop. We go, Poppy's hooves clopping on the tarmac, a stereophonic counterpoint to the fencing work on the other side of the Escley, me holding the pony's leading rein, Tristram holding Edith's lead. The hedges on the thin lane, naked of leaves and flailed by the cutter, have the sterility of wire brushes.

I dread these trips to the village shop. I can't buy anything for myself, except a newspaper, and Hope's has the sort of stock one actually fancies; it is a little Waitrose. This is the upside of the valley being enfiladed by moneyed incomers: the local shop sells more than McVities Fruit Shortcake and Happy Shopper tins of beans. Tris and Freda go in to buy Tyrrells crisps and organic strawberry milk drinks. The pony, dog and I are parked outside, by the Hope family's irritatingly perfect sheep.

On the walk back home, just as we reach our own land, I notice a dead hedgehog on the mud-sprayed verge. Presumably the hedgehog had been woken accidentally from its hibernation, or due to global warming had not yet gone into its winter sleep; whatever, it failed to cross the road safely. Edith, inquisitive, pricks her nose on the spines.

There is nothing wrong with eating hedgehog – Romany gypsies, who cooked hedgehogs by wrapping them in clay and putting them in the fire, used to laud its similarity to pork – but I have not sunk so low as to eat Mrs Tiggy-Winkle roadkill. At least, not yet.

—

Sitting in the low, washed-out winter sun I consider, for the first time, poaching. From the bank just below the house I can see through binoculars (the same Boots-own-brand 10×30 I have had ever since I was a child) three mallard resting on a pool in the Escley on my neighbours' land. An untimely tawny owl too-witts in Quarry Wood. I observe the wild duck for an hour or more, but they show no inclination to stray my way and I'm about to surrender to crime when I see by events on the other side of the Escley that I may get lucky. High up at Oldcourt the farmer is walking down the steep valley side with a sack of feed for his flock of white ewes. His collie dog is running on ahead. The duck raise their heads. Since the wind is blowing faintly upstream, the birds will likely take off into it because of the 'kite effect' it gives them. They will come my way.

Oh shit! They're lifting off the water now. My way. Stumbling to my feet, I take a stance. Do it right: legs slightly apart; relax; safety off; shuffle slightly so that the left foot is pointing at the approaching birds; eyes over the muzzle; lock on bird, take the front one, it is the easiest; mount the barrels on to the bird's head; follow it. The bird is flying very high, say fifty yards. Swing through. Pull the trigger.

And miss. The joy of a double-barrelled shotgun is that you have another chance. Oddly enough, one's second shot is often better than the first. Taken in haste, it is less pressurized, more instinctive. The leading bird is almost exactly overhead when it is felled from the warm bright sky.

The mallard plummets to earth so close to me that I have to jump out of the way.

Christmas Eve. Chestnuts roasting on an open fire, Bing Crosby on the CD player. All I need is the sort of red V-neck sweater that affects the TV colour balance and the cliché would be complete. It is late, the children are in bed, Penny and I are wrapping the last presents to put under the tree. I have my menu finalized for the big culinary day: wild mushroom soup with a garnish of crushed hazelnuts and brooklime (the very last I can find in the ditch); roast duck with elderberry wine and hogweed mash; honeyed chestnuts for pudding. The duck, which has been hung for three days, is now sitting naked in slightly salted water to reduce the faint liverish tang that can sometimes come with a mature bird. All is well.

At 6.30 on Christmas morning the phone rings. I expect it to be an eager grandparent/parent wishing us a 'Happy Christmas!' Although the caller is a parent-cum-grandparent, she does not have a message of good cheer. It is my stepmother, to tell me that my eighty-one-year-old father has fallen in the kitchen and broken his hip. The ambulance has just taken him away.

We manage to put on a good show of opening presents with the children, but then I have to dash to Hereford County Hospital. By 9.30am I am beside my father's bed with my stepmother. My father is being stoical but is clearly in great pain. Things decline. He has a stroke and lapses into unconsciousness. By mid-afternoon, he is plugged into a tangled sci-fi nightmare of oxygen, drips and monitors. I have had only one cup of rosehip tea all day. Stress and lack of food are not boon companions. Come the evening, when my father stabilizes, I am so light-headed I cannot safely drive the twenty miles home. 'John, you must eat something,' says Joyce, my stepmother. 'Mum,' I say, 'I think you're right.'

Adam and Eve in the Garden of Eden were brought low by a fruit, probably a rosy red apple. My fall comes with the most mundane and suburban of food and drink: a cellophane-wrapped cheese sandwich and a coffee in a plastic cup with a cardboard handle.

On Boxing Day my father pulls back from immediate danger and my yuletide lunch is finally cooked. Served up on an oval meat dish, surrounded by a ring of hogweed mash, and placed on the white linen tablecloth, my duck in elderberry wine gives me a twinge of pride at the luxury. Certainly it does not pale in comparison to the cod au gratin the rest of the family are having. Even my one green vegetable accompaniment, steamed sorrel – baby leaves hunted down in the mass of Road Field, like finding needles in hayfields – bursts with culinary voluptuousness.

Looking across the table, 'Can I try some of your duck?' asks Tris.

'Me too,' Freda echoes.

I cut off two slices and spoon on some juice.

And say nothing when they exclaim that it is 'awesome' and 'delicious'. This is the winter of my content.

Roast duck with elderberry wine and hogweed mash

After hanging, gut and feather, and leave in slightly salted water for a day if you think that the duck is advanced in age. A piece of hogweed root put into the bird before roasting will also absorb some of the liverishness. Rub salt into the skin. Put salt and a glass of elderberry wine into the cavity of the duck, alongside the hogweed. Roast for about an hour, depending on weight, basting frequently in the winey juices. Serve hot with the juices poured over it, together with a dish of bramble jelly.

*Hogweed (*Heracleum sphondylium*) can be decidedly difficult to distinguish from any number of umbellifers in winter, since the differences between it and them – size, stalk markings, flowers, leaf arrangement – are eradicated by seasonal dying-off. The umbellifer in midwinter is often nothing but a bunch of dried stalks sticking out of the ground. So take from a place where you know only hogweed grows; there are umbellifers that are drop-dead toxic. Hogweed roots can be stored in the dark, entombed in earth or sand. The roots of the plant – which has the country name of cow parsnip – can be roasted but you will need the teeth of a beaver to eat them. Neither does orthodox boiling do much to tackle their immense woodiness. Best of all is to wash the roots then grate them, or at least their softest parts. Boil the gratings in salted water and* *you are left with something pleasantly like sweet potato.*

Oddly, when hogs are fed hogweed they will not eat it. But then they will not consume parsnip either.

The other forager's usage of hogweed is the steaming, braising or boiling of its young shoots, which are then reminiscent of celery.

Honeyed chestnuts

5oz/150g chestnuts
½ cup honey
1 tbsp water
Peel the chestnuts and steam them for 7–8 minutes over a pan of simmering water.

Put the honey into a saucepan, together with the water. Heat and stir until the mixture is syrupy. Tip the chestnuts in and stir with a wooden spoon to coat them. Lift the chestnuts on to a wire rack to cool.

When cool, dry them off in a low oven for 5–10 minutes.

To eke out the Boxing Day mallard I put its disintegrating carcase, a prop for a Stephen King novel, into the cauldron. In too goes a glass of elderberry wine, a tablespoon of salt, four tablespoons of chestnut purée, two cloves of ramsons and a handful of the precious dried chanterelle mushrooms gathered from Road Field back in October.

After two hours of simmering, it's palatable broth, but nothing more.

Four o'clock in the morning. I'm jerked awake as if someone has applied defibrillators. My heart is pounding its way out of my chest and there's an excruciating pain in my kidneys. I'm weightless on my back, nauseous, unable to stop myself shivering uncontrollably. Every particle of the bedroom is infused with neon violet.

I don't think it's food poisoning. I think I've eaten a poisonous mushroom. I want to ask Penny to phone for an ambulance but absurdly don't want to alarm the children at Christmas time. As if discovering the cadaver of their dead father would be better.

For hours I shiver and hope, promising myself that if the symptoms worsen it's 999 time. They don't and as morning eases into the bedroom I realize that I'm not going to die yet. My heartbeat is normalizing and the purple haze is thinning.

The nausea is made of sterner stuff and I'm ill for days.

—

My father lying in a hospital bed, sickly, almost perfectly camouflaged in the jaundiced yellow light of the ward. 'Couldn't you find out something about the family's history, John? Go on, it's the sort of thing you can do.'

I've absolutely no interest in tracing my roots. What could there be to discover? We have been forever peasant farmers, sometimes owning a small farm but usually tenanting, and younger sons have spun off into lesser, straitened trades such as game-keeping. There's talk of the line having the occasional 'priest' (C of E) and I could possibly make a decent tilt at being related to Blanche Parry, Elizabeth I's lady-in-waiting, but that's it. It seems to me that the modern genealogical industry is founded on the fool's-gold hope that the seeker is the lost heir to an earldom or the descendant of some eighteenth-century someone. The truth that lies at the end of the ancestral taproot is likely to be more mundane.

There's another reason why I've never wanted to investigate my family past. Since both my mother's and father's maternal lines come from the next-door villages of Kilpeck and Much Dewchurch I've always assumed inbreeding.

Still, it's difficult to deny a possibly dying man his wish. That evening I press on the PC in my son's room and google 'Verry', my grandmother's maiden name.

Bingo. A Verry descendant in New Zealand, Adrian Verry, has constructed a website detailing the family history back to 1520 when the Flemish 'Verriors' arrived in Much Dewchurch and took on the tenancies of three local farms. With some shock I realize that one of the farms is Pool Farm, directly opposite the Rudolf Steiner school the children used to attend when they were smaller. Another circle.

Following the family tree down to modern times, I find my great-grandfather and great-grandmother, listed as William and Harriet Verry of Upper House, Aconbury. To supplement his income from this small farm, William Verry had, it seems, a couple of sidelines, soldiering and stonemasonry. I'm intrigued by the stonemasonry, since my mother's maternal line, the Bamford-Parrys, were farmers and stonemasons too. 'Not so strange a coincidence,' points out my wife Penny, 'since their farms probably had stone quarries on them. Ours had, after all.' She's right.

Next day my cousin Roger phones to find out about my father's health and I mention to him the Verry website. But he's not persuaded that the 'Verriors' were Belgian. 'No, no, Auntie Edie's gone right back, way before the 1500s. The Verrys are Norman . . . you can tell by the red hair in the family.'

Like William Rufus, king of England. Later in Hereford public library I pull down *A Dictionary of English Surnames* by P. H. Reaney and R. M. Wilson. Sure enough, the origin of 'Verrier' is old French and the first Norman Verriers in England were here by 1100.

The surprise comes later, on the phone. Although long divorced, my parents' lives are oddly synchronous. My mother has been contacted by a cousin, who happens to have done her family tree back to 1614, when the Amoses were farmers and corn mill-owners in the Leysters in north Herefordshire. 'The funny old thing,' she says, 'is that the family used to be called Aymes. Your dad's got Aymes from Leysters in his line.'

Another circle.

People wonder why I'm not Belsen-thin.

I have a guilty secret. In the dead of night in this dead of winter I sit and drink a half-bottle or more of one of the wines I've made – sloe, 'hedgerow', apple, elderberry, whatever. And when you think of it, wine is nothing but calories in water.

Alcohol also removes any self-discipline I have, so sometimes I pad to the kitchen and open a jar of honey and sit and eat it, a louche Winnie-the-Pooh.

A CALENDAR OF WILD FOOD AT TRELANDON

December

Mallard, nettles, rabbit, pheasant, hogweed,
dandelion, sorrel, rosehips, brooklime

O N NEW YEAR'S DAY my kidneys are pulsing with the pains of a thousand tiny dagger prods; I do not know the cause of the agony but, aside from the ingested poisonous mushroom of the previous week, the most obviously guilty items in my diet are excessive meat and excessive sorrel. Not only does sorrel contain oxalic acid, I am mainly eating the sorrel I have preserved in cider vinegar. To give my kidneys some respite I undertake a cadastral survey of the edible winter greens on the farm. Up fields, down ditches, around the copse, along hedges and riverbanks I search in the short daylight, filling a carrier bag with specimens as I go. Although I find nettles, plantain, goose grass, Good King Henry, docks, dandelion, sorrel, hairy bittercress and ground ivy, all are stunted or, when bitten into, unpalatably bitter because of the concentration of acids that occurs in midwinter. They are tiresomely stringy too. Even the plants growing in the temperate clime of the Copse Field ditch are useless; they are under inches of flood silt. Only the dandelions and sorrel in Road Field, which is still a deluxe baize despite the six months that have elapsed since it was cut for silage, pass the taste and consistency test. More sorrel, though, is hardly what I need. But is dandelion the answer? In France, dandelion is sometimes rudely known as *'pissenlit'*, on account of its diuretic qualities. All parts of the plant, no matter how prepared, have this side effect.

For three days the only greens I eat are dandelion leaves, the pert ones from the heart of the rosettes. Of dandelion John Evelyn, the diarist, wrote: 'With this homely salley Hecate entertained

Theseus.' So I have them as 'salley', with a dribble of cider vinegar and a pinch of salt, and when I tire of their bitterness I chop them up and add a touch of clear honey to the dressing. And when I weary of dandelion leaves as bitter-sweet salad, I blanch them in cold water for a day before steaming them as you would spinach. And eventually I try the leaves as soup.

After three days of the dandelion regime, my kidney pains diminish, but whether this is due to time, the placebo effect or the dandelions I cannot say.

Dandelion soup
7oz/200g young dandelion leaves
½ tbsp duck fat
1 clove wild garlic
1 dandelion root, diced
1.3 pints/750ml gamebird stock
salt

Chop, parboil and drain the dandelion leaves. Melt the duck fat in a saucepan, add the wild garlic and fry gently. Add the diced dandelion root, cover the pan with a lid and sweat on a low heat for 5 minutes. Add the parboiled dandelion to the pan, stir in the stock and bring to a rolling boil. Cook for 15 minutes. Season with salt.

The leaves of the dandelion can be dried to make a tea, by steeping 1 tablespoon of dried leaves in 1 cup hot water. Aside from medicinal grounds, though, it is difficult to see why anyone should bother with something so insipid.

Sheep, like Saxons, never make straight roads. I am following the meandering track of the sheep through Bog Field because, pummelled by hooves, it is firmer ground than that around it. In this time of rain, Bog Field more than lives down to its name;

an unwary step off-track has resulted in my wellington being sucked off by the mud. Nothing moves on land, on the river, or in the air.

This is the day when I decide that I will use long nets to catch rabbits. I have been out by light and by dark for three days but the perpetual rain and wind is making the rabbits skulk and my view of them obscure. But I will have to buy some nets from the agricultural merchants in Abergavenny first.

I'm driving in my car, halfway down the valley, just where the border detours off the Black Mountains towards the Monnow river. Floodwater has made the lane skating-rink slick. A cock pheasant, hidden in the hedge, waits for my approach and runs out in front of me. I stamp on the brakes, the Audi skews and skids and I come to a haphazard rest sideways across the lane. Thankfully there was no vehicle in front or behind me. But why did I brake for the pheasant? Why did I risk human life for a bird I spent the earlier part of the day hunting?

Unharmed, the pheasant strolls off unconcernedly through a crop of winter wheat, eyes left, eyes right, looking for food.

To use a long net you need to know your rabbits, because the net must be positioned across their bolt route home. So with the twenty-five-yard net in my hands I set it in a straight line about fifteen feet out from the warren in the hedge at the top of Bog Field. Tied to fencing stakes, which have to be pounded in with a sledgehammer, the net is gathered up from the ground for its entire length, like a row of women hitching their skirts, so that the rabbits can pass under it. The rain scorns me as I toil, especially when I have to reset the net because it is too taut and any rabbits running into it would be sprung backwards to Norfolk. At length I finish, and leave the net for the rabbits to become accustomed to.

Two nights later, I go out into the raining raven-dark of Bog Field with a pencil-beam torch and silently untie the gathered drapes of the net so that it falls fully to the ground. Theoretically, the rabbits are now beyond the net, hunkered down in the rough grass until peril passes. What they do not know is that danger is not yet upon them. I return to the yard, pick up a metre length of 25mm blue plastic piping and sneak into Bog Field about twenty yards below the net. Sloshing parallel to the net I bang the ground with the pipe, which 'whooms' in the dark. The rabbits run, run, run. In an instant I can hear the thrashing of little legs in nylon; turning on the torch, I rush to the net to see two rabbits caught. They struggle. The more they struggle, the more they become tangled. Soon they are so swaddled by the net that they cannot move.

What most rabbit catchers do at this point is force back the coneys' heads and break their necks. Fuck that, I think, as I pull Tris's Webley .22 air pistol out of the Barbour's poacher pocket. It is already loaded. I flick off the safety catch, push the barrel to the nearest rabbit's head and bang! just like Brigadier General Nguyễn Loan executing the Viet Cong prisoner in Eddie Adams's famous 1968 photograph. Then I reload and do it again.

For the rabbits, from being driven out of their cover to being killed took under a minute. But it was a minute too far. For days afterwards I see the torch-lit images of the entangled, petrified, panting rabbits on my retinas. There are good ways to die, but lying in bondage in a net waiting for your neck to be broken or your brain to be purged by a pellet is not among them. The best way to die is to be shot, unsuspecting; failing that, to be shot running or flying free will do.

The proof is in the eating. Despite hanging for three days, the flesh of the rabbits is metallically tainted by the stress they felt in that single minute of entrapment.

I resolve never to use the nets again.

All colour has drained from the land. The world is in mono-
chrome. Grey lines of hedges criss-cross pale fields, with
occasional interruptions by patches of grey woods. The treeless,
dead heather-clad top of the mountain is a band of mourning
black. 'The Black Mountains look very black today, Mother,' we
say, in an echo of a joke from *Ripping Yarns*. In the 180-degree
view from the house down the valley there is one tiny daub of
colour, as if tinted into the landscape by a movie colorizer. This is
a clump of fir trees, still bright green, perched halfway down the
long sloping side of Merlin's Hill. Think of an English winter and
you think of red – red for Father Christmas, robins' breasts, hunting jackets (unless you are my farmer grandfather Joe Amos, who
wore mustard yellow), the cheeks of choirboys, mulled wine, holly
berries. The actual colour of a late English winter without human
agency is no colour at all. Nature's puny efforts at bright cheer fail
to figure. The holly berries have been gobbled up by passing trios
of blackbirds, and cock robin cannot find a place that is dry
enough or sheltered enough in which to sing. Anyway, only
mature robins get to sport the blood-red chest; by the time the
stoats, the weasels, the pine martens, the rats, the grey squirrels,
the kestrels, the sparrowhawks, the magpies, the jackdaws, the
carrion crows and the ravens on the farm have robbed the robins
of their eggs, their fledgling sons and their daughters, few robins
make it past juvenility.

There is a room in the house which is forty foot long, known as the
big sitting room. Its windows have yet to be glazed and its doors
to be hung, but it does have a roof. The children, when the
Longtown wind is not invading the room, use it to play badminton,
with the heavy oak beams in the roof adding an idiosyncratic

gambling element. In narrow winter days viced by blackness, I use the room to train Edith by the light of an anglepoise lamp tied to a beam. We are in the big sitting room a great deal. We are practising RETRIEVING, which consists of sitting the amber-eyed Edith in front of me, and me lobbing the green canvas training dummy to the far end of the room and ordering her to bring it back. This she does every time, with a pleasure that makes her body S-bend with wags; the problem is that she always drops the dummy a yard short, instead of bringing it to my outstretched hand. To remedy this fault, for days in a row I try Keith Erlandson's advice to run away from the dog while calling its name, but still Edith delivers short.

With such a persistent offender, drastic measures are called for. So I take a leaf out of Erlandson's *Gundog Training* and try a species of the 'forced delivery'. I apply 'a measure of discomfort to the foot, ear or lips of the dog so he opens his mouth in protest'. Into the open mouth goes the dummy. Then the dummy is taken out and the discomfort stopped. The dog comes to believe that its pain can only be ended by the trainer taking the dummy out of its mouth. Soon the dog is positively clamouring to give the dummy to the trainer's hand.

At least Erlandson does not suggest biting the dog on the bottom lip, a method favoured by some trainers; much as I love Edith, I know that she, like other country dogs, is a germ-manufactory on four legs. The English countryside only looks like a pleasant land; underneath it pullulates with pathogens. A year or so back, a local farmer contracted hydatid disease, in which cysts containing tapeworm larvae grow inside the body, from his sheepdog.

Edith's ears are too velvety soft to bear hurt, so I settle for pinching her bottom lip between my thumb and forefinger. Within three days she delivers direct to my hand.

The four dogs are sprawled in front of the fire sleeping, Tris is sprawled in the blue leather armchair reading James Bond, Freda is sprawled on one end of the sofa perusing horse-tack catalogues and Penny is sprawled on the other end engaging with Zadie Smith. I had been perusing Thoreau's *On Walden Pond* – because I should, shouldn't I? – but in a fit of New Year mental tidying have decided to work out how much my wild living is saving the family budget. So now I am sat on a hardback wooden chair, leaning on an occasional table which is covered in bits of paper, a biro in hand. Over the snoring of Labradors, the splutter of the fire, the purgatorial sighs of the wind outside, there is the sound of my pen frantically scratching. When I have deducted £5 for shotgun and air-gun ammunition, plus £5 for honey, I calculate that I have lightened the housekeeping by £50 per week. (I *was* expensive to run since, as my wife lamented, I uniquely considered claret to be a household essential.) This is not a great sum, but it is not a bad sum either.

With my mind on housewifery, I decide to take stock of my supplies, which are all located in an old pine linen cupboard in the unfinished big sitting room. With the hindrance of a wind-up torch that constantly needs its handle turning I peer into the shelves, which, in their array of bottles, jars, boxes, tins and bags, resemble those of a witch's provisioner.

Ignorance is bliss. My provisions are less than I had fondly thought. They comprise:

4 jars crab-apple jelly
2 jars bramble jelly
1kg (roughly) hazelnuts in sacking
3 Kilner jars pickled sorrel
12 bottles sloe wine (not yet drinkable)

2 bottles elderberry wine

6 bottles sloe wine

5 bottles cider vinegar

7 flagons cider

½kg chestnuts in a cardboard box

2 jars dandelion coffee

3 tins rosehip tea

1 wooden box hogweed roots

½ carrier bag dandelion roots

1 Kilner jar pickled mushrooms

½kg dried mushrooms in a plastic jar

1 small bottle hazelnut oil

2 cups duck fat

The blackberry cordial has long gone. Two bottles of rosehip cordial sit in the recesses of the top shelf but these have clouded and browned and are suitable only for use by Lucretia Borgia.

In the cow byre hangs one rabbit.

And that is it.

When I was a boy my bus journey to school took me to the top of Hampton Park Road in Hereford and past Plas Gwyn, Elgar's old house. From its windows the composer enjoyed, as I enjoyed through the bus windows, a view clear across twenty-five miles of Herefordshire to the Black Mountains, which rear up on the horizon. That strange blue-black wall entranced me and I had childish thoughts of adventures beyond it, because the mountains seemed to be life's imitation of the division between the bucolic Shire of the hobbits and the forbidding Mordor in Tolkien's *Lord of the Rings*.

Now that I live in the very shadow of the Black Mountains, on one of the small hills which run like waves slap into their eastern sea-wall, I still think of the land beyond – which is the sparsely populated vastness of mid-Wales – as a place of mystery. But in living under the Black Mountains, I have come to understand that they dominate as well as demarcate. In winter's beating rain and wind we cling to the mountain and its foothills as children, on their fronts, try to cling by fingers and shoe-tips to the slippery surface of the playground slide. The land gives no succour, it only gives water, water which floods and dampens, water which mixes with the clay soil to make a red mud that sticks and stains, clogs and slips. Above us a claustrophobic roof of black cloud settles on the valley, cutting off the sky. The brooding mass of the mountains encircles the view to the front, and the entrapment is made complete by Merlin's Hill and the narrowing of the little Escley valley behind the house.

My mood takes on the hue of the dark mountains.

While he was having his hip op, my father's heart stopped beating. Although he was resuscitated his blood pressure will not normalize. On some days it is so low that, if it was any lower, it could not be plotted on the graph by the hospital nurses. There is no lower. There is dead.

January, will you ever end?

Every morning, even though I can hear the sound of battering bastard rain, I force myself out of bed, dress and take the shotgun out. (Shooting with the Weihrauch has become impossible, for the rain occludes the telescopic lens and the wind veers the pellets.) As Edith and I step out into the great void of outdoors, one bird is there to greet us, always. *Peeeio.* The mewing buzzard, on its giant moth wings, is always the first of the daytime shift of hunters to clock on. I hope he or she has more luck than I, since my average kill in this time of famine is one bird or rabbit every two days.

All I see in two hours of walking in the seeping cold is the occasional low-level, hedge-hopping blackbird, a fleeting wren in the bankside scrub, and a clutter of jackdaws tossed across the sky; the excitable flocks of redwings and fieldfares, having eaten all my berries, have gone south. With an empty game bag, I beat my way home but stop, out of curiosity, to watch the floodwater rage down the drainage ditch in Copse Field. The water is churning two feet deep. Then something red, redder than the clay ditchwater, catches my eye; it is the thin corpse of a fox, snagged against a clump of brambles, holding fast despite the current trying to move it on.

Life is precarious in winter for the hunter just as it is for the hunted. There is one killer that does not discriminate between herbivore, omnivore and carnivore: the weather, and its handmaiden, hypothermia. Predators have another problem in winter. Some prey species have cannily gone into hibernation.

I would like to hibernate, in a vast bed with a Norwegian duvet a foot thick, in a house with central heating.

On a day conspicuous by its sunlight, I'm in the kitchen hydrating some mushrooms when the dogs start barking madly. Looking out on to the yard I see an unfamiliar red Toyota Hi-Lux pick-up park and two young men step out. There's a moment of double-take, since the two men are almost identical in their oval faces and in their green waxed-jacket dress sense. They also happen to be the sons of the vicar, the Reverend Frank Rodgers. Owen and Ben Rodgers, however, have not come to save our souls, they have come to kill mink. They are employees of the Monnow river conservation project, and are exterminating the alien black mink, escapees from fur farms of the 1950s, in order to protect the local brown trout, water vole and otter populations. They have recently trapped thirty-eight mink on the Dore river.

Since we know each other by sight only, they negotiate cautiously, for I could be an animal rights type relocated from London.

'We were wondering,' asks Ben Rodgers, 'if you had any riverbank?'

'About half a mile,' I reply.

'Could we trap here?'

'I'd be delighted if you could.'

When we arrived at Trelandon there was a family of mink living in the decrepit outhouse at the buildings' western end. Mink are loathsome, slinky, vicious and over here, but you do have to admire their *cojones*; one time, when I was lying under the International 484 tractor on the yard, trying a repair, I was suddenly aware of a shadow to my right. Turning my head, I saw a mink a yard away, its emotionless, black-bead eyes gazing directly into mine. The world contracted to a soundless capsule on a concrete yard in wan sunlight. The mink looked at me, I looked at the mink. Trapped under the tractor, I became petrified that the mink was going to attack my face. I thought about inching my fingers to reach the hammer and maybe chucking this at the animal but could not force my paralysed body to make even this small movement. So I just lay there, until the four-inch-high mink decided that it had tormented me enough and walked off. A thrush in the Scots pine fluted a song of salvation. Eventually the mink family found the builders as disruptive as we did and moved away.

How, I ask the Rodgers boys, are the mink trapped? Ben explains that they tether a floating raft in the river; on top of the raft is a soft clay plate. Mink, being inquisitive, climb on the raft – and leave footprints on the clay tablet. If mink are present, the detecting device is replaced by a live trap, in which the mink are hustled to one end and shot. Ben and Owen Rodgers go off to set the raft on the river and I return to my mushrooms.

Later, just before nightfall at 5pm, when the foxes are grey shadows on the far sloping bank of the Escley, I walk down to the river to view the raft, which I find tethered by blue nylon rope to an alder in a stretch of slack water. On top of the raft is a square wooden burrow containing the all-important soft clay plate. Perched on the burrow is a clod of long grass, giving it a mop-top a Beatle would recognize. If I was a mink I would certainly investigate such a phenomenon.

Curiosity killed the cat. Curiosity will also hopefully kill the genocidal mink.

—

Not that I would ever forget my daughter's birthday, but Nature anyway provides a reminder. The little bell-flowers of the snowdrop open today, for her birthday, just as they did on 19 January in the year she was born. Freda wants a miniature Shetland pony. When I calm down enough for her to explain that she has found a pedigree colt advertised in *Horsemart* for £150, and she will put in a hundred pounds of the money from her Christmas haul, this doesn't seem such a bad idea. So off we drive to Lincomb in Worcestershire on a dulled-out Saturday afternoon, towing the pony trailer, which I've hastily repainted (in navy blue) because Freda thought it wasn't smart enough for a new pony to see. In the back seat of the Audi sit Tris, Freda and Freda's friend Allegra, who are all in high spirits, the girls gently teasing Tris because he's a boy and, even better, a teenage boy stuck in his school uniform because he has just been picked up from Saturday morning school. ('Boys need extra school on Saturday, don't they, Mum, because they are not as smart as girls . . .') Tris, who can be insufferably charming, is taking it on a smiling chin.

When we arrive in the village of Lincomb at three o'clock, and eventually find the right 'field by the track with a silver Land Rover parked by it' we are met by Sandy, a pleasant fortysomething horsey woman, who explains that she has two miniature Shetland 'boys' for sale and Freda can take her pick.

'I can't decide which one to sell,' says Sandy, leading us up the track, 'so I need someone to make the choice for me. But one of them has to go, to pay the vet's fees.'

'Tell us about it,' I say. 'Tris here wants to be a vet, so we're hoping to live it up in our dotage.'

By now we have reached a small paddock under the wood. 'There they are,' says Sandy, pointing into the field. The girls go 'aaahhh' and 'oohhh'. Tris says, 'Is that them?' Penny says, 'Where?' and I can't see anything except a couple of sheep.

Good God. Sandy rattles a bucket of horse cubes, and what I thought were two sheep trot over. Whinnying.

'Will they grow?' asks Penny, mesmerized, as they snuffle around our feet eating the tipped-out cubes. 'Oh, no, not much,' Sandy says proudly, 'about an inch. They are almost fully grown.'

'They're cute, aren't they,' says Tris.

'Gorgeous,' says Penny.

'Fantastic,' I reply.

We leave Freda alone to make her choice between a palomino named Willow and a piebald named Rocco. She doesn't need long. Because she is kind and wants something to pet, she chooses the smaller colt, the bundle of fur on legs that is Willow.

The shy Willow has to be gently coaxed to the trailer, where he halts at the ramp. So I lift him up ('I'm strong enough to carry a horse,' I joke to the kids) and when he sees the hay net inside the trailer his appetite gets the better of his nerves. As I check that the tailgate is properly secured and the trailer lights are working, Sandy gives Freda a present, a brand new show bridle for Willow.

'You can put him in competitions now and get plenty of rosettes,' says Penny.

'Cups,' says Sandy, 'you're aiming at cups.'

On the slow drive home, the speed kept down to 40mph so that Willow is not tossed around, my mood is so good that I can even tolerate the kids' request to listen to Radio 1 on the car radio. As someone who believes that popular music effectively ended when the Clash disbanded, this is a concession indeed.

'You have to admit,' says Penny after the artist known as Mika has falsettoed his way through 'Grace Kelly', 'that it is catchy.'

'So was the bubonic plague,' I point out.

I continue with what I think are my witticisms about contemporary music ('Is that rap with a silent c?'), when the Audi's headlights illuminate a fallen bird on the bend of the B-road somewhere near Tenbury Wells. A roadkill pheasant.

Penny tenses beside me. I know what she is thinking: will he stop and pick it up and embarrass Tris and Freda? Will he ruin a perfect day? At the moment the children are oblivious, chattering. I drive on. My luck is in. A lay-by comes into view just yards further on. I pull in. Penny is silent.

'I'm just going to check that Willow is OK,' I say jauntily to all.

Dashing back in the dark, I almost trip over the ragbag of feathers. Grabbing the bird by the wing I know instantly by the weight and size that it is not a pheasant. Running back to the pony trailer, I hold the bird against the rear lights.

A grey partridge.

Because I said I would and because I should, I check on Willow, who is eating away contentedly. I stash the partridge down behind the wheel arch of the trailer.

Back in the car, I mutter, 'Partridge,' to Penny. 'Put where?' she mutters back. 'Behind trailer wheel arch,' I reply in this strangled, kids-must-not-hear language.

At home in the cow byre, I examine the partridge under the overhead light; the bird is almost unscathed by its meeting with a vehicle. Only bruising around the right eye gives away the cause of death.

The grey partridge (*Perdix perdix*) is a bird of cultivated land and a stranger to Trelandon, although I did once see a covey scuttling across the road in the bottom of the valley. Actually, the grey partridge is a rarity almost everywhere these days, its numbers devastated by agricultural intensification, herbicides and rotten, wet summers. Unhappily, the bird sits on the British Trust for Ornithology's red list. So I take some time to study the bird in the hand, admiring its orange head, its grey dumpy body, the bright brown bars on the wings, and the perfection of the chestnut horseshoe on the lower breast, so strongly marked that I think this must be a cock (partridge cocks, unlike most game cocks, are spurless). Stretching out the wing, I can see that the first flight feather tip is pointed, not rounded, the sign of a young bird. A bird, then, perfect for roasting.

Roast partridge with elderberry wine gravy

Grey partridge is best after just two or three days' hanging, unlike its red-legged cousin (introduced into England from France in 1673) which needs a week. Like all small game birds, partridge is very lean and will dry out quickly, so do not overcook as many bug-fearing people do. Partridge is one of those birds which need to be skinned, not plucked.

1 grey partridge
2 crab apples
4oz/110g duck fat
1 tbsp bilberry or wild cranberry jelly
2.5fl oz/75ml elderberry wine

Preheat the oven to 375°F/190°C/Gas Mark 5.
    Rinse the bird and pat dry.
    Place two halved crab apples inside the bird, and season the skin with salt.

Place the partridge in a non-stick roasting pan with the duck fat and cover with aluminium foil.

Roast for 25 minutes, basting three or four times along the way, and removing the aluminium foil for the last 5 minutes.

Transfer the partridge to a serving plate and keep warm. Pour the juices from the roasting pan into a saucepan and add the bilberry jelly (better still, wild cranberry) and the elderberry wine. Simmer over a gentle heat until the jelly has dissolved and the sauce has reduced. Strain, pour into a sauce boat and place alongside the partridge.

Serve with watercress or hairy bittercress salad.

Roast partridge is equally good cold. Again serve with a jelly; a sharper one such as redcurrant would be particularly suited to the occasion.

The liver, kidneys and heart of the partridge should be kept for game pâté.

On 21 January there is, at last, dryness after the rain. In the dying of the day, as the light seeps away, like water into sand, I hear the call of a male pheasant close by. Then a vibrating whirr of wings and a crash of branches; the pheasant has gone to roost in the etiolated hazel trees which march down from the house to the bloated Escley. At this moment the pheasant will be hyper-alert; later he will be less cautious, trusting in the cape of night for his protection.

By the time I go out with the Weihrauch, the moon floodlights the valley, painting my wellingtons in glam-rock silver and trans-figuring Poppy the pony into a white china statue. My silhouette is drawn precisely. So is the pheasant's in the wiry winter branches. As I approach he fatalistically lowers his head as though placing it on the executioner's block. I stand underneath the tree and shoot him through the eye from two yards' range.

Ill met by moonlight, the pheasant tumbles from the tree without a sound, to lie at my feet, his bill slowly opening and closing as life departs.

—

At the top of Copse Field is a wide pan of a ditch under the hedge, which is known to us as 'the Newt Ditch', on account of the smooth newts (*Triturus vulgaris*) that flourish there amid the lank grass, the club rushes and the dark alcoves of the back bank. The ditch would more accurately be termed 'the Frog and Newt Ditch' because it is primarily a spawning ground for common frogs (*Rana temporaria*); the carnivorous newts are there merely to snack on their amphibian cousins. But catching newts with a net, putting them in jam jars with string handles and marvelling at them before returning them to the water is a family pastime, just as it was a boyhood love of mine, and so the Newt Ditch it is. With the frog spawning season almost upon us, I decide to check the Newt Ditch to see that all is well. Disaster. At some point in the autumn, the cattle must have trodden down the ditch's shallow front edge and rainwater is leaching out over the field; the lower end of the ditch is empty.

So I lumber to the house, load myself like a pack-horse with spade, bow saw, bits of planking and an axe and return to the ditch, where I dig out a new front wall of mud, reinforcing it with the planks, which in turn are held in place by staves cut from a hazel tree. Pressed by the early coming of darkness and the incessant rain I labour hurriedly, but even so my trousers soon become so sodden by rain and splashed ditchwater that they puddle my wellingtons from inside. All my 'come and have a go' taunts at winter have crashed into vainglory. I want to creep off home and I do, as soon as I have finished.

And yet, as I sidle through the rain, head hunched into my neck *à la* Quasimodo, I know that on this day, 27 January, I saw the first light of spring at the bottom of the well of winter. Floating in the stunted grass of the ditch was one forlorn lump of frogspawn. The frogs have begun their reproductive cycle. Life is starting up amid death. I am getting through the winter. There is a spring in my step.

Mooching through the woodpile at the top of the yard, seeking a prop for the sagging roof of the stable, I catch a view of the western end of the house and there, growing in the old stone wall of the outhouse, are slender little green plants all in a proud row in the drizzling rain. About corn salad, *Valeriana locusta*, the herbalist Gerard commented, 'it serves in winter as a salad herb among others none of the worst', which is fair comment. The tangy taste of the oval leaves is best described as 'pleasant', unless

you have been hankering for salad in endless dark days, as I have, when it can pass for 'fantastic' with the addition of a hint of cider vinegar.

Corn salad is sometimes known in England as lamb's lettuce because it appears at lambing time.

Springtime.

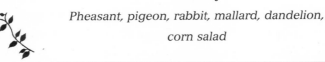

A Calendar of Wild Food at Trelandon

January

Pheasant, pigeon, rabbit, mallard, dandelion,
corn salad

OVER THE NIGHT of 31 January the wind attacks the house. Alone in the dark on a bare hillside, we feel as though we have been singled out for special treatment. At length, the house concedes, first a handful of slate tiles and then the cow-byre door. A long death rattle: then the door is blown screaming off its hinges into the night.

When I arise in the morning at six o'clock, the wind has not abated; if anything it has got worse. As I stand in Bog Field, pulling apart a silage bale to put in the cows' metal ring feeder, tree branches break off and plummet down around me. To get Tris and Freda into the car for school I have to hold its doors open with two hands, in case the doors whip closed as the children scramble in.

Winter might be on its way out, but its tail still stings. A gust of wind engulfs me with such force that my breath is taken away and I panic, fish-mouthed, as I fight the feeling of suffocation. There is something in the air other than fear, though; there is sadness. Today is the last day of the shooting season and I had hoped for one last hurrah, one last chance of shooting a pheasant. And Edith, I had thought, might even manage the honour of the retrieve.

But there will be no shooting today, not in this weather, not with this wind.

Inside the safety of the house, behind walls thirty inches thick, I contemplate a day without meat, although I do not contemplate it for long. By mid-afternoon, after trying to fill the chasm of my stomach with boiled hogweed roots and honeyed chestnuts, I ping open one of the three Kilner jars in which I have preserved duck in its fat. These jars were meant for desperate times in spring, when the only legitimate quarry is rabbit and wood pigeon, not for the last day of the game season itself. As soon as the jar is open, I cannot stop myself from eating the contents in a sitting. Afterwards I feel a guilt which is vaguely familiar. Then I have it; it is the same guilt you have as a child when, sitting on the bus hired for an excursion, you eat the Cadbury's mini-rolls intended for your picnic lunch before the charabanc has even passed the school gates.

Preserved duck

This recipe, which is derived from the French peasant confit d'oie *(preserved goose), is easiest at the onset of winter, when wild duck is at its fattiest. The* confit *takes 3 days to prepare. This is how food preparation used to be before refrigeration: time-consuming.*

1 wild duck
¼lb/100g salt
pinch dried wild thyme
1lb/450g duck fat

Cut the duck into quarters. Mix the salt and thyme together, and rub into the duck. Put the duck into an earthenware or china bowl, add the remaining thyme and salt and cover. Leave for 24 hours.

Gently melt the duck fat in a large frying pan, and add the pieces of duck. Turn down the heat to very low, and cook softly for 2–3 hours, until the juices run clear when the flesh is skewered.

Take out the duck pieces, and cut out the bones and gristle. Pour the molten duck fat into the bottom of a Kilner jar; when this has solidified, carefully pile the duck pieces in the centre of the jar. They must not touch the glass sides. Pour liquid, cooling duck fat into the jar until the duck pieces are covered. Set in a cool place for two days.

Pour more liquid duck fat into the jar to cover any air holes that have appeared. Allow to set. Then top up with liquid duck fat until there is a solid layer of fat at least half an inch/1cm thick at the top of the jar. Put a new rubber ring on the Kilner jar top and seal down.

In the absence of a Kilner jar, a glazed earthenware jar will oblige. To seal, use several layers of greaseproof paper tied around with string.

The confit *will keep for a month, perhaps even two, in a cool place.*

The game season is a week over. Not that it matters, for almost every day of the first week of February has brought storms which make bird shooting impossible. When I do venture out, on two nights when the wind pauses for breath, to shoot rabbits with the Weihrauch, a torch fixed to a DIY stand to illuminate the killing field, the fields shine with suppurating water.

I've eaten another of the Kilner jars of duck *confit*. Alas, the method might be airtight but not foolproof. I've done something wrong, and the remaining jar is growing something suspiciously like botulism. Out it goes.

The confessions of a hunter-gatherer: I've eaten more than the duck *confit*. I've consumed almost all of the food listed at the New Year. The drink too. The elderberry wine is gone. Only the scrumpy remains. The thought of an evening without alcohol jitters me more than the idea of a day without food. Something has to rub the rough corner off this life. Such a thought, I know, has occurred to many previous residents of Trelandon. Because I know their drinking habits.

Until the 1960s the households in this forgotten valley buried their refuse 'out the back'. Penny's vegetable garden is built on a midden. Dig a foot down, then up come lemonade bottles with glass stoppers, cider flagons, brown beer bottles, tobacco tins, bits of Georgian clay pipe, broken willow-pattern china, leather boots, clay jars, 1930s cough-mixture bottles, Victorian inkpots, belt buckles, bits of oak cask which once held God knows what, and more than sixty miniature bottles of Johnnie Walker whisky so far, and counting.

In casting my mind to the back garden, I remember the bits of rotten beehive we found beyond it in the orchard undergrowth.

Beehive.

Bees.

Honey.

And the next connection is easy.

Mead.

Mead
Adapted from Herbs for Daily Use *by Mary Thorne Quelch, 1941*

According to Quelch, her recipe for mead was given her by a Romany acquaintance. Unlike many mead recipes it does not rely on spoonfuls of yeast and yeast nutrients, assuming that wild yeasts in the air and 'just the honey and water' will do the trick. You do, however, need a source of honey that is as little processed as possible. Raw honey is best.

Quelch's ratio of water to honey is three to one. As long as this proportion is observed, mead can be made in any amounts you care for. Put the honey and water into a stainless steel pan and bring to the boil, stirring as you go to ensure that the honey and water are properly mixed. Skim off any scum. Keep it simmering for an hour, adding a little water if necessary. Allow to cool, then strain the must into a demijohn.

*Put outside in the garden with a piece of muslin over the open
neck. The muslin needs to have holes small enough to keep
out flies, but big enough to allow in the airborne yeasts (which
are micro fungi). After a day, bring inside and fit fermentation
lock. Mead requires a relatively warm temperature to ferment,
around 80°F/27°C.*

*My first vat failed miserably to ferment. So I remade it
later in February, when the weather was fine and dandy and
the yeast was flying. That took.*

*Since raw honey contains a relatively low level of nutrient,
full fermentation may take months. The mead produced will
also have a relatively low alcoholic content for a wine – which
is, essentially, what mead is – at around 10 per cent. Bottle
when the process is definitely completed. Store in a cool dark
place. Drink after a fortnight at the bare minimum.*

*A stronger mead could be made by decreasing the
water:honey ratio, or by adding some preserved fruit. The
latter would add nutrients and acid, both of which would feed
the yeast to a fuller, faster fermentation. In farmhouses of old
England, another variant was to add cowslips to the must just
as it was taken off the heat.*

———

By my calculation I have eaten fifty-eight rabbits since October. I
have had rabbit roasted, grilled, kebabed, stewed; I have had
rabbit in cider, I have had rabbit in elderberry wine. I have
had rabbit for breakfast, brunch, lunch, high tea, dinner and
supper. I have tried to disguise the taste of rabbit with mushrooms, wild garlic, wild thyme, rosehips, crab-apple jelly and
bramble jelly. Rabbit, rabbit, rabbit. Just the word makes me
heave. Everywhere I go I trail a cloud of rabbit. To escape from the
smell I throw my clothes into the machine to whirligig at 60°C in
Ecover bubbles, but I can still smell rabbit. Is something stuck to

my coat? Have I brought something into the house on the sole of my wellingtons? I put the coat and wellingtons into the cow byre, open the house windows to winter's clinical winds – but no, the aroma of rabbit cages my head yet.

In an effort to serve up rabbit in a new and interesting manner I sit in the kitchen with my head in my hands and Prue Leith's *Cookery Bible* in front of me. This is perversity, since Leith's rich, Frenchified style of cooking ('There never was a good cook with a Calvinist heart') is a pole away from mine, which, given my resources, is of the type to make John Knox glad. Thus I flick the pages aimlessly, until I catch her recipe for Peking Duck, which glazes the duck with honey. Rabbit glazed with honey? Why not.

Roast rabbit with honey glaze

Take a skinned rabbit and soak it in a cold salt water solution for one hour, then pat it dry. Brush the rabbit with generous amounts of clear honey and leave to dry (it won't dry off completely, but tacky dry will do). Repeat. And repeat. Place the rabbit in a roasting pan and cook at 350°F/170°C/Gas Mark 4 for about an hour to an hour and a quarter.

The crisp, brown sweetness of the outer flesh is sublime; so is the contrast with the inner flesh, made white by the soaking in salt water.

Since the recipe turns out so well, I OD by having it three times in a row, which palls its pleasure.

I have one last culinary idea for rabbit. Pâté.

It is a variant enough to get me over the psychological hurdle of another day with rabbit, another day until I can kill something else.

Rabbit pâté
1 rabbit
1 rabbit's offal
mixed herbs (wild thyme and chervil)
2 cloves wild garlic
salt
duck fat

Paunch the rabbit, but do not discard the liver, heart, kidneys and lights. Skin and behead the rabbit, and cut the meat from off the bones in small strips. Put the meat and the offal into a frying pan with the wild garlic. Lightly fry, adding the mixed herbs just before the meat is completely cooked through. Put into a blender with 2 large pinches of salt. Whizz. Put the mixture into a heat-proof dish with a lid and cover. Steam in a bain-marie for two hours and allow to cool with a heavy weight pressing down on the pâté.

One of the most useful aspects of this recipe is that it uses the rabbit's offal. I used to boil up the discarded innards of rabbit, pheasant and duck and feed them to the dogs, but this has become a generosity too far.

In a break in the weather I take the Weihrauch down to Copse Field. There, with the rain dripping from the roof of branches, I sit and wait in the hide on the bank. The hide works to perfection. I'm the invisible man. A succession of animals, once deemed edible but now forbidden on the plate, parade by. A green woodpecker – the poor man's duck – busies itself poking about in the meadow, before flying off with a manic laugh. A grey heron lands beneath me, walks on its ungainly stilt legs and fishes; as late as 1917 T. Cameron was proposing the heron as a meal fit for a hungry man if (a rather big if, one feels) it was plain-boiled for eight hours, after which it would be 'only very slightly fishy'. Song thrushes and blackbirds both make an appearance, both of them at one time roasted or 'pied' by the English. Directly in front of the hide, across the narrow finger of meadow, the barbed wire at the base of the copse fence is strung with the grey and white bristles of the badger; almost certainly the first inhabitants of Trelandon, like other West of England peasants, used badger fat for cooking. The hams too would have been eaten. According to Cameron, 'The hams, when cured by smoking – over a fire of birchwood for preference – after the manner used in curing bacon, are a decided delicacy, and may then be cooked and eaten either hot or cold.'

Only at last light does my legitimate quarry make its appearance, leaping through the bare treetops on his way home to the dray in the elder tree before me.

The grey squirrel stops for a cautionary look around. Unfortunately for the squirrel the telescopic lens on the rifle gathers light and I can see him as clear as at midday.

Seeing him lying dead at my feet, with the overbite of death, I remember why I've never eaten squirrel. They have the faces of rats.

Slitting the squirrel open I find its stomach full of hazelnuts. Pre-stuffed, so to speak. Casseroled in cider, the squirrel tastes better than I suspected. It has some of the succulent, white delicacy of roast farmyard chicken.

Squirrel casserole
1 squirrel, quartered
¼ pint/150ml cider
¼ pint/150ml rabbit stock
pinch wild thyme
2 dandelion roots
2oz/55g duck fat
salt

Cut the dandelion roots into neat cubes. Rub the squirrel quarters with salt. Brown the dandelion and squirrel together in the duck fat, then transfer to a casserole dish. Sprinkle with the wild thyme. Add the cider and stock. Place the lid on the casserole and cook at 300°F/150°C/Gas Mark 2 for 3 hours.

Introduced into Britain in the nineteenth century, the grey squirrel is a common food source for predators in these dregs of winter. Unlike its native red cousin, the grey does not hibernate. Fired up on the success of the dray-side shooting, I sit next morning on the bank of the river, across from the wooded quarry, listening and watching for squirrels. Over the plash of the water, I hear one chakking away, and stalk it to a towering ivy-clad oak. High up, the squirrel does not deign to present a clean shot. Nor does the next one I track: although the squirrel seems perfectly silhouetted on the open winter limb of the ash, the .22 pellet is deflected by a twig and the squirrel bounds free.

The grey squirrel might be plentiful, but it is not easy to hunt. I know of one other winter quarters for squirrels on the farm, a hollow limb in an apple tree in Bank Field, and set myself up for another *Day of the Jackal* assassination. Lying behind a fallen tree trunk smoothed shiny by time, I have a perfect view of the entrance hole into the limb. Although I'm upwind of the dray, my smell is likely masked by the odour of sheep on my waxed jacket from lambing. Somewhere away in the bland mist a buzzard keens.

There's a movement at the base of the apple tree. A white chest appears, but it belongs to a stoat. A glance at my watch. I've been out for three hours. Inside my head there is a universe of blank space. My arms tremble. My blood sugar levels are way too low. I give up.

Lunch is cold pheasant, a present from my aunt Margaret, a bird shot on the last day of the season in north Herefordshire.

She has skinned not plucked it. I don't blame her. I pile on tablespoons of crab-apple jelly. When Penny is out of the kitchen I filch a round of brown seeded bread from the tin. Oh! Aside from the embracing arms of my wife and the holding hands of my children, I have never known such softness. There is a long, elasticated moment of temptation before I pass the bread down to the elderly, trusting Hatty, with her beseeching Labrador eyes. This is the truth I know: I'm getting tired, too tired for morality. I have accepted Aunt Margaret's pheasant without a qualm; and that round of bread almost passed my lips. A thought assembles itself confusedly in the depths of my head: curious that bread, the stuff of communion, should be such a devilish temptation to me.

This is the other truth I know: if I hadn't heard Penny walking back towards the kitchen I would have eaten the bread.

When I resume my vigil at the fallen trunk, a squirrel appears almost immediately, a motion of liquid mercury running along the grass. I sight the entrance hole in the end of the limb. As soon as the squirrel's head appears in the cross hairs, I fire. The shot, dispensed a fraction of a second too late, ploughs into the squirrel's back, knocking it to the ground.

Under the spread of the dormant apple tree, the squirrel whirls on its back, powered by adrenalin and fear. As quick as I can I run to it, loading as I go, to administer the balm of death. That I am seeking the squirrel's euthanasia is, of course, beyond its comprehension. The squirrel is struggling to keep its life. Consequence: the squirrel won't keep still. In a panicky, untidy manoeuvre I put my foot on the squirrel's chest, bring the barrel of the rifle to rest on the toe end of the wellington and shoot through the squirrel's neck into its head. At this the squirrel stills, but even so I shoot into the squirrel's brain one more time, in leaden overcompensation for my failure to deal a clean kill.

On the scales, the squirrel weighs in at 2lb, half a pound heavier than yesterday's catch. Such a weight suggests a veteran. The proof comes when I try to pull the pelt off and a tug of war follows, a certain sign that fur and flesh have been attached together for a season or more.

On the 6th the rain halts and in the red dawn the mountain glows like coal in a fire. The sheep decide to celebrate. I see one of the spotted Jacobs, separated off from the main flock, straining to look at the sky: a characteristic pose of a ewe about to lamb. Sure enough, by the time I walk across to where she is standing beneath the sprawling hazel hedge, the green water bag is protruding from her vagina. I walk up to Road Field in the triumphal sun to check the other sheep and by the time I've walked back the Jacob has two greasy black lambs on unsure legs standing before her.

The first lambs of the year are born. Another sign of the coming of spring. On the following day, I check the Newt Ditch where there are thirty pieces of spawn congealing together in a Pangaea of amphibian embryos.

For a fortnight the weather is the best for February I can recall; at night the temperature drops to −6°C, frosting the landscape in enchantment, and I hunt rabbits in the vast open fields by moonlight, the only sounds the whispering of the gently flowing Escley, the crunch of frost beneath my feet, the wooing of the tawnys in Quarry Wood, the satisfying 'crack' of the Weihrauch and sometimes the thin, tearing wail of a rabbit losing its life to another predator; by day the sun shines hazily high in the sky and it is warm enough for shirt sleeves rolled up. Celandines and dandelions flower in Copse Field and in the hedges honeysuckle leaves start to sprout. By the 11th there are fifty-one pieces of spawn in the ditch. So loud is the factory din of the mating frogs in the evening that it can be heard at the house, 600 yards away.

—

Tisk. Tisk. Tisk. A robin endlessly repeats its alarm call in the hedge bordering the Grove. *Tisk. Tisk. Tisk.*

It is around eleven o'clock and Edith and I have tramped the forty acres, top to bottom. We have sat and observed, we have skulked and planned ambushes, but we have seen nothing to shoot at except three wood pigeons flying too fast across the face of the sun. So chill is the baby-blue air that it drills into my finger ends and will not let the ground defrost; there are still little dishes of ice in the hoof marks of the cattle.

Edith's head has dropped, so I feel in my pocket for some dog biscuits, which she eats off my hand. I take off my shooting glove and put my right hand under her front right leg to warm my fingers. A fair exchange of food for heat.

Looking down towards the bog I know that there is something there, something hiding at the back where the crack willows flop over. But what is it? Another rabbit probably. And if it is a rabbit from the warren whose burrows in the Grove hedge I am presently standing outside, it might be induced to run for home along the dry bank at the bog's edge.

'Let's go, Edie,' I say, and we start downhill towards the bog, tacking left. I need to work round behind whatever is in the bog, so that I am shooting up our own land and not into the Grove's field. Shooting behind a fleeing rabbit is not ideal because it lessens the chances of a clean kill: the target area is smaller, the prey is going with the direction of shot. But it is this shot or no shot. At the back of the bog we skirt along the Copse Field hedge towards the rabbit. Twenty yards into the bog and nothing has moved.

If I go any further in, I am going to be hopelessly stuck, because the firm ground runs out. This is the mouth of the bog, where it gathers its surplus water before allowing it to seep into the drainage ditch of Copse Field below it.

Time to send in Edith. 'Edith, go on!' I point to the corner of the bog under the willows. Edith looks up at me sheepishly.

There is something about Edith that I have not dared tell anyone, for fear of ridicule. Edith does not like getting her paws muddy. Faced with a puddle, she will jump over it; faced with the bog, she will leap with balletic grace from one clump of rushes to the next.

Edith does not want to go into the nasty wet smelly bog. I do not want to repeat the command because if one repeats a command the dog has negotiated with you. Dogs should not negotiate. Dogs should do. I remain quiet with my finger pointing.

Edith begins her audition for the English National Ballet Company. An arabesque. A glissade. A quite lovely tour en l'air. An absolutely remarkable pirouette piquée. By now Edith has danced to the far corner of the bog. Edith is not entirely lacking gundog genes. She stiffens. She smells the air.

The snipe rises. *Creech. Creech.* The snipe zigzags through the air in twisting flight, barely above the rushes, goes straight, then performs a vertical lift before flicking left over the hedge into the Grove's field.

Edith's contempt for my failure to fire at, let alone hit, the snipe is boundless. She shakes her head in disbelief. I signal her to come back, which she does with a series of grands jetés en avant.

'Edith, the bloody game season is over! It's against the law to shoot snipe now.'

Edith says nothing. Edith thinks there is not a pussycat's chance in hell he would have hit that snipe, it must have been pushing 60mph.

The robin has hopped down the hedge to add his voice. *Tisk. Tisk. Tisk.*

Obviously, this is one of those days when surrealism reigns. As I make my excuses to Edith, a lone Canada goose – the first I have ever seen here – flies overhead on long steady wings. Officially deemed a pest species, Canada geese can be shot the year round. But this one is already over the Grove's air space. I do not mention the goose to Edith.

I have always felt cheated by the bog, which stretches to two stagnant, marshy acres but has never, ever shown the slightest inclination to pull a wading bird. Until now, that is, when the season is over.

Snipe are crepuscular and nocturnal. In the creeping in of the dark, my breath whitening the air, I return to Bog Field with binoculars in the hope of seeing the snipe feed. But it has gone. Snipe, like woodcock, are creatures of mystery. Here today, gone for ever tomorrow.

Spring quickens its advance. On 14 February the first daffodils open on the track. A week later I count seventy-one lumps of spawn in the Newt Ditch. Blackthorn buds are tumescent and the elders are throwing up their red shoots. They look good enough to eat: but they taste disgusting and I spit, spit, spit them out. In the great beds which border the back of House Meadow and Little Field the young nettles are an inch high. Spring is erupting.

I go and lie amid the celandines in Copse Field, the great bowl of the Black Mountains, Merlin's Hill and Trelandon bank around me, and allow the soft sun to warm me. This is the first time I have stopped for reflection in over a month. The complaint that modern life leaves no room for rest, no cloistered space for thought, laughs in my ears; for a month my world has not stretched beyond the prosaic mechanics of food and drink, the obtaining and preparing thereof. Is the gun shooting true? Will the rain break? Where are my thermal socks? Have I casseroled the rabbit to leather? There are primitive hunter-gatherer tribes in the Brazilian jungle that have no metaphysics, because they have neither the time nor the energy to speculate about existence. Life is simply what happens in this moment in this place. I think I understand. With next to nothing in the larder, I have spent the last four weeks surviving from one day to the next, nothing more. I have been on the auto-pilot of instinct. Even the visits to my father, now transferred to a community hospital in Leominster where he is repeatedly con-tracting MRSA, have taken on the aspect of blind duty because I cannot bear to wonder what his – our – future is. I am too young to lose a parent, because one is always too young to lose a parent. I resolutely do not think about his health, and if worry about my father threatens to break in I pummel it back and seal up the wall with English cold blood.

And what do I think about, stretched out in the yellow flowers, as Nature microscopically works and awakens around me? I think about my hands. To know something 'like the back of your hand' is to know something intimately, but I do not recognize the back of my hands. They have been worn by the elements into elderly brown leather, parched and cracked, impersonations of discarded brogues. I think about wood pigeons, and how glad I am that I have shot so few, because from here to September they are my one game bird. I think: I have made it through to spring.

More, much more than this, I think: I know why I'm here, doing this.

Energized, I spend the evening in the kitchen decanting and bot-tling the sloe wine from last autumn. It is, of course, the maker's prerogative to test his fermentation. His duty even.

I had a small fantasy that I might have a glass of sloe wine with tonight's meal of kebabed pigeon, but this is shattered into fragments by a single tentative sip. The sloe wine is raw. It needs time. Some things cannot be hurried. I am the object of time, just as I am the object of Nature.

Listening to the dawn chorus on the last day of February, I notice that the buzzard is absent. I hope that it is well and is merely scouting pasture fields new, or – and I quite like this notion – that it is having a well-deserved perch-in. Whatever, the buzzard missed an avian symphony, for all the birds of the valley flew to vantage points and sang to welcome the day and to stake their breeding territory. This was surround sound Dolby would have admired, although most of the birds congregated at the wooded bottom of the farm along the Escley. The thrush family were the virtuosos, while the crows performed drum and bass.

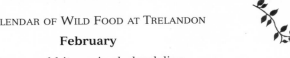

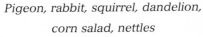

A CALENDAR OF WILD FOOD AT TRELANDON

February

Pigeon, rabbit, squirrel, dandelion,
corn salad, nettles

SPRING

S ALAD DAYS ARE HERE again. Wandering through the pig pen, on 6 March, I find that the Somme-like expanse of mud that the Gloucester Old Spots left behind in autumn has produced a mass crop of hairy bittercress. A drab little green plant with minute diamanté flowers on slender stems, hairy bittercress is not well served by its name, being neither bitter nor hairy. It tastes like peppery rocket. One can only wonder at the happenstance that caused 'roquette' to become the staple of the Waitrose class and not hairy bittercress. Like New Zealand gooseberries (aka kiwi fruits), it is a plant in need of renaming.

Hairy bittercress is one of the first wild salad plants to push through the warming spring earth; it is also one of the best.

Winter does not go gently. A day of stinging snow flurries leaves the mountains and Merlin's Hill dusted in white. Typically, this is the day when one of the ewes decides to go next door to the Grove and have her lambs there; she then comes home, leaving one white and one black lamb behind her. By the time I find the curly-coated abandoned lambs in the snow they are desperately dehydrated. I carry them under my arms to the house, where I syringe colostrum and glucose down their throats, and put them in a cardboard box beside the Aga. Despite everything I do, they die. Lambs rarely come back from the far edge.

That night, by torchlight, we round up the sheep and put them into the paddock, where they can take shelter behind straw bales. The lambs we dress in natty plastic foul-weather jackets, save for two which, when we run out of the shop-bought models, are put in carrier bags with a hole for the head. There is a certain irony, we feel, in seeing lambs wrapped in the legend *Tesco*.

On the next day the spring sun melts the snow before my eyes, even that which lies in the deep west shadow of the trees, and like the plants of the earth I want to push up into the vernal air. During the long days of winter I walked around shrunken into my coat, but today I walk tall and warm. The world of the upper Monnow and its tributaries seems completely different from this heightened perspective; I had forgotten what a big airy landscape this is.

In sheer exuberance I run free down Bank Field, gun in my right hand, *Last of the Mohicans* style, Edith bounding beside me through the picture-book celandines until, puffed, I sit on a long log beside the river. The river is almost instantly responsive to the weather and is rising perceptibly with melted snow water; by midnight it will rage in the vociferous manner of surf pounding a winter beach in Pembrokeshire. But for now it is only flexing its oiled brown muscles, rippling and rolling as it parades downstream in the sunshine.

I want a day off – well, an hour – and so decide to leave the gun behind a tree and walk the farm over, instead of slinking and sidling through it like a weasel or a fox. As I stride out over broad acres, Edith running free on her own holiday jolly, the thought strikes me that an Englishman's home might be his castle, but it is his land that is his kingdom. Soon I am warming to my theme, my stride is getting longer, and I feel like a colossus marching across his dominion.

While it is revolting to say it, the ownership of land does feel good. James Brown trips into my head. I feel good, I feel good, I feel good.

Somewhere off in the still, naked trees by the river a woodpecker issues its manic mocking laughter at such pretension.

On this green hill, far away, we are at least two weeks behind the botanical clock of even the neighbouring valley. Only now, in mid-March, are the great beds of nettles which band the Pony Paddock really pushing up. There are enough to pick – and you just pick the top leaves, like tea – for a meal of early spring greens. (One can steal an advance on Nature, as Andrew Fairservice, the old gardener of Lochleven, did in Walter Scott's *Rob Roy*, by raising the nettles under glass.) Probably nothing I do amazes my friends more than the eating of nettles, but a quick steam or boil removes the sting, leaving a brilliant green vegetable that tastes like bitter spinach, though with a rougher consistency. I pick a second full carrier bag for another purpose: to make a vat of nettle beer.

In the kitchen, as I add a carrier bag of nettles to a boiling cauldron, Tristram comes in and says archly, 'Has one of the dogs peed?' He has a point. The drawback of nettles is the smell of urea. It never goes, even when the dark amber liquid is drained and fermented into beer, even if ground ivy – the medieval brewer's standby, hence its alternative name of 'ale hoof' – is added. A piss-up, indeed.

Nettle beer

This is simplicity itself.

2lb/900g young nettle tops
8 pints/4.5l water
6oz/170g honey
1oz/30g ground ivy

Wear rubber gloves to pick the nettle tops. Wash and drain them, plus the ground ivy. Put the nettles, ground ivy and water in a large saucepan or cauldron and bring to the boil. Boil for 15 minutes. Strain the liquid and add the honey. Stir with a wooden spoon until the honey has dissolved. Allow to cool and pour into a brewing vat. Cover with a layer of muslin or net curtain, tied down so that it doesn't dip into the liquid. Leave outside for a day, so that the wild yeasts of the air can slip through the cloth and land on the liquid. Bring inside, cover with an additional layer of cloth, and leave in a warm place – about 70°F/21°C – for at least 3 days. Strain into sterile wine bottles and cork loosely. Or you can use old plastic mineral water bottles, which work well. Store in a cool, dark place. The nettle beer will be ready in a week. Serve chilled.

Alas, I rarely achieve alcoholic consistency with nettle beer; sometimes it has the immobilizing capacity of curare, sometimes it is no more dangerous than ginger beer. A more stable brew could undoubtedly be gained by substituting sugar for honey, and fresh yeast for wild yeast.

Nettle beer is a pleasant, refreshing drink, and allegedly good for one's health; English cottagers swore by its ability to cure gout and rheumatism. Aside from ale hoof, other traditional wild flavourings for nettle beer are dandelion, burdock, clivers (goose grass) and meadowsweet.

To use nettles as a vegetable, they should be washed and then put in a saucepan with a cupful of water and cooked with the lid on for about 15 minutes. Nettles, for the unwary, are slightly laxative and old nettle leaves, especially in winter, contain high amounts of cystoliths (crystals of calcium carbonate), which make them grittily unpleasant.

When my octogenarian father and stepmother decided that they could no longer garden in the manner to which they were accustomed (herbaceous borders twelve feet deep) they moved into a purpose-built retirement apartment in the middle of Hereford and put pot plants on the twelve-inch-deep windowsills. A cardboard box marked 'very old photos' was given to me for safekeeping during the removal process. Presumably there were boxes marked 'old photos', 'quite old photos' and 'newish photos' somewhere else.

I still have the photos. What correctives to memory's tricks the photographs are. There is one of me aged ten (surely only a 'quite old photo') in Clarks sandals outside the barn at Hampton Park with two puppies, which I would have sworn from memory were black Labradors, but actually have white paws and chests, suggesting miscegenation with a collie. There is me aged nine in my school uniform; what I fondly imagined was a friendly sprinkling of facial freckles turns out to be a mass band across my nose and cheeks giving me a decidedly racoonish look. I would not have believed that the boy in the picture was me, except that I could make out my YOC (Young Ornithologists' Club) badge on my tie. Mostly, however, the photos are as described on the lid, taken broadly between 1943 (my father, a seventeen-year-old volunteer in his Fleet Air Arm uniform) and Daguerre's heyday. My father has written 'Me' on the backs of pictures of himself, endearing but not much help to a genealogist, and he has identified some relatives, but there are galleries of ghostly unknown ancestors.

I spasmodically hunt through the photographs, looking for the obvious: clues to my identity. There are a few rich red herrings, such as the Probert cousins from Monmouthshire, every inch 'Society' in their 1920s flapper hats and white silk stockings, and Great-aunt Ruth Dymond with her wrappings of furs (she emigrated to Canada and married a speculator who made a fortune in gold or oil or some other mythical wilderness substance). Mostly the photographs are what I would expect: they are very down home. Spreading them out on the sitting-room rug in their hundreds, I find scores of my father as a boy beside the 1930s English seaside (Weston-super-Mare, making good use of a souwester, year in and year out), and there are several of the Verrys on their farm at Little Birch, tucked up under the trees of Aconbury Wood. There is a photograph of my uncle Gordon; it is taken in the quad of the boys' school he won a scholarship to, and which I also attended, although not in such glamorous circumstances.

Above all, there are masses of photographs of my paternal grandfather Thomas, who prophetically called himself 'Will'. All of my grandparents were born on the land but Will, you feel, never liked animal shit on his shoes. Will, with his Edwardian waxed-curl-ended moustache, Will who was always dressed in suited perfection, Will who was elected to the diocesan guild of bell-ringers, Will who bowled for Herefordshire against the touring South Africans in 1936, Will who became a director of Hereford United.

Sometimes I play a game with the children, or indeed the dogs. Staring. He or she who blinks first is the loser. Even in death, even when confined to a piece of card as he is today, I cannot outstare my grandfather. Will is determination made incarnate. I cover up the photographs of him. I do not have Will's power, but I do, if I face the facts, have a shade of his willpower; I would not have got through the winter without it.

While I am pondering my genetic inheritance, I realize that a buff envelope that I thought contained photographs actually contains papers. Pulled out and spread open they make interesting reading, as in the Chinese curse, 'May you live in interesting times.' As my mother had suggested on the telephone back in December, my father's family do indeed have 'Aymes' in the line. My great-aunt Sarah, Will's sister, married into the Aymeses. Gordon, the scholarship boy, was even given a third Christian name, Aymes, to seal the connection. I'd always thought that if there was a blood connection between my parents' families it would be through the maternal lines, since you could throw a stone between their ancestral farms at Much Dewchurch and Kilpeck; but no, the connection comes through the paternal lines. And is thankfully too distant for me to worry that I am going to sprout a third eye or some other mark of inbreeding.

⁓

For us, the sound of spring is not the cuckoo's call. It's the corneting of the curlew.

On 13 March, the same day that the thicket beside the river becomes illuminated at ground level by the flowering of fragile white wood anemones, I fancy I hear a curlew but above the raking wind I can't be sure. Two days later, the wind eases away and I then definitely hear the call of the wild. Looking around the 360-degree sky I spot the brown curlew, its long decurved beak silhouetted clear against the white cloud as it issues its mournful wail. *Curlee, curlee.*

More curlews come in from the Welsh seaside over the next week, the males performing their undulating flight-dance, their songs winding up into a reverberating trill. My spirits soar up to meet the curlews. Spring is sprung. More, it is so good to have the uncommon birds home safe. Eventually, when the grass flushes later in the month, two pairs will scrape depressions in Road Field, our highest land, and despite being Europe's biggest wading bird – the size of a duck – will sit almost unseen in the lengthening grass, the cows eating carefully around their olive, brown-blotched eggs.

At the shingle bank by the waterfall, the level of the river has fallen so much in three days that, for the first time since autumn, I can access the lesser burdock (*Arctium minus*), which is just beginning to sprout above the pebbles. I dig down with a narrow spade intending to extricate the roots. Even in the mewing wind, which is catapulting the jackdaws around the March sky, I soon overheat because the shingle is nearly impervious to the metal blade. I switch my body into machine mode but let my mind tune into birds sheltering in the bankside bushes and trees around me: an insistent whistling blue tit works the hazel, a nuthatch walks down the alder trunk picking and prodding, a chaffinch collects dried grass from the moraine of flood rubbish caught in the wire fence, because the nesting season is under way in earnest. These are not exciting birds, but ticking off rare species is not what I'm interested in: I am fascinated by the birds' diligence. Shamed, or perhaps inspired, by their industry I carry on digging until it darkens and the birds go to bed, and two hours have passed, and when I strike the spade into the stones sparks flash into the night. And I have so many burdock roots piled up that I have to fetch the tractor and load them into the link box on the back.

In Japan burdock roots, thinly sliced and boiled, are a popular vegetable and the plant is grown commercially. An equally ancient usage of the root is in the making of dandelion and burdock beer, said to have been invented by the Italian theologian St Thomas Aquinas in the thirteenth century, when he walked from his place of prayer and, 'trusting in God to provide', concocted the drink from the first plants he encountered in the countryside. So stimulating did St Thomas Aquinas apparently find dandelion and burdock beer that it helped him formulate the theological thoughts that culminated in his masterpiece, *Summa Theologica*. Somewhere further along the historical line dandelion and burdock beer was transmogrified by the British into a non-alcoholic soft drink but it is really a type of light mead. The 'pop' version, which is carbonated and tastes similar to Coca-Cola, may be bought from suppliers upmarket (Fentimans) and downmarket (Tesco), though I fancy that it is localized in popularity to the west and north of England.

Dandelion and burdock beer

4oz/110g dandelion leaves, chopped
4oz/110g fresh burdock root, chopped
2 tbsp dry cider
1lb/450g nettle leaves, chopped
8 pints/4.5l water
1¼lb/550g honey

Put the nettles, dandelion leaves and burdock into a stainless steel tureen (or similar) and add 4 pints/2.25l water. Bring to a boil and simmer for 30 minutes. Add 1lb/450g honey and allow it to dissolve. Take off the heat and strain to remove the solids. Pour into a brewing vat and add the remaining water and the cider. If you are intending to use wild yeast at this point, you will either have to add skins of crab apples or leave the brew outside, with a muslin cover, where wild yeast can land on the surface of the liquid. (Alternatively add wine yeast or brewer's yeast, following the instructions on the packet.) Leave it to ferment in a warm place for 3 days. Pour off the beer and bottle it, adding a teaspoon of honey per bottle.

Leave the bottles undisturbed until the beer is clear, which will take about a week.

Dandelion and burdock beer has a very short life and needs to be drunk immediately.

The usefulness of burdock is not limited to its roots. In the later spring, its ribbed stems can be peeled and the innards steamed; their flavour has a note of peardrop to it. In looks, burdock is similar to rhubarb, for which it is sometimes mistaken.

—

There is a bend at Penbidwal, on the way to Monmouth, that we christen Kamikaze Korner because of the tendency of pheasants to commit suicide there. So, although the game season is gone, I am still eating the occasional *phaisanus*. On one such day of easy roadkill pickings, and when the rain is torrential, I decide to stay in the dry beside the Aga all afternoon and experiment with a solution to a pressing culinary problem: my lack of flour. I try drying (in the Aga) then grinding dandelion roots, which do make a flour of a bitter sort. As do burdock roots. And then I recall once having eaten pastries made from chestnut flour on holiday in Italy. So I take a handful of chestnuts from the larder, which at five months old are so dry they may fairly be termed desiccated, crack the peel off them and put them in the electric grinder. The resultant flour is yellow and sweetly gorgeous. And all my remaining chestnuts go the same way.

Later in the year, I make flour from fat hen seeds and from acorns, but neither is a match for chestnut.

—

It rains. Dear God, it rains. And that is the problem with March, surely the slowest month of the year to pass: it teases and gives the come-on but never quite goes all the way in delivering springtime.

I spend two hours in the morning trying to shoot rabbits, but retire before the onslaught of water. Sitting in the kitchen drying off, drinking dandelion coffee, I carry on reading *Rogue Male* by Geoffrey Household; inevitably the parts which lure me in most are those in which the hero, the would-be assassin of a European dictator (Hitler, effectively), hides up in the English countryside from the goons, and lives off the land. In the manner of Yosser in the 1980s TV tragedy *The Boys from the Blackstuff*, I think, 'Gis a job. I could do that.' It must be the bleakness of the weather, because I come over all survivalist and start remembering another TV show, *Survivors*, from the 1970s, which had an End Days scenario concerning the dropping of a vial of germs by some white-coated lab worker. Could the survivors of this plague then scavenge enough from Nature to subsist? Gis a job. I can do that too. Appropriately, *Survivors* was filmed on location in Herefordshire. Actually, some of it was filmed in Withington, where my retired Amos grandparents lived, enabling me to lie on the floor and watch *Survivors* on TV and afterwards look out of the sitting-room window at exactly the same scenery.

On the sort of fresh, bright morning when the oxygen-heavy breeze seems to have been imported from the seaside, I go out on to the yard to admire the white blackthorn blossom, which is happily exploding in every meadow hedge for miles down the valley. There are no leaves in the hedges yet; blackthorn flowers precede all the deciduous botanical life of the English hedge. The scene of darling blackthorn buds in March is almost 'perfick', save for one irritating blot on the landscape, which constantly draws my eye. Unfortunately the blot belongs to us.

As I always say, 'You're not real country unless you've got a few scrap cars lying around.' We have two, a silver Subaru estate with defunct suspension and a bronze Honda Accord, which my parents bequeathed us a year or more ago. Pompously, and probably erroneously, I considered myself too young for a Honda, and the children were so embarrassed by it that they flatly refused to be driven to school in it. They almost cheered when it failed its MOT because of rusty arches and was deemed to be forever unsuitable for the road. Still the Honda did sterling service in a financial crisis and, if the children never wish to be seen in public in it, they are quite happy to drive it around the fields, and then park it neatly at the bottom of the yard afterwards.

The Subaru, stranded unmoving and unmovable in the paddock, is, even I have to admit, a hillbilly eyesore, down on one corner with its headlight hanging out. Finally I revolt at the Subaru's decrepit state and pull it up on to the yard with the tractor, with a view to asking a scrap merchant to collect it.

Now this is weird. As I'm searching for the Yellow Pages, a seven-ton lorry appears on the yard, from which steps down a pale young man with startling night-black hair. I'm not a great believer in crystal balls, but the gypsy scrap merchant's visitation surely cannot be coincidence? Can it?

He gets straight to the point. 'Want to scrap that?' he says, pointing at the Subaru.

I am so befuddled by his mysteriously apposite timing that when he says, 'Forty quid,' I reply, 'OK.' No haggling, nothing.

He asks if I can load it on the back of his truck with the tractor, which I try to do, driving the muck fork on the front loader into the side windows of the Subaru, but although the International 484 can lift the car it cannot lift it high enough to get it on the truck's back. He is not one for wasting time, so he says he'll go and find someone with a Matbro with a telescopic loader.

While I am waiting for the gypsy to come back, revelation strikes at last. He must have called at Old Court or the Sett, on the hill opposite, when I was pulling the Subaru out of the field and literally seen his chance.

The March weather is contrary. One day it is spring sunshine and the hills are alive with the sound of lamb music and the beat of fieldfare wings (now going northwards, to the land of summer); the next day snow lashes the air, and the land locks down in a silent memory of winter just past. But through everything the heavens can conjure, still the land ineluctably greens. The tipping point comes on 20 March, when the first tight, tumescent buds of hawthorn leaves appear on the hedges. Walking up the track, with pairs of curlews sailing down the fields calling for dead souls, and a female wheatear eyeing me warily from a fence post, I pick hawthorn leaves as I go, which is a quintessential but forgotten country pastime. Before the age of affluence hawthorn leaves were considered a useful wayfarer's snack; my mother munched hawthorn leaves as she journeyed home from the village school in the 1930s. Young hawthorn leaves were then sometimes known as 'bread and cheese', although they taste nothing like these foodstuffs. On the tongue they have a definite, pleasing nuttiness.

On my mind, the hawthorn leaves have the effect of a balm, for the balance of my relationship with the land around me will now subtly change. Over winter I have taken from Nature. When Nature comes into leaf, it gives. The knowledge that for the next months Nature will give and give again its greenery has the reassurance of a hug from your dad when as a child you scraped your knee.

Of course, since Nature was the mother of the idea that there is no gain without pain, no blackberry without a scratch from the bramble thorn, the greening of the pleasant land presents me, one of life's carnivores, with a challenge. Which is: how to use all the bounteous greenstuff?

Stuffed bistort leaves

A plant of wet meadows on high hills, bistort is the prime ingredient of the dock puddings traditionally made at Easter tide, hence the plant's local name of Easter giant. At this time of year, the bistort's leaves are an excellent wild green but after early spring they become bitter on account of their high tannin content. Unfortunately the plant's arrow-head leaves are not fantastically distinctive and when the bistort sends out its notable pink brush-like flowers in summer it is too late to eat it. Such is Nature's Puckish sense of humour.
Serves 4

12 large bistort leaves
1 tbsp hazelnut oil
1 bulb wild garlic, crushed
1 tsp dried wild thyme
8oz/225g minced squirrel
2oz/60g ground chestnuts
salt

Cut 12 of the biggest bistort leaves you can find and lay them in a large heat-proof dish. Cover with boiling water and leave for 10 minutes. Drain, dry and place on one side.

Preheat the oven to 400°F/200°C/Gas Mark 6.

Heat the oil and gently fry the garlic, thyme and chestnuts. Add the minced squirrel, stir, remove from the heat and allow to cool.

Lay out the bistort leaves and place a tablespoon of the squirrel stuffing on each leaf and roll them up. Place the rolls in a greased dish. Cover and bake for 30 minutes.

In the absence of bistort, dock or curled dock can be used for the leafy wrapping of the stuffing.

On Easter Sunday, the Easter Hare comes, as he always does, and hides presents and Easter eggs for the children. Usually he leaves them in the garden, but this year he has hidden them down by the Elephant Tree bend of the river.

At 7.30 I go into Tris's bedroom and shake him gently by the shoulder. 'Tris,' I say, 'Easter Hare has decided to be more challenging this year and has put his presents for you down by the river.'

'Easter Hare,' says Tris, the duvet snug around him, 'is having a laugh.' Eventually he gets out of bed. Freda, who is ten and a big believer in Easter Hare, has been awake since six. Down to the river we troop, wrapped in multi-layers against the pure clear cold, with an optimistic wheelbarrow for the gifts. While the children run around, hunting gifts under hedges, in trees, on the shingle island, Penny and I stand in wide-eyed wonder at the beauty of the mountains, with their caster-sugar sprinkling of snow.

Later, after the traditional Lewis-Stempel Easter Sunday egg-rolling competition (hardboiled, pushed with a stick down the bank in a race: the winner he or she who finishes first with an intact egg), I go down again to the river to savour the view of the Black Mountains in white, and ponder the way snow always changes the perspective, so that the mountains look higher, even Himalayan.

Suddenly, in the corner of my eye I notice a grey blob on the river. A duck. I drop to the ground. I have the Weihrauch with me. OK, it's outside the duck-shooting season, I say to myself, but would anyone know if I shot the duck? There is not a soul to be seen in the lifeless fields around me, after all. Or maybe I should take the moral course and just stalk the duck, for the practice?

When I look back on this moment, I am still not sure what my motive was as I crawled Indian-style through the grass, my trousers absorbing the thin decaying snow, until I reached the bank. With my head behind a convenient fence post, I gradually fed the Weihrauch's barrel through the wire, before pressing my face against the post and peering with one eye down to the river, ten feet of red sandstone cliff below.

In the twinkling sunlight on the water, a male mallard paddled to and fro. From behind a fallen trunk, his mate sailed out to join him. Together, they up-ended happily, before drifting down beneath me.

Never in my life have I been so close to wild mallard. Shoot or not shoot?

Not shoot. They were too blissfully unaware of lurking death and the scene was so perfect that I felt as though I was the first intruder in Albion.

On the last day of March, the weather achieves that soft humid warmth so characteristic of the English spring, and we take a midday family walk to Longtown castle, up and over the spur which separates the little fold of the Escley from the little fold of the Monnow. Naturally, I do not entirely relax from registering the state of wild foodstuffs as we walk up the track to the lane; tucked discreetly in the emerald verge under the hedge are the leaves of wild strawberry and creeping everywhere in the hedge's lee is ground ivy, its tiny violet flowers held valiantly aloft. Across the lane we are off our own land, and I'm off duty, and since I hardly ever leave the farm, save to run the kids to the school bus, the expedition has something of a holiday adventure about it. The way to the castle is officially a bridle path, but its deeper, old self is still evident: it is the continuation of the peasant road which runs to the quarry at the bottom of Trelandon. The tread of centuries of hooves and cartwheels have gouged the bridle pathway down into the earth, so that for much of its length one cannot see over its high sides of clay and black leaf mould. While we are walking along in the old dark of the bridle path, an obvious thought articulates itself: I do not live in modern time, I live in Arthurian time. Because Trelandon is so quiet, so unaffected by traffic, I cannot tell by exterior noise whether the day is a working day or a weekend day. Everywhere I have ever lived, even in the depths of the country, commuter traffic has marked the weekday from the weekend day and the holiday. Not here. One day sounds as silent as the next, endlessly so, endlessly so, just as it must have done in slow-moving medieval times.

Longtown castle is no Camelot. Perched on an earth motte, it consists of a rare round stone keep and is bare Norman military function writ in sandstone. Even eight centuries later, it still grimly dominates the top end of the valley. Or at least it does in my mind's eye. For the children it is a playground, the grass-topped motte being quite excellent for rolling down.

⌒

Ambling around the farm, the celandines pushing up beneath my feet, I pop two pigeons on the wing in quick succession in afternoon sun so bright I've got the shades and the shorts on. Bang. Bang. Dead-eye John! Of course, anyone who has shot as many birds and beasts (140 plus) as I have in the last six months *should* be getting towards sharpshooter status. But it is not merely practice that is improving my shooting, it is attitude. Or more accurately, lack of attitude. As a shooting uncle once said to me, the best advice a shooter can follow is that of Obi-Wan to Luke Skywalker in *Star Wars*: 'Use the Force, Luke.' By which my relative meant, get inside the moment, go with your instinct, be natural.

⌒

When it happens I think, oh shit! I'm going to prison for this.

As much for personal enjoyment as larder necessity, I take a turn around the farm in the lengthening evening. But of course shotgun and dog come with me. As I walk the wooded edge of the river and bask in the rose light of the setting sun, I suddenly sense that an animal has tensed with alarm. I flick off the Baikal's safety catch and raise the gun. Out of the trees a pigeon flees frantically, a silver arrowhead traversing the pink sky. It is only when the pigeon flips in flight to curve around me that a warning sparks across my brain: the bird has no white wing-bars. It is not a wood pigeon.

But by then it is too late, the kill instinct has already mounted the shotgun to my shoulder, pulled the trigger and ended the bird's flight. Down it crashes, with all the grace of a shot-to-pieces First World War triplane hurtling to earth. I stand there stupefied, but Edith rushes off and brings the bird to me, her tail wagging with pride. I don't really want to receive it, whatever it is, but Edith places the bird neatly on my upturned palm.

Shit. Shit. Shit. The bird looks like a stock dove, which is a protected species. I want to toss the bird into the depths of the Escley, but then worry that it will wash up on somebody's land, who will start a criminal investigation to find THE DOVE KILLER. For one mad moment I consider weighting the bird down with stones, but dismiss this as too melodramatically gangland. So I decide to take the bird home and eat the evidence.

Under the light of the bulb in the cow byre, I look at the bird again, and a thought occurs to me. Maybe those black borders on the wings aren't very black, and perhaps the green sheen on the neck isn't very green. And what *is* a stock dove, a bird of arable lands and parklands, doing up here in the hills? So, on second thoughts, I determine that the bird is a feral pigeon, which is a legitimate quarry bird. Of course, one does not wish to waste a pigeon, so I eat it anyway (roasted) and dig the plumage into the ground, because birds' feathers make such mineral-rich compost. And there the matter lies.

In my worry about the provenance of my pigeon, I have not entirely overlooked Edith's successful retrieve. There are some cavils, such as the fact that she did it without my asking (a fault known as 'running in' in gundog circles) and that the retrieve was all of twenty yards, but full marks I think for realizing that the bird was, like the dummy she has worked with for weeks, a thing to be brought to the master's hand. Definitely paw steps in the right direction.

Warm burdock and pigeon salad
Serves 1
4oz/110g burdock root
2 pigeon breasts
1 handful mixed spring salad (chickweed, hairy bittercress, corn salad)
1 dollop goose/duck fat

For the dressing:
1 tsp hazelnut oil
pinch salt
1 tsp elderberry wine
1 tsp pan juice

Clean the burdock root and slice into long matchsticks. Simmer in salted water for 15 minutes, allowing the water to evaporate. Meanwhile cut the breasts off the pigeon, put the carcase aside for soup, and wash the salad leaves.

When the burdock is nearly boiled dry, heat the fat until it begins to smoke and fry the pigeon breasts for about 2 minutes each side, which will leave them pleasantly, bloodily moist inside. (If you want to follow contemporary health and safety advice and so overcook your game that the juices run clear, you will need to double the time the breasts are in the pan.)

Take the burdock and the pigeons off the heat and leave both to cool for 5 minutes. Mix the salad dressing, not forgetting to add the teaspoon of pan juice.

Put the burdock matches on a plate, pile on the salad, and then carefully lay the sliced pigeon on this green bed. Dribble the salad dressing over.

A CALENDAR OF WILD FOOD AT TRELANDON

March

Pigeon, rabbit, squirrel, dandelion, corn salad, hairy bittercress, nettles, hawthorn, bistort

S OMETIMES FORAGING, LIKE charity, begins at home. No sooner have I got out on to the yard in the morning and enjoyed the tender fragrance of daffodils on the air than a shower capriciously opens above me. Well, it is 1 April, All Fools' Day. So I decide to explore for plants in the sheltered, tussocky overgrown area between the back of the house and the orchard. Where the earth was once excavated for a water pipe I find an elongated carpet of chickweed, some of which is bravely displaying the species' distinctive pentagonal white-star flowers. Although chickweed is a tough little plant, it does not enjoy the frosts of the hills, and this is its first resurgence since winter. As with so many other 'weeds', chickweed was once a hawked vegetable on England's streets and markets, but for most of us today it is the gardener's bane. If one views *Stellaria media* as an enemy invader, eating it is delicious revenge.

To save on root-washing, cutting chickweed with scissors or a knife is advised.

Chickweed soup
With a flavour similar to round lettuce chickweed is most often used in salads, but it can be served hot as a green vegetable. Or as the principal ingredient of a light, bright green soup, perfect for early spring.
Serves 4

1¾ pints/1l game stock
1 clove wild garlic, crushed
2 bunches chickweed, chopped
pinch salt
1 diced root burdock/wild parsnip

Pour the game stock – pigeon is ideal – into a heavy saucepan, and bring to the boil. Add the burdock/wild parsnip, the salt, the garlic and the chickweed, turn down the heat and simmer for 10 minutes. Put the mixture into the blender and liquidize. Return to the hob and heat through.

A good base for soup in its own right, chickweed also combines well with other wild vegetables. Try adding nettles, sorrel, hairy bittercress or watercress.

From Road Field, there is a spectacular view down the valley to the angular Skirrid mountain, which rises gauntly into the clouds. Since I am gawping at this Borders Bali Ha'i in the morning haze, I fail to look where I am going and almost tread on the pear-shaped curlew's egg which is lying in the perfect middle of a mole hill. Curlews do not lay their eggs on mole hills and I cannot account for its being there, unless by a fluke the mole earthed up under the curlew's nest.

While I high-mindedly hope that the curlew parents can still hatch the speckled, spotty egg, the basest part of my being licks lascivious lips and thinks, it looks good enough to eat. Then it occurs to me that a whole wild food source is denied me by law, for just about all birds' eggs in Britain are protected. Soon I can think of nothing but eggs and the various wondrous ways they can be prepared.

Eggs I must have.

A plan is hatched. For every wild bird's egg I find I will

compensate myself, on a pro rata scale, with a domestic hen's egg. On second thoughts this, like some of my other 'plans', does not seem such a 100-watt bright idea: since Lucky, our pet chicken, ran out of luck and became a fox's midnight feast we have no egg provider in situ. Anyway hen's eggs don't seem authentic. But duck eggs do, especially since there is a mandarin mother currently sitting on a clutch by the twin oaks. Accordingly, I traipse the children to Hereford poultry market early on the first Wednesday in April. 'It will be interesting,' I tell them.

On the outskirts of Hereford, I stop at a Tesco's superstore cashpoint. I daren't check the balance and, feeling like a criminal, tentatively tap in a request for £100. The display curtly tells me that I have insufficient funds. £80? No. We settle on £60, the machine and I.

The poultry shed at Hereford market is a 1950s brick and asbestos hangar, with reinforced glass lights in the roof. Sawdust covers the floor. At 9.30 on the morning of a sale, the noise is Dantean. Three hundred lots of chickens, geese, pheasants and quail are stacked in three tiers of wire cages around three sides. Every inhabitant is protesting its capture. The children blanch visibly as they walk through the door.

In contrast to the sheep farmers in the neighbouring hangar, with their uniform of blue Dickies boiler suit and blue Land Rover 90s parked herringbone-style outside, the crowd in here is diverse. Teenage hoodies with eyebrow studs are crammed shoulder to shoulder with elderly Welsh smallholders across from Powys. What they have in common is their marginality. The profits in poultry farming, unless done on a massive scale, are tiny, to be measured in pence, not pounds. With the price of wheat so high ('£180 a tonne!') they are slimmer than ever.

A young mother tugging an infant parts the crowd with a 'Sorry!' and a smile, so that he can see the cardboard boxes of peeping yellow chicks at the far end of the central table, a free entertainment on an Easter holiday morning. My children and I follow in her wake.

There is a secret to buying at an auction: go early so you can view without pressure. It's also useful to know something about what you are buying. We used to have a flock of thirty chickens, Araucanas, Minorcas, Marans and Light Sussex, laying a selection box of green, brown, white and pink eggs. But ducks? My knowledge begins and ends at the fact that male ducks sometimes have a curly feather in the tail. Five minutes before bidding starts I'm only halfway round and a definite panicky feeling is rising. My mind is blank as to whether Aylesbury ducks are the eating sort or the egg-laying sort. Two Khaki Campbell ducks stand aristocratically oblivious to the two cockerels in adjacent cages above them, who are trying to murder each other in a cloud of feathers.

A man with the grey slicked-back hairdo of a boxing trainer is standing to the side of the Khaki Campbells, making notes on a piece of paper. 'Excuse me,' I shout above the din of fowl and people, 'do you know anything about ducks?' The children shrink with embarrassment behind me. 'These any good for eggs?' I bellow, pointing at the Khaki Campbells.

He pulls the cage open with his left hand, shoves in his plate-sized right and squeezes one of the astonished ducks. Swiftly closing the cage, he turns to me and smiles kindly. But broadly. 'No good for you. They don't quack.'

My face must have betrayed my confusion. He adds, 'Only ducks quack. Drakes don't.'

I grimace an acknowledgement at my ignorance.

As the bell clangs for the start of the auction, I spot the cages of Penrhiwgarn Poultry Supplies of Crickhowell, NP8 1LL. Penrhiwgarn Poultry Supplies must cater for people like me. On their cages of ducks they have put a helpful notice: 'White Female Laying Ducks. Ideal Free Range'.

Lot 87 is the one I quickly decide on. A top-tier crate of three brilliant white ducks with yellow bills and beady eyes.

The auctioneer mounts his podium. He is a cut above us, on his platform, in his tweed jacket. Pulling at the cuffs of his jacket, he leans into the microphone and speaks so fast I can only catch 'ten per cent buyers' premium' in the first minute.

'I swear he doesn't really say anything,' observes Tris standing next to me.

A white-coated assistant opens a cage and holds a bird aloft. 'Whatamibid, whatamibid . . . two, two and half, three, three and half, soldat three pounds . . .'

Even with such a rattling delivery, it takes ages to work through the lots. Tris spots a space on a table and there is real relief as we three sit down to wait for lot 87 to come up. The auctioneer reminds us of his exalted position by sniping at a young boy holding on to the side of the podium for a better look. 'No one allowed up here but me.'

I'm surprisingly nervous as the bidding moves towards the lot I want. My mouth dries in that manner known to every English person who has ever had to do anything with the face of the crowd upon them. The bidding is over in a flash. As the auctioneer starts on lot 85 I suddenly realize that I have to bid for it instead of 87, because the winning bidder can option lots 86–7. Up goes my hand, not unfortunately in the cool, minimalist manner of the auction veteran but in the flagpole style of the teacher's pet. 'Please, miss, I know the answer . . .'

Lot 85 goes to 'Seven and half, over here', 'over here' being me. Lot 85 being four white female egg-laying ducks, for which I have paid £7.50 each. I decline the option on the other ducks. I wanted three ducks. I've got four. I'm a duck up.

To get the ducks and their cardboard carrying box out of the auction room is to get them past a security system more stringent than an airport's. First I must pay at the adjacent office. In return

I get a bill of sale in triplicate. One page of this the office retains. The other pages I give to the burly doorkeeper, who duly checks 'Lot 85: Four white ducks' against the contents of the box by opening the top. For a moment I think the ducks are going to make a flap for it, but he's done this a thousand times before and shuts the lid in time.

'That's lovely, boss,' he says, handing me my page of the bill and releasing us to go on our way.

At home I ask the children to dig a pond for the ducks, expecting a puddle big enough for the ducks to bathe their eyes in (which is essential) but they exceed my wildest expectations and excavate in the unforgiving clay an oval pond six feet long, four feet wide and two feet deep, complete with a stone island in the middle. It is then that I remember that children are happiest when working, and when working with mud in particular. As they labour for two days solid in the thin sun, earning blisters on their hands, the first bumble bee and the first red admiral butterfly of the year make their début, while the blackbird cautiously flits past to gather dry grass from the pig paddock for the nest she is building on a shadowy beam in the unfinished sitting room. The children have cunningly positioned their pond below a field drainage pipe which juts out of the orchard's earth bank, so that the next time it rains the pond will fill.

This being the uplands of western England, we do not have long to wait; the rain comes the next day and the pond is replete within hours. The little white ducks take to the pond like, well, ducks to water, and swim in happy circles. A week later, when I open the duck house at seven o'clock in the bright spring morning, there in the interior gloom shines a bright white egg. I could sing for joy, but the skylark ascends fluttering into the sky and does the job for me.

I rush the egg into the kitchen, somehow paranoid that if I am not quick enough, it will disappear in a cruel trick, and boil it for four minutes. Curiously, I have never eaten a duck egg before; they do not have a good culinary reputation and are mostly used by the catering trade. What does my duck egg taste like? Exactly like a good free-range hen's egg but with, if anything, a smoother finish. Soon the ducks are giving me three eggs a day, and I have an embarrassment of egg dishes I can make.

Then comes the catch, because I cannot justify sitting around waiting for domesticated ducks to provide my food for me. So I determine that I can only eat one duck egg for every two wild birds' eggs I hunt down. The next weeks are bliss, as I track the mallard's shallow nest in the leaf litter on the bank by the Elephant Tree, the pigeon's rickety nest of sticks in the ivy tree by the orchard, the skylark's scraped hollow in Road Field, the swallow's painstaking mud bowl in the roof of the outhouse, the tightly woven hay dishes of the blackbirds and song thrushes in the hedges, and the tiny soft cushion of the jenny wren poked into the crumbling stone wall of the utility room.

Then I spy on the rough nests of the house sparrows in the roof of the kitchen, I locate the nest hole of the greater spotted woodpecker in the dead elm by the river, I observe the mud hole of the kingfishers on the red riverbank, stinking with pushed-out black fishy excrement, I look up at the careless twig raft of the jackdaws in the chimney, I hunt down the pheasant's scratched hole under the hawthorn bush, I trove the redstart's secret abode in the tree stump and, easiest of all, I see the deep, plush dish of the blue tit, with its moss and wool lining, because it is constructed inside our wooden postbox at the top of the track. Over the letter slit, we tape a notice for the postmen: 'Birds nesting! Please leave post in carrier bag below.'

Sorrel with eggs
From The Compleat City and Country Cook, *1736, by Charles Carter, reprinted in Roger Phillips's* Wild Food
'Your sorrel must be quick boil'd and well strained; then

poach three Eggs soft and three hard; butter your Sorrel well, fry some Sippets and lay three poach'd Eggs and three whole hard Eggs betwixt, and stick Sippets all over the Top, and garnish with slic'd Orange and curl'd Bacon or Ham fry'd.'

Sippets are fried bread. But even without the bread and butter, even without the garnish of pig meat, the combination of sorrel and egg is delicious. Jason Hill recommends folding raw sorrel leaves into an omelette, an idea I have adapted to serve 1:

2 duck eggs
pinch salt
small knob duck/goose fat
1 tbsp water
handful of young sorrel leaves

With a fork, whisk the eggs and water together. You want something that is blended, not foamed. Season with salt.

Heat a heavy frying pan until it is smoking hot, then drop in the duck fat. When the fat has melted – which will be very soon – pour in the egg mixture and swirl this around so that it covers the entire bottom of the pan. Cook for 30–45 seconds over medium heat.

With a wooden spatula gently lift the edges of the omelette so that the liquid egg runs underneath. Add the sorrel and cook for a further 30 seconds, repeating the lifting of the edges.

While the top is still faintly runny, fold the omelette in half and turn it out on to a warmed plate.

Sans sorrel, the above recipe for omelette is my standard model. It works well with wild garlic shoots, with mushrooms, with watercress, at the rate of one tablespoon of filler per omelette.

There are a few little local difficulties I'll have to admit to. I have run out of duck fat and hazelnut oil. I have finished the crab-apple and bramble jelly. I have cleared the cupboard of rosehip tea. Actually, now I come to itemize my larder, there is nothing left of the supplies gathered in during the autumn, with the exception of the sloe wine, one bottle of blackberry wine, one flagon of cider and the chestnuts, now changed into precious flour. I am back living hand to mouth, day to day, and in such verdant, vernal times this is not impossible, not even particularly difficult – with one exception: the absence of fat or oil to cook with. For the last days I have had food steamed, stewed, boiled, casseroled and raw but actually some things were meant to be fried. So, the next time Penny goes to Waitrose I add 'goose fat' to her list.

I have failed to live off the land. After six months of wilding I have resorted to buying Nigella Lawson's culinary favourite, goose fat, from a shop. Although I should feel despondent, I don't. In retrospect, to limit myself to foraging and hunting on my own forty acres was just one of those rule-setting, control-freak measures to which I am prone. I should have poached hazelnuts from my neighbours, from the lane, from up on the mountain.

And there is one paltry mitigating factor I propose again in my defence. The wildlife protection laws. As I write, a brace of mallard are sitting on the river, a showery rainbow overarching them. I might shoot them for their flesh and their fat, but I can't because of the law, which protects them from shooting in inland England for the closed season of 1 February–30 August, so that they are able to breed and grow in peace.

—

The April showers swell and muddy the river. On the Escley the trout-fishing season began on 3 March, and so far I have not dipped my rod into the water. My reason is that the river has been running too high and too brown, like it is today, but a nagging doubt is enlarging in my head. I am scared of failure. I've always been a hotshot with a gun. With a rod I'm the model for the compleat tangler. My boyhood summers were long silent humiliations as Tim, my best friend, reeled pike, perch, eels and trout out of the Wye and I caught nothing. Nothing at all. Not until I was sixteen did I catch my first fish, a pitying mackerel in the Irish Sea.

I lack faith in fishing.

The fifth of April is a bright, bright, sunshiney day. Tris, Freda and I arm ourselves with nets and march on the Newt Ditch with the lazy Saturday afternoon sun at our backs. When we stick the nets into the mass of floating grass and club rushes, clouds of frog tadpoles rush to be caught, but we cannot find a single smooth newt. I am about to wail, 'My newts have gone!' in a manner Wodehouse's Gussie Fink-Nottle would understand, when Freda says, 'Got one!' And she has: a small brown newt is sitting cold-eyed in the wet bottom of the net, and she delicately picks it out and places it on her other, upturned hand. We take turns at admiring its petite prehistoric lizardness before placing it back in the water, where it hangs suspended for a moment, then oars its tail and heads to the depths. After catching two, Tris wanders off home for an electronic screen fix, but Freda declares, 'I could do this all day,' as she stands in pink-spotted wellies with heron-type patience in the ditch waiting for a newt to make a betraying movement in the lengthening shadows. But eventually she becomes hungry, and we make a turn for home.

In the corner of my eye some dancing specks catch the sunlight above the Escley in Bank Field. Can this Brownian motion be house martins, this early? We walk towards the brook and, sure enough, in the sky-blue sky, house martins are wheeling and diving. Swallows too, their scarlet heads and forked tails clearly visible; the Victorian naturalist Gilbert White believed that swallows hibernated in winter in air bubbles in the sea, the truth being scarcely less mundane, in that they fly all the way to Africa. The house martins and swallows have never arrived back this early before – usually they come on 20 April – and I want to scream at them, 'Go back, go back!' I wish they had, because that night it snows and in the white of morning I find a swallow spread-winged on the soft linen bed of death.

Nothing can stop my good mood, even the death of a swallow in snow. I wish I had poetry in my head, instead of rock songs, but rock songs it is. These spring days I'm stuck in 'The Wild One' by Iggy Pop . . . 'Ooh yeah I'm a wild one.'

There is one poem I know well. It is *The Shepherd's Calendar* by the rustic madman John Clare. This is the verse for April:

> And fairey month of waking mirth
> From whom our joys ensue
> Thou early gladder of the earth
> Thrice welcom here anew
> With thee the bud unfolds to leaves
> The grass greens on the lea
> And flowers their tender boon receives
> To bloom and smile with thee.

In the third week of April, spring quickens its pace. No, it overruns the place with a force that awes, powered by heat and showers. Plants sprout everywhere, even through the concrete on the yard. The celandines now mat the lower fields, there is a hallucinogenic haze of bluebells in the thicket along the river, while one pink campion makes a brave advance stand in the Grove hedge. But the plants I 'thrice welcom' are the edible ones: the bright yellow primroses on the banks of the ditches, the lady's smock in Bog Field, ramsons in the shade of the river trees, and everywhere there is garlic mustard. So named because its pale leaves have a strong garlic taint when crushed, garlic mustard has been used in sauces for centuries, hence its alternative name of 'sauce alone'. Just as it does not lack for taste or stature (it grows several feet high), garlic mustard does not lack for names, because it is also known commonly as Jack-by-the-hedge. About garlic mustard Culpeper's *Herbal* advised, 'Reader, just try a little in your next salad.' Rightly so.

Jason Hill's *Wild Foods of Britain* also recommends using the roots of hedge garlic: 'The white, tapering roots taste rather like horseradish slightly flavoured with garlic and may be grated into a salad or pounded with oil and vinegar into a good substitute for mustard or horseradish.'

Salad, the truth be told, is my favourite foodstuff. I could eat it all day. And pretty much do. So to go gathering salad in April is not unlike being set free in a sweet shop as a child. I can hardly bear to be in the kitchen, I can hardly be bothered to cook. My trug overfloweth with salad greens.

Spring salad
garlic mustard (Jack-by-the-hedge)
hairy bittercress
hawthorn shoots
young dandelion leaves
cider vinegar
hazelnut oil
salt
honey

Wash and shred the leaves. Make a vinaigrette from the cider

vinegar and the hazelnut oil, ignoring the standard
proportions of 1 vinegar to 3 oil because hazelnut oil is so
strongly flavoured; try instead 1:1. Add a pinch of salt and
an iota of clear honey, working this in with a wooden spoon.
Transfer the ingredients to a screw-top jar and shake to salsa
music. Toss the salad in 2 or 3 tablespoons of emulsified
vinaigrette.

The delicate but peppery leaves of lady's smock also
make a good salad ingredient, although combined
with hairy bittercress the mix becomes unpleasantly
hot.

In the green glow of the copse, the red buds of the elder are
bewitching. Raw, as I know from my previous encounter with
them, they are vile, but optimism overtakes me and I refuse to
believe something so good to look at can be quite so useless, so I
fill a plastic food bag with them, shaking off the shiny April
shower drops. The archetypal spring smell of moist earth and
warm plants is intense in the copse and I linger and linger until the
wood anemones close one by one for the night. At home, in the
kitchen, I become intent on finding some old recipe that will
alchemize the elder buds to culinary gold. In this I fail, yet Jason
Hill's recommendation that they should be turned into a pickle
does at least make them edible.

Elder bud pickle
Adapted from Jason Hill's Wild Foods of Britain, 1944

Place the washed elder buds in a jar with shavings of horseradish or Jack-by-the-hedge root; pour over them a boiling
mixture of equal parts vinegar and dry cider and salt. Put into
the oven for an hour to infuse. Seal and store.

St George's Day, 23 April, is traditionally the date on which the mushrooms bearing the dragon-slayer's name first flourish in the grassland. This year, confused troops of fairy ring mushrooms (*Marasmius oreades*) appear instead, but I forgive them, for they make good pickings too. There is a care to be taken with fairy ring mushrooms, because they are similar in looks to *Clitocybe rivulosa* and *Clitocybe dealbata*, both of which are little-hope deadly. The circles of brown fairy ring mushrooms in the glistening grass, assembled like so many military formations on a Napoleonic battlefield in Prussia, stretch for twenty yards or more and I pick sixty with ease.

Fairy ring mushrooms are much recommended by the old books for their ease of drying (just string 'em up high), but I want them for a liquid solution to the tastelessness of too many of my dishes. I want them for mushroom ketchup.

Odd stuff, ketchup. Originally 'ketchup' was a brine of pickled fish but by the eighteenth century it came to mean any long-lasting brine or vinegar-based sauce. Its culinary heyday came with the British Raj, when it enlivened meals on the long voyage to and from India.

Mushroom ketchup

1.5lb/700g mushrooms
2oz/60g salt
¼ pint/150ml cider vinegar
¼ pint/150ml elderberry wine
2 cloves wild garlic, crushed

Chop the mushrooms and place in a china or earthenware pot. Sprinkle with salt. Leave for 2 days, but do stir occasionally. Heat the vinegar and add the wild garlic. Leave to infuse for 2 days. Mash the mushrooms and add the infused vinegar and the wine. Simmer until the mixture is like, well, ketchup, which should be in two hours or so. Sieve and pour into hot bottles, allowing the ketchup to almost reach their tops. Seal, then sterilize by placing the bottles on a folded cloth in a saucepan and filling this with enough hot water so that it reaches to 1in/2.5cm from the bottles' top. Boil softly for 30 minutes. The ketchup should keep for months in a dark, cool place.

One brisk afternoon we decide to climb the mountain *en famille*. Although from the east the Black Mountains seem to be a single wall, they are really made up of several hills joined together, and we take the footpath by the cliff known as Red Darren. The children ascend like goats; Penny and I stop breathless several times 'to admire the view'. On reaching the top at 605 metres, we sit in the springy beds of purple heather and fortify ourselves with Kendal mint cake and apples, or at least Penny and the children do; I take repeated nips of dandelion and burdock from a hip flask. None of us can believe the hue of the sky, which is the artificial blue of photographs taken by cheap disposable cameras. On a clear day you can see for ever. Almost. Before us the view stretches east for forty miles or more, and only ends because of the curvature of the Earth. From this vantage point, Herefordshire lies beneath me and I can see almost every-where my family have lived in the last half-millennium: Marlas, Little Birch, Common Hill, Much Dewchurch, Withington, Bromyard, Wormbridge, Hampton Bishop, Much Cowarne, Bishop's Frome. Only Kington in the north, where my Lewis great-great-grandparents lived, is denied me, occluded by the bulk of the mountain above Craswall.

To prevent me from coming over all sentimental, a peregrine falcon goes into a distracting stoop in front of us, before flaring out of the dive hundreds of feet later empty-footed. A red grouse, panicked by the peregrine's shadow, rises up from the heather and whirrs away at low level. Oh, the things you see when you don't have a gun and the season is closed! The bird show over, we follow the flat marshy top of the mountain northwards until we come to the top end of the Olchon Valley, where the Black Hill has joined the mountain and the land has risen to 703 metres. And we are the highest people in southern England, higher than the poor deluded walkers on High Willhays on Dartmoor who believe that they have that pleasure. It is fantastic but true; in this little-known valley in this little-known county of England is the nation's highest point below the Pennines. As we savour our elevated position, a feral white mare and her foal come over the brow of the mountain from the direction of the Vision Farm, the sometime home of the illustrator Eric Gill, and drink in the bog pool, their reflections looking glass-precise.

—

I love the smell of silage in the morning. At dawn, the frost still fixed on the ground, I unwrap the last bale from its plastic sheath and feed it to the patient, breathy cattle. Despite the spate of frosty mornings the grass in the meadows is flushing, because nothing can keep spring down. There is enough lush green grass out in the fields now to feed the cattle, and they will have no need of preserved grass. This afternoon I will lead them down to Copse Field from their winter compound in the dry top of Bog Field, calling, 'Cows, cows,' and as soon as they reach Copse Field they will do what cattle always do when released from confinement, even a rather loose house arrest of two acres such as ours have endured for the winter. The cattle will thunder around, their tails in the air or near-horizontal behind them, frisking and jumping, with their hooves kicking up great divots of turf, and I will be pleased for them and sorry for the pristine sward.

If I miss feeding the cattle twice a day, I shall be glad of the time saved, time to be devoted to food I can actually eat, such as wild garlic (*Allium ursinum*), whose heady pall now lies thick in the Finger thicket in the April wet. The garlic spreads incrementally year on year and its long luxurious lily-of-the-valley leaves have now invaded Copse Field, and to protect it from the cattle, sheep and ponies I have moved the boundary fence to enfold the bulge. (I leave some garlic accessible to the stock; they are geniuses at self-healing, and will nibble the garlic if ailing.) In enclosing the garlic I am aware that I am on the cusp of farming and that, ten thousand years ago in Mesopotamia, some similar action began the cultivation, as opposed to the collection, of food. Neither is wild garlic the only plant that I give a helping hand to, because I have already cut the grass back underneath the track hedge to allow the ground ivy to flourish, and cut down cow parsley which threatens to outdo Jack-by-the-hedge. I am also aware that some wild plants thrive on the cultivation of the soil, even if this cultivation is non-intentional; the pig paddock, turned over and over by porcine snouts until it is quite tilled, is currently cropping profusely with docks and plantain, as well as hairy bittercress.

So strong is the garlic smell of ramsons in March and April, when it comes into flower, that a fox passing through it is sure to lose any hounds on its tail. All parts of the plant – leaves, stems and bulb root – may be employed as domestic garlic, although the bulb root of ramsons is fiery on the tongue. The leaves are milder and, chopped, can be added to almost any dish, including green salads. Dipped in egg and fried they make a reasonable appetizer.

A Calendar of Wild Food at Trelandon

April

Pigeon, rabbit, dandelion, fairy ring mushrooms,
corn salad, hairy bittercress, docks, ground ivy,
nettles, hawthorn, sorrel, Jack-by-the-hedge, primroses,
lady's smock, elder buds, chickweed, ramsons

MAY DAY ALWAYS was a day for loose morals. Traditionally it was the day when villagers danced on the green around a priapic symbol of fertility (the original pole-dancing) and fairies played tricks and offered temptations. So, at least I have history on my side when I am seduced on the back lane between Ewyas Harold and Longtown by the beguiling sight of wild hops climbing up the steel guy rope of a telegraph pole. I have never seen hops closer to Longtown than this, because exposed cold clay will not support them.

I stop the jeep on the verge and walk over to rub a hop leaf between my thumb and forefinger. This is not a Proustian moment, for I well know in advance where the smell of hops will transport me: to my childhood, to the house of my Amos grand-parents, whose lives were dedicated to, and ordered by, the farming of *Humulus lupulus*. Even when Joe and Margaret Amos retired they continued to deck their house in Withington with hops every year, stringing them up in the sitting room, the dining room and the hall, but they need not have bothered, because after a lifetime the sharp fragrance of hops had entered their clothes and I fancy their skin.

As a boy my grandfather smoked dried hops, rolled up in pieces of newspaper; as a man he graduated to Woodbines, choosing this brand, I always suspected, because it had the hoppy word 'bine' in it. The 'bine' is the climbing stem of the hop plant. As a boy he ate hop trimmings in spring as green vegetables, and as a parent he served up hop shoots, cooked like asparagus, to his five daughters, but I do not think that as a grandfather he ever put hops on my plate, or that of my cousins.

Standing on the side of the lane looking at the sky-yearning tendrils of the hops – the word hop is from the Anglo-Saxon *hoppan*, to climb – I know that I cannot resist them, for the sake of the old ways. Because I want to draw closer to my grandfather. And this, I suppose, is the moment to confront the past.

As I child, I hero-worshipped Joe Amos, known to his grand-children as 'Poppop'; I was egged on in this slightly by my mother, who suffered from the same syndrome. It was easy to hero-worship Joe Amos, who was known to his labourers as 'the Whippet', for his extraordinary speed of walking; there was noth-ing strained about this turn of speed, even when he limped slightly in middle age, because Joe Amos was a natural aristocrat, always perfectly poised in motion and at rest. With big eyes and small legs I would accompany him around the farm at Withington, where, despite being officially retired, he was called in to oversee the hop growing and the picking of the cider apples, and where he commanded operations with the straight-backed efficiency of a Guards colonel. He knew everything about farming, everything about the natural world. Despite leaving school at thirteen and being hard pushed to read the *Daily Express*, Poppop was as sharp as a barber's razor; he could famously retain the hours and the rates worked by his men for a week, then spiel them off to my grandmother to do the books.

I think my grandfather liked me almost as much as I liked him. He made me my first bow and arrow, and he once gave me a brown ten-bob note. (This gift of 50p startled everybody in the family, because he was not rash with money.) To this day I can feel his stubbly evening cheek as I kissed him before bed when I stayed with them, which was often, because my parents both worked and then they divorced.

When I was eighteen my grandfather said one sentence which, while it would be too much to claim that it ruined my life, cruelly diverted it. I had gone to see my grandparents on the evening before I left for university, thrashing my Honda CB 125 motorcycle to Tenbury Wells. They had recently moved into a smaller, modern abode which, after decades of living in old houses where the wind whipped under plank doors, they found to be bemusingly free of draughts. As we sat drinking ginger tea in the sitting room with its alien, perfectly fitted carpet and picture windows, my grandmother posed the question, 'Will you come back to Hereford?'

Before I could put down my tea and answer, Poppop interjected, 'Oh, Jahn'll not come back to 'ereford.'

I *almost* burst with pride that my grandfather thought that I could make my way in the wider world; I actually zigzag-fissured inside with despair because I knew that I could not come home without disappointing him. I was the first person in the Amos family to go to university; oh, I had an Aunt Daphne who went to teacher-training college, but I was the first to go to an actual university. Like many who do not enter the supposedly hallowed portals and dreaming towers of higher learning, my grandparents believed that a university education was the first-class ticket to a better life than one spent down in the drudgery and draughts of the country. And so I attended university (three of them actually), did more and more rarefied research into history, hated every second with the exception of those shared with my future wife, and departed further and further from my essential self, which I left behind me in a small county in the west of England.

I couldn't come home until I had persuaded my wife to give up city life. I couldn't come home until my grandfather died.

I hold a hop shoot in my hand. Forgive me, Poppop: I had to rejoin my alienated self, I had to become whole again. I had to come home. I think he'll understand, maybe even approve, because I did manage to achieve some success in the rarefied outside world. I was a Published Author.

Everything is clear. It is not the life of its seventeenth-century peasants I want to emulate at Trelandon, it is the life of my own grandfather, the way he – and my grandmother – lived by the seasons even in the 1960s and 1970s, as they made their own fruit wines, brewed beer, picked cobnuts, and hung hares for so long in the larder that if one brushed underneath bits fell off. More than that, I want the peace of my childhood, when all the meadows were sunny and daisy-filled because the deluge of my parents' divorce had not yet crashed over the horizon.

Hop shoot soup

2 handfuls young hop shoots
2 cloves wild garlic, crushed
2 pints/1.1l game stock, preferably pigeon, partridge or pheasant

Gather the young shoots in April or early May, when they are at their most tender. Tie them in bunches and lay them in salted water for an hour or two. Drain and chop. Gently brown two crushed cloves of wild garlic, then add 2 pints of game stock (preferably pigeon, partridge or pheasant) plus the hop shoots, and simmer for 45 minutes. This makes an admittedly thin but tasty soup; natural thickeners are remarkable by their absence, but you may wish to try adding grated hogweed root at the cost of 'sweetening' the soup.

Of course, the easiest method of preparing hop shoots is to lay them in salted water as above, then steam until tender. Some recipes advise boiling rapidly.

Hops have a chemical affinity for eggs. To make a hop shoot omelette: chop a handful of hop shoots into 3in/7.5cm lengths and gently brown in duck/goose fat in a pan; meanwhile, lightly beat 3 duck eggs and flavour with a pinch of salt; add the beaten eggs to the pan and fry the omelette in the Italian style, cooking it through and serving flat, instead of half-frying and folding over, because the shoots need the additional tenderizing. A slushy-topped frittata can be put under a grill for 2–3 minutes to set. Serve the omelette with a light white wine, such as dandelion.

Dandelion flower wine
2lb/900g clear honey
6 pints/3.4l boiling water
2 pints/1.1l dandelion heads

The essential ingredient for dandelion wine is a sunny spring day in early May, when the flowers are in full bloom. Cut off the resplendent yellow heads, being careful to leave the green stalks behind, and place in a fermentation bucket. Add the boiling water, then mash the heads with a wooden spoon. Cover with muslin and leave outside for four days in a cool place so that wild yeasts in the air can reach the flower water. (Alternatively you may wish to add a sachet of wine yeast and simply cover with a lid.) Strain and add the honey, which you will need to work in well with a wooden spoon. Pour the must into a sterilized demijohn, sealing with an airlock. Leave in a warm room until fermentation is complete. Siphon into another sterilized jar, leaving the sediment behind. Top up with cold boiled water and bung well. The wine should be stored in a cold place until it clears. Bottle and serve at Christmas.

Dandelion wine has a sharp, medium-dry flavour. Its

*sometimes resinous taste can be reduced by cutting off the
green calyxes from the flower heads, as well as the stalks.*

Before the Second World War, cowslip wine was a favourite
home-made tipple in the cottages of the English countryside, but
the flower has so declined due to modern chemical farming
practices that you will struggle to find the necessary numbers in
the wild to make wine. And if you do, people will waggle their
heads. Of course, if you sow some on your own land – you can
buy packets of cowslip seeds – or your land is covered with them
anyway, as Trelandon is, the flowers are there for the picking. A sensible rule of thumb is to pick every other flower, allowing half go to
seed.

So sweet are the yellow bobbly flowers of the cowslip (*Primula
veris*) that the nectar can, it is said, be sucked straight out of them.
The flowers make a pleasant addition to salads and mead; less
delightful, but useful, are the cowslip's young blue-green leaves,
which can be employed as salad or a boiled vegetable. Take a
moment to smell the plant before you consume it. What does it
remind you of? After a second you will get the answer.

It is the smell of a newborn child.

The primrose is closely related to the cowslip, although as its
name – *prima rosa*, first rose – suggests it is earlier to appear.
Primrose flowers were also used to make wine, but as a mere
handful of primroses inhabit the farm, I am unable to gather the
half-gallon of heads needed. In addition to making alcohol,
English country folk put primroses in salad (leaves and flowers),
over meat (flowers), turned them into sweets and into a tea to cure
rheumatism and insomnia (the leaves and root). One thing they did
not do was bring a single primrose flower into the house, for this
was unlucky and heralded a death. They also tried to stop children
eating the flowers, because if they did so the children would
develop the power to see fairies.

In early May we rejoice in temperatures that touch 80°F, and Freda is able to swim in the glassy pools of the river. How green is my valley? Utterly and gorgeously green, except for the hawthorns, whose branches are sprinkled tight with sugary white blossom. Greenest of all are the young leaves of the oak, which can be turned into a light white wine (in the ratio of leaves to water of 1:1), under which I sit in paternal guard over my mermaid daughter in air that is thick with the scent of cut hay. In this English heaven I chew a piece of grass, make a daisy chain, and watch the jackdaw on Willow's back pulling off his hair for a nest-lining. Eventually, even the aquatic Freda tires of swimming and with her Saxon hair flattened wet to her head, a towel around her shoulders, we walk up Bank Field to the house in the blue-steeped haze.

As we climb the bank, she asks me to stop shooting rabbits on the yard. 'They are only baby ones playing,' she says, with pleading eyes. Who wants to spoil an unutterably perfect evening? Not me. 'OK,' I reply.

So next morning, while it is still dark, I drive the tractor into House Meadow where I plan to use it as a mobile shooting lodge. There I sit in the cab, sipping a flask of chickweed soup, as the land awakens around me. Blackbird sings first, followed by robin, and at six fifteen the swallows and house martins come chattering out from under the eaves of the house and climb into the cerulean sky in search of their winged breakfast. Down on the dewy green ground, the rabbits too come out to eat. But I don't get to shoot. A low brown weasel, calm as you like, trots up behind a fresh young rabbit – I want to yell to the rabbit, 'Run!' – jumps on its back and bites into the neck. Only now does the rabbit react, kicking out, squiggling, rolling, but the snaky weasel, clutching tight, does not let go and sinks its fangs in again. The rabbit ceases to move. Off pops the weasel assassin, pulling its prey into the hedge. The other rabbits have long vamoosed, and will not come out again for hours.

I too was frightened by such a virtuoso display of Nature red in tooth and claw.

Herby squirrel burgers
Serves 4

1lb/450g lean minced squirrel
1 egg, beaten
1 tbsp hedge garlic, chopped
2 tsp equal parts wild thyme and wild chervil
pinch salt

Mix together the egg, meat, herbs and salt in a bowl.
   Shape into flattened patties and fry or grill until cooked through (about 5 minutes a side). Serve with a green salad.

Surely with a stream of my own I can catch a trout? Especially a stream described by the *Field* in 1904 as 'one of the best in south Britain'. In Victorian times the local vicar, the Reverend Eagles, took almost a thousand trout a year from the Escley and the other two upper tributaries of the Monnow.

By the beginning of May I have run out of excuses not to be fishing. The late afternoons are perfect for the pursuit. Under the trees, vortexes of mayfly hang in the stolid heat above the water, which is running sepia-toned but clear enough to see the bedrock stones, coated in their antique brown silt.

I know where the trout lurk because I've seen the master at work. The heron fishes the slow pool on the bend near where twin alders, which the children call the Elephant Tree, dangle their feet into the brook.

Since trout tend to face upstream I work my way up along a strand of silt on the river's edge, always keeping an alder between me and the pool. The shady scene has the sort of private, fecund, dank beauty Holman Hunt and the Pre-Raphaelites would have approved of.

On reaching the alder, I peep around its trunk at the pool. Bingo. In the daubs of sunlight I can see a big diamond-backed trout working the water, its monstrous prehistoric maws sucking in flies as they drop to the surface.

I retrace my steps as daintily as a man in a minefield and then cut across the field to go above the bend to where the brook runs over great tables of bedrock. Standing in my wellingtons in the water I prepare to make my first cast. This is the most open part of the river. Even so I manage to snag the fly on the hazel bush behind me.

After I retrieve the fly my right wellington mysteriously springs a hole and water trickles in to above my ankle. Nevertheless, I make some promising casts, letting the line and fly float down over the pool.

And then I hear them coming. *Huff, huff, huff, huff, huff.* Two black Labradors, pink tongues hanging out and tails wagging, come racing down the field. Edith and Bluebell. Edith splashes through the water to greet me. Bluebell jumps straight into the pool, where she swims in circles, nose out of the water the way women bathers do when keeping their coiffure dry.

In the words of the rappers Baha Men, Who let the dogs out?

I'm back the next morning. I cast thirty times to no avail with a Coachman fly, and then change to a Greenwell's Glory. Nothing, save for snagging the Glory on the alder above the pool. I know the trout is still there because of the occasional ripple in the water. I try a dry fly. I try a lure. Nothing. I fantasize about connecting mains electricity to the pool and electrocuting the trout so it floats to the surface belly up. I dream of chucking in a stick of dynamite.

Is it, I consider, legal to put down seine nets? I wonder if I could allow for deflection and shoot the monster with the twelve-bore.

A morning of my life passes fishlessly before me. The only excitement comes after I've packed it in.

As I walk through the remnant of old apple orchard on the bank side, darkness descends at midday. A red kite, off its normal beat on the Black Mountains, flies thirty feet over my head, its wings casting a long shadow. The world stills in an instant. The blue tit stops her whistle, the pigeon halts mid *coo-coo*, even the river seems to hold its breath. The kite scours on by. After an interval for safety's sake all the birds around me burst into song. We survived.

The trout is my Moby Dick. I return to the Escley the next morning to continue the contest. As I approach the pool I can see the house martins swooping over its surface in Battle of Britain acrobatics as they pursue their winged victims.

But it's the early hunter that gets the trout. On the dark sandstone strip to the side of the pool, a brown trout head lies, severed but provocative. Around it are the unmistakable spoors of an otter.

We have otters. I don't know whether to celebrate their arrival or curse it.

In Road Field a skylark springs up and begins its vertical ascent, singing as it goes; inspired, another skylark takes to the air, until they are both trilling in the heavens. The birds dwindle to mere specks, causing my eyes to water with the strain of trying to identify them against the hazy white. I am standing beneath the two and it seems as though a canopy of enchantment has been suspended above me.

The birds, fluttering, descend rather more quickly than they soared up, but not for a second do they halt their exuberant twittering, which has so inspired poets, led by Shelley:

> I have never heard
> Praise of love or wine
> That panted forth a flood of rapture so divine.

The skylark is the subject of the French song 'Alouette, gentille alouette', which appreciates the bird in a rather more basic way. Translated, the first verse is:

> Lark, lovely lark
> I am going to pluck you
> I am going to pluck your head,
> I am going to pluck your head,
> And the head, and the head,
> O-o-o-o-oh

In the remaining verses, the other parts of the skylark's body are plucked prior to its roasting. It strikes me as rather amusing that generations of British schoolchildren are taught the song 'Alouette' in utter ignorance of what it means. Skylarks were widely eaten across Europe – Britain included – until relatively recently, and I can remember seeing rows of them grilled outside a fashionable restaurant in Palma's old quarter in the late 1970s. But it seems crass to think about skylarks as food when they have so divinely entertained me, and I concentrate on why I am here, which is to pick nectar-rich cowslips in the feel-good heat.

And there are other birds to distract me on this May morning. A cuckoo calls somewhere up the Escley, and the scythe-winged swifts, which have only just arrived, are flying in screaming hyperactive circles around John and Claire's tall chimneys.

Beside a puddle on the track house martins are landing, filling their beaks with mud and flying up to the eaves to continue their mansionry.

—

Is there *anything* lovelier than a quiet English country lane in May? I'm standing on the lane, ostensibly tightening the stock fence to prevent the sheep pushing under, but I'm absorbed in the way the colours of the verge-side flowers tone, with each other, with the grass. Dandelions, red campion (my favourite flower) and delicate white stitchwort abound under the thrusting cow parsley, which is already beginning to reach out over the tarmac. And there's the rub; when the cow parsley invades the road, the council mows the verges dead flat. Only for a few miserly weeks is the lane allowed to blossom before the corporation reaperman comes along in the interests of the motorist's visibility.

A green Land Rover Discovery puffs up the hill in the huzzing heat, stopping when it reaches me. It's Ken, a neighbour from along towards Michaelchurch Escley. He winds down the window and asks me how it's going. I complain about the sheep – always a safe topic in the country: we all curse sheep – and, as he runs a few himself 'to keep the grass down', I ask him how the lambing went.

But Ken doesn't want to talk about lambing. Ken wants to talk about incomers from London. He double-checks that I'm not from off ('But you're local, aren't you?') and then tells me how his neighbours from London complain if he leaves any equipment in the field next to them, how they want a telegraph pole moved because it's in their view, how they don't like the mud on the lane.

'And why do they bloody smile all the time?' Ken asks, his florid face tight with tension and far off smiling. I'm about to tell Ken that they smile because they have the best of all possible worlds. They have moved to Arcadia. But they do not need to make money from living here. The money still comes from London, from his job, from the useful little flat they bought to rent out in Islington.

But Ken has started up again. Some of his observations are very precise. 'You know, the London kids never sit next to ours on the bus to school . . .' He shakes his head at this.

Then he shakes his head at himself. 'Bloody hell, what do I sound like? I'm off before I bang on any more.'

The Disco's diesel engine putt-putts into life and Ken drives off, a hand lingering out of the window in a farewell salute.

The lane returns to tranquillity. I let my attention drift to the spotted flycatcher which is leaping off a fence post at passing insects. I feel discomfited; I should have been generous in the defence of those from off. After all, you can't blame people for wanting to live in beauty.

My excuse for not doing the right thing is that my mind was elsewhere. Where do they go, all those people who *leave* the valley? When I reach the house, I flick through the phone book to see if any Landons still live locally. They do not. Back in Stuart times, the Landons must have been a big local clan because at least three places are named for them. Later in the week, I check through issues of *Kelly's Directory* in Hereford reference library, but the Landons are missing from this register of tradespeople and householders. In the papers of the Marquis of Abergavenny, the major landowner in the valley, I find one last mention of the Landons in 1878, when John Brace ('otherwise Landon') surrendered the tenancy on 9 acres, 3 roods and 1 perch of land at Llanveyno, under the Cat's Back.

———

Cow parsley (*Anthriscus sylvestris*), which stands sentinel on country lanes from April to June, is the close wild relative of chervil (*Anthriscus cerefolium*) and is to be counted as one of wild England's tastiest herbs, with definite notes of aniseed and myrrh.

The fresh, lacy light-green leaves can be chopped and added to salads and omelettes; they dry well too, and buck up all manner of winter soups and stews. Try to pick early leaves; by late season the taste has coarsened.

Alas, cow parsley is similar in appearance to a number of umbellifers which are toxic, among them hemlock (as used by Socrates for his suicide) and fool's parsley, so one has to be *absolutely* sure that the white-headed, ferny-leaved plant before one is cow parsley, aka wild chervil, and not a deadly impostor. The main difference between cow parsley and its poisonous kin is the stem: in the case of cow parsley this is furrowed and slightly hairy; the stem of hemlock is smooth and spotted with purple; the stem of fool's parsley is thin and hairless. But you need a good guidebook. And if in doubt, do not pick.

—

'It joyeth in watery ditches, in fat and fruitful meadowes,' wrote the Stuart herbalist Gerard, and that exactly describes the country in which common comfrey thrives. There is a clump stretching to three feet high and three feet wide in the drainage channel below the duck pond, known to us as the Mekong Delta in honour of its broad slushiness. Covered in white fur, the large leaves of *Symphytum officinale* are unpleasant to pick with naked hands, though I find their fresh, soapy scent – reminiscent of something from the Body Shop, aloe vera maybe – addictive. 'Comfrey' is from the Latin *confevre*, to grow together, and the plant's local English names – knit-bone, nipbone – are more reminders of the herb's medieval reputation as a gluey bone-setter. Long before, the Roman scientist Pliny extolled the sticky virtues of comfrey but as a binder of food, not bones. 'The roots be so glutinative,' wrote Pliny, 'that they will solder or glew together meat that is chopt in pieces, seething in a pot, and make it into one lump.' They do. But comfrey has more, much more, than glutinousness to recommend it; it has more protein in its leaf structure than any other British wild plant.

The wild cook can prepare comfrey leaves in various ways. When the plant is sprightly in spring, comfrey leaves, boiled in slightly salted water, make a fine green vegetable, as do the stalks before flowering; the latter should be blanched and cooked in the manner of asparagus. In pinched times the roots, boiled, have been used to make wine.

And then there are comfrey fritters.

Comfrey fritters
Serves 1

1 duck egg yolk
pinch salt
2 dollops goose fat
2 tsp hazelnut oil
3 tbsp warm water
comfrey leaves (a handful)
2oz/60g chestnut flour

To make the batter, mix the hazelnut oil with the flour in a shallow bowl, then add the egg yolk and salt.

Dip the comfrey leaves into the batter and fry in hot fat, turning once.

A CALENDAR OF WILD FOOD AT TRELANDON

May

Pigeon, rabbit, sorrel, dandelion, corn salad, ground elder, sow thistle, dock, ground ivy, nettles, Jack-by-the-hedge, primrose, lady's smock, chickweed, fat hen, cow parsley, comfrey, burdock

SUMMER

THE TWO HAY MEADOWS, Road Field and Little Field, are crested red with gone-to-seed sorrel. Underlying the sorrel are bright yellow buttercups. While I admire the two-tone scene, a buzzard cruises down Road Field, four curlews hotly mobbing it. The curlews are the ungainly string bags of bird aviation compared to the compact Lancaster bomber menace of the buzzard, but even so they drive the predator out of their breeding zone. At this victory, three of the curlews break off, but the last keeps up its attacks on the buzzard. The buzzard, its patience taxed by the pin-pricking, suddenly rolls on to its back and bares its talons at the curlew, catching its chest. Feathers fly, and the curlew tumbles down the hazy sky before righting itself and flapping off on wings too rapid for such a languorous day.

—

In the first week of June my father is transferred, after much anguish for us all, from hospital to a nursing home. By one of those small circles of which my life is made, Hampton Grange Nursing Home is situated almost directly opposite my childhood home. Such a familiar location is, I think, some comfort for my father in alien times and the view down to the river Wye and across to the wooded slopes of Dinedor from his ground-floor room is almost exactly that from the end of our old drive. On my first visit to him there, while we are talking, three pink-blushed wood pigeons alight on the pale post-and-rail fence outside his open window, almost close enough for me to touch, which prompts me involuntarily to utter the family saying, 'Oh, the things you see when you don't have a gun.'

The Trelandon wood pigeons would never knowingly allow me so close. Of all the game and quarry species on the farm, they are by far the most difficult to shoot. Wary and far-sighted, wood pigeons often break for sanctuary, in a panic of flashing white-barred wings, long before I get into the killing range. Besides, a wood pigeon on the wing flies faster, curves quicker, than almost any other British bird and more than once I have mistaken a wood pigeon barrelling along for a sparrowhawk. Although no one who pays to shoot driven, high pheasants would want to admit it, the humble, free wood pigeon likely presents the most challenging target for the gun.

The best way of shooting wood pigeons is to ambuscade them. In winter I sometimes stand under the oaks in the darkening evening and shoot through a skylight in the canopy as the pigeons come in to roost, though one has to stand corpse-still, because even the slightest movement will catch their bionic eye. One really should wear a veil over the face, though this feels unsettlingly perverted. I also have some plastic decoy wood pigeons which I arrange in a feeding circle around scattered corn on the meadow, while I lie low and camouflaged. For reasons I can never fathom, sometimes the decoys attract pigeons but usually they do not. Tris and Freda, indeed, dismissively refer to them as my patented pigeon-scarers. So my favoured method of shooting wood pigeons is to sit patiently with a pair of binoculars and note which tree they are using as a lookout, then drag the cattle ring feeder to within twenty yards of it. A cattle ring feeder looks like a giant hamster wheel lain on its side, and usually I move it with the tractor, though sometimes I yoke myself to it and pull it like Captain Scott with a sledge. Then I cover the top and sides with an ancient, green tarpaulin, making sure to arrange it so that there is a small loophole facing the perching tree. The catch is that I can never take Edith with me, because she simply won't sit still enough for long enough.

Today, the perching tree is an old favourite, the stark dead elm at the bottom of Bank Field. Climbing inside the ring feeder, I tie the nylon tarpaulin tight behind me and sit down on a canvas fold-out stool. There is enough green-hazed light for me to pass the time by reading *Birdsong* by Sebastian Faulks. Pigeons rely on their eyes; the noise of turning the pages of a book does not put them off. By the time Stephen Wraysford has seduced Madame Azaire and the gathering heat of the late morning has made the hide breathless, I can clearly hear the whirring descent of a pigeon. Putting the book down, I kneel before the loophole and feed out an inch or two of the shotgun's barrel. Flies drone around the cowpats as I imperceptibly angle the barrel upwards, past the elm's Indian-goddess arms, until the pigeon is behind the rib of the gun. A sitting pigeon at twenty-five yards, with unblemished blue sky behind it, has little chance and both pigeon and part of its wooden perch are knocked off by the blast of No. 7 shot. Inside the metal-barred walls of the hide, the noise of the cartridge's detonation is ear-ringingly loud, causing me to wonder why, oh why, do I never remember the ear-protectors.

It takes me at least ten minutes to find the pigeon, which has dropped into the Escley and been borne downstream till it caught on the side stones, a gentle grey bundle betrayed in the tree gloom by its startling white collar patches. Taking the pigeon back to the hide, I continue with *Birdsong* and, as an idler's luck would have it, another pigeon does not interrupt me until Stephen and Isabelle abscond.

There is no closed season for Britain's ten million wood pigeon. *Columba palumbus* – the wood pigeon is blessed with the one Latin tag that is fun to say – may be shot at any time under a general licence by an authorized person. They cannot be killed for sport, they cannot be killed intentionally for the pot. They can only be killed to stop the spread of disease or prevent damage to crops. Thus today, as on every day that I shoot pigeons, I was only doing my bit for the arable farming industry locally. That the pigeons ended up in a casserole was an incidental by-product of my do-goodery, or so I tell the RSPCA inspector who comes to call in my mind.

Out of curiosity, before entombing the pigeons in blackberry wine, I cut open their crops. These are full of destructive insects. It is not always so. In winter, when acorns have been in short supply, I have found wheat shoots from the fields in the lower end of the valley in their crops.

Pigeon with lovage

Most 'wild' lovage, and this includes ours, is actually an escapee from a herb garden. Such feral lovage is bigger (reaching 12ft tall) than the genuinely wild version of the plant which inhabits Scotland, but both versions have the same odd flavour, which is of celery dipped in brewer's yeast and lemon.
Serves 4

6 pigeons
2 tbsp goose fat
2 pints/1.1l dry cider
small bunch lovage
pinch salt

Brown the pigeons in the goose fat. Put them head down in a casserole and cover with the cider. Put a dozen or so lovage leaves in the pot, and cook slowly at 300°F/150°C/Gas Mark 2 for two hours or more.

I double-check the illustrations in Roger Phillips's *Wild Food*. It's hogweed (*Heracleum sphondylium*), I'm pretty sure, which is edible, as opposed to giant hogweed (*Heracleum mantegazzianum*), which is not. I've been dithering here beside the track and its incessant clicking grasshoppers for half an hour, checking hairiness of leaves and stem size with more precision than a forensic scientist. This is madness, because I've eaten hogweed umpteen times before and we don't actually have giant hogweed on the farm.

Yet the spike-leaved plants are very tall, almost two metres high. One might say giant even. My excessive caution has a cause: something I have eaten recently has produced another bout of poisoning. In the end I decide that the only reliable method of identification is to cut down a plant with the billhook. Sitting on the verge next to the lanky foxgloves I dab the back of my left hand with milky sap from the cut plant. If it's the giant variety my skin will blister in the sun.

This seems a foolproof method of identification until I wonder how long I should give the skin test. Is the blistering immediate? After half an hour? The guidebooks fail to inform me. I settle on fifteen minutes, and spend the time watching the puffs of cloud make shadows on the long wall of the Black Mountains.

Nothing happens to my skin.

On the way back to the house with a carrier bag full of hogweed stems, I notice that the ponies have pushed through the bed of thistles which borders the shallow ditch at the top of the paddock. When I follow their route I find, to my astonishment, that the ditch, usually hidden from view, is massed with watercress in white flower.

A century and a half ago watercress was grown commercially in Britain, to be sold on the city streets by child vendors (for a heartbreaking description of the life of a girl watercress-seller see Henry Mayhew's *Life and Labour of London's Poor*) as an inexpensive source of vitamin C. The cultivated version and wild version of watercress are identical: they are both *Rorippa nasturtium-aquaticum*. Probably watercress's very cheapness turned people against it; by the late 1970s it was reduced to being a garnish on the plate in naff steakhouse restaurants, whereas it can be boiled as a green vegetable and its shoots put in salads, soups and omelettes.

Ploshing into the ditch I pick a handful of springy watercress leaves and indeed use them as a filler in omelette. The pungency of watercress is sublime to those of us who like hot stuff, but raw watercress should only be eaten when it comes from a flowing stream. As I eat the omelette a worry grows in my head: was the water in the ditch *flowing*? I abandon the omelette and walk out to the ditch, where the water is . . . trickling. Worse, much worse, there is a sheep standing in the ditch, chewing the watercress heads with the grinding sideways motion beloved of ruminants. That is the other thing about watercress: it should only be taken from flowing water from which cattle and sheep are barred, because otherwise the 'nose-twister' cress (which is what *nasturtium* means) can harbour the larval stage of liver fluke. Which can parasitize humans.

Oh shit, how could I have been so stupid. My Homer Simpson desire for a nice lunch has possibly infected me with a worm that will multiply by the million and eat my liver alive. I try not to panic but do definitely, decidedly fret. Did I wash the watercress well enough? How much realistically did I eat? For days I check for rashes and feel my liver.

There is one other danger for the careless from watercress, which is that it may be mistaken for the toxic *Apium nodiflorum*.

Fool's cress has umbels of flowers down the stem, opposite the leaves. The small white flowers of the watercress, however, are carried on the stem tips.

Watercress soup

This is undoubtedly the safest and tastiest way to use watercress gathered in the wild. Against the usual rule of foraging, one should pick the older leaves of the plant, for these have the stronger taste.
Serves 4

¼lb/110g watercress
¼lb/110g burdock root
1 dollop goose fat
1 pint/600ml water
pinch salt

Chop the watercress and burdock root. Place the burdock root in a saucepan with a dollop of goose fat and cook gently until it is soft. Add a pint of water and bring to the boil. Add the watercress and a pinch of salt and continue to boil for 3 minutes, then simmer for 10 minutes. Liquidize. Chill. Serve with a sprig of much-washed watercress. This is the gazpacho of the English wild food larder.

'They are like hefted sheep, your family,' says Penny.

Hefted sheep are hill sheep that are genetically conditioned to stay within a certain locality. We have been talking about my cousin Roger Williams, who has thoughtfully given my father two paintings to hang on the wall in his room in the nursing home, one of a village church, one of a Gloucester Old Spot pig. Roger lives slap bang next door to Hill Farm at Much Dewchurch, where the Verrys were farming in the sixteenth century.

'That has to be the world record,' I say to Penny, 'in moving the least distance from an ancestral home in half a millennium.'

'You haven't exactly gone far,' she points out. 'And your dad is a whole mile from where he was born. Even if you leave Herefordshire you come back, your lot. You really are like hefted sheep.'

On a sultry evening, the heady scent of honeysuckle wafting from the lane hedge, we drive around to the village hall for an exhibition of local history. We are not the only ones; cars overflow on to the road and the hall, a cramped 1930s construction whose one virtue is its small wooden stage, is sweating with villagers. On display boards there are a hundred or so photographs of Longtown and its environs in the last century; in appearance the village, which in recognition of its name straggles for about a mile along one road, has changed little. The life of the village, though, has altered almost beyond comprehension; a hundred years ago Longtown was self-sufficient, bustling with a baker, two iron-mongers, a tailor, a C of E church, three pubs, a school, major livestock fairs every 19 February, 29 April and 19 November, with a statute fair on 21 November. Today you can drive through Longtown at midday and struggle to see a soul, even though it miraculously retains one shop, one pub and one primary school. And driving is the problem, because you can not only drive through Longtown but away from it, to work and shop in Hereford, Hay, Abergavenny, wherever.

On the last red display board I find what I was looking for: a photograph of Trelandon. The black-and-white photograph, from circa 1900, is of Emily Broome, the farm's servant girl. She is look-ing after a brood of urchins. She looks miserable. See Emily play? Not much.

For a week I try fishing the bend pool but no sooner do I succeed in getting a fly on the water than something interrupts the session. Tris drops by to ask if he can borrow the air gun to shoot up plastic Ecover bottles. ('They're meant to be refillable,' I protest.) Gwyn, who rents the land next door, comes into the field to round up a straying white ewe and her lamb, his sheep distinguished by a black marker line across their backs. Then a tropical hallucination occurs: in a passable imitation of a hummingbird, a juvenile kingfisher flutters in my face before careering across the stream to a low branch, almost within touching distance, where it sits like a hungry child and cries *tichst, tichst* to its parents.

Like the medieval London apprentices who complained about being fed salmon so frequently, I also discover that one can have too much of a good thing, in this case the sight of a kingfisher. The endlessly repeated call of the kingfisher kid grates my patience, but more problematically the bird's parents won't come to feed it while I'm so close by.

I kiss farewell to another day's fishing.

Then, early one Sunday morning, my fishing at the pool is terminated for an unexpected reason. I've taken the gun down to Bank Field to hunt squirrels in the hazel trees and am patrolling along in the faint mist when a green Daihatsu 4×4 comes skimming down the field on the other side of the river.

To have company was unexpected and I'm far from certain, now I come to think of it, whether shooting vermin on a Sunday is legal. Certainly shooting game is not.

The Daihatsu parks and out steps a man with a tight flat cap pulled low on his head. He marches towards me, down through the shallows, the water crashing under his boots, and up the bank on to our land, shouting, 'Hello! Hello!'

One thing you can be sure of is that someone who marches on to your land is very, very angry.

His eyes bright under his tweed cap, he says, 'Powell,' as he sticks out his hand.

'Lewis-Stempel,' I reply, rather fluffing the handshake as I swap the gun to my left hand.

'Saw you'd cut down some bushes on the bank,' says Mr Powell, 'and I thought, there's a sporting man. A man doing a bit of fly fishing.'

I have a horrible, glum feeling about where this is going. Mr Powell confirms it. Instantly. 'The thing is, you see, I own the fishing rights.'

This is big but not entirely unexpected news. When we bought Trelandon we were informed by our solicitors and the estate agent that the fishing rights had lapsed in about 1945. Probably.

I'm reeling under the news – oh hell! I've started punning under stress again – but Mr Powell has more complaints to make. 'I hope I'm being polite?' he continues, setting his feet apart. 'Now, about your sheep coming across the river on to my field there. No use you denying it, I've seen them . . .'

This is too much. I say: 'Yours come on to my land all the time. If you look at your fence, you'll see that I cut down the bushes to plug the gaps to keep your sheep in.'

Mr Powell is not interested in listening to me. Instead he tells me, 'This is how we do things in the country . . .'

So this is what it feels like to be an incomer. I've been damned by my mouth. Thirty words and Mr Powell has concluded that I'm 'from off'. I say nothing because I want the conversation to die as quick a death as possible. He suggests renting out the fishing rights to me, adding, almost friendly, 'It won't cost thousands.' I admit to, and apologize for, poaching (he might have seen me, after all). Mr Powell is a decent enough cove. Unfortunately fences make for difficulties with neighbours; in local-speak they are known appropriately enough as 'argies', as in 'argy-bargy'.

Before we part with another fumbled handshake, I ask Mr Powell to show me exactly the stretch he is claiming the fishing rights to. This extends to about 400 yards at the bottom end of Trelandon, alongside Copse Field and the Finger.

Since I don't have hundreds of pounds to give to Mr Powell, it is time to move on up the waterfront, to the 400 yards at the northern end of Trelandon, where the fishing rights are unclaimed. Probably.

> Now summer is in flower and nature's hum
> Is never silent round her sultry bloom
> Insects as small as dust are never done
> Wi' glittering dance and reeling in the sun
> And green wood fly and blossom-haunting bee
> Are never weary of their melody
> Round field hedge now flowers in full glory twine
> Large bindwell bells wild hop and streakd woodbine
> That lift athirst their slender throated flowers
> Agape for dew falls and for honey showers
>> John Clare, *The Shepherd's Calendar*

The hedgerows of the farm are lush with honeysuckle, guelder rose, wild rose and round, beaming lamps of elderflowers. On the evening of 17 June I begin picking the fizzing heads on the east side of the hedges, where they are ripest. The heads are intoxicatingly fragrant and sugar-sweet on the tongue when munched raw, a sort of English delight, although one has to be careful to shake off the multitudes of insects which hum on them. Elderflower cordial and elderflower wine are familiar drinks for English summers, but another, and to my mind better, way of preserving the plant's sparkling flowery essence is elderflower champagne. It is English summer in a glass bottle.

Elderflower champagne

8 large elderflower heads
¼ cup wild rose petals
2¼lb/1kg clear honey
4 tbsp cider vinegar
16 pints/9l cold water

*Put the honey into a saucepan, add 1 pint/0.5l of the water
and gently heat until the honey melts.*

*Remove any insect life from the elderflowers, preferably by
gentle shaking, not washing. Put the flowers and rose petals
into a large vessel. Pour on the water and add the vinegar and
the melted honey mixture. Put a lid over the vessel and leave
to stand for 24 hours. Stir gently with a wooden spoon at least
twice.*

*Using either chemical tablets or boiling water, sterilize the
receiving bottles. (If you use chemical tablets of the camden
ilk, rinse the bottles afterwards so that the chemicals don't kill
the wild yeast in the elderflower champagne mixture.)*
*Take the lid off the vessel and use a small jug to bail some of
the champagne mixture through a sieve and into a bottle.*
*Once all the bottles are full, cork (or cap) them and place them
somewhere cool. An outbuilding is ideal.*

*The champagne is ready for drinking after a fortnight, yet it
does improve with age and will keep for months, even years.*

Although I have talked of hedges, the joy of June is the amount of
food the fields are providing me with. To date, the edges of things
– hedgerows and the thicket along the river – have been my main
victuallers but in the month named for Jupiter's wife the meadows
are overflowing with edible plants. There are the usual suspects –
nettles, sorrel, Good King Henry, plantain, dandelion – but now

these are joined by red clover, wild thyme, yarrow, rough hawkbit and bush vetch. The clover makes wine or flower fritters or a flower salad (try it with honeysuckle and borage), the thyme a herb flavouring for meat, the yarrow a tea, the hawkbit a green salad, and the little pods of the tangled vetch give minute green peas.

There are also grasses galore – tall fescue, timothy, cocksfoot, tufted hairgrass – which I have earmarked for a little DIY threshing and winnowing when their heads are full and dry, which is not quite yet, and I check them every day with the dutifulness of those who farm their descendants, oats, wheat and barley, rubbing the heads through my fingers in a thoughtful manner. On these daily trips through the hay meadows the pollen from the buttercups paints my wellingtons a startling gold.

Yarrow tea

Yarrow's Latin name, Achillea millefolium, commemorates the use of the plant by Achilles to staunch his soldiers' wounds at the battle of Troy. Yarrow has an equally long-standing claim as the psychotropic enabler of prophecy; the counting of forty-nine dried yarrow stalks is the traditional method of divining the I Ching, the ancient Chinese Book of Changes. The herb, with its white heads and green feather-boa leaves, makes nice tea too.

Pick 3 long leaves of yarrow and infuse in a cup of boiling water for 4 minutes. Strain and serve. Sweeten with honey if required.

The tea can be made equally well with dried yarrow leaves.

Extended use of yarrow, it might be noted, can cause sensitivity in the eyes and skin.

—

Midsummer's Eve and in the fairy light there comes a moment of magic that would bewitch Puck himself. From a small wood on Merlin's Hill, the liquid song of a nightingale sounds clear across the still air of the valley.

Usually I find midsummer, to borrow Vita Sackville-West's phrase, a 'small despair', because from this day forth the darkness begins to grow more lengthy each and every day. But not this year. If one has fed oneself by the seasons – admittedly with a little help from one's relatives, from careless drivers and from one visit to Waitrose – then one knows the rhythm of natural life, and that the truth of natural life is both mundane and joyous.

The darkness comes.

It goes.

And that is it.

—

On 27 June, my birthday, I hunt over the high shelves of my food cupboard for some titbits to make a celebratory meal and deep on the top shelf I find a dish of forgotten hazelnuts. These I crack open for breakfast, and when there is only a child's handful left it occurs to me that, damn, I could have made a nut cutlet for lunch.

Perhaps a nut and pignut cutlet would serve? Pignuts are a true delicacy in the wild food larder, with a taste that hovers between sweet coconut and parsnip. They grow, with their fragile umbelliferous heads gawking over the grass, scattered in a long swathe along the bottom of Bank Field, where I protect them from the cows by an electric fence. One needs to see the pignut flower to be able to trace down to the single, delicate tapering root at the end of which, three to four inches below the ground, lies the brown pignut tuber. Caliban in *The Tempest* used his nails to dig up pignuts; in the hard red clay of Bank Field Penny and I use a trowel.

So time-consuming is the locating and extracting of pignuts that usually I regard them as a special treat, to be taken singly and eaten raw. With Penny's help, the rate of removal ups to a record-breaking pignut every three minutes. Being a woman she works systematically through the swathe, a carrier-bag turban around her head as protection against the warm drizzle; I wander hoping to slay a monster. By luck, not judgement, I do: a middling pignut flower leads to a pignut the size of a golf ball, the biggest pignut I ever did see. A birthday present from Nature.

One should use a brush and water to scrape off the earth but I use my thumb, believing that a little Hereford dirt is good for the immune system. Penny compliments me on my caveman table-manners. 'Nice hat,' I retort. 'You were wearing something similar, I seem to remember, on our first date.' It was raining then too.

'Yes, well on our first date you were wearing arty black and urbane opinions. I should do you under trades descriptions, because at no point did you mention tweed, countryside or reversion to type. Besides,' she continues, as we labour up the bank through the thistles, 'you had longer hair then. Thicker too. You get sunburn on the top of the head now, don't you? Perhaps *you* should have the carrier bag.'

Ouch.

With the bounty of pignuts I set about making the nut/pignut cutlet, which proves to be so filling and rich that it keeps me going until the day's end. Penny joins me in the meal – though I rather miserly insist that she provide her own hazelnuts from out of her baking supplies for her cutlet – which, accompanied by a glass of elderflower champagne, set out on a linen tablecloth and eaten with silver cutlery, passes for the height of luxury.

Nut and pignut cutlet
Serves 1

½ cup hazelnuts
⅓ cup cleaned pignuts
1 cup mushroom stock
pinch salt
dollop duck fat
1 duck egg

Grind the hazelnuts and pignuts together, while the stock simmers. Add the grindings, salt and egg to the stock and beat together. Take off the heat and leave for at least 30 minutes to allow the liquid to seep into the nuts. This helps reduce chewiness.

Heat the duck fat in a frying pan until smoking and spoon in the nut mixture. This should be moulded into a thick patty shape with a wooden spatula. Turn down the heat a touch and cook for 3 minutes, then carefully turn the patty over and cook the flipside for 3 minutes. The patty will not keep a perfect form but it will, thanks to the binding stickiness of the egg, keep a respectable shape. Serve with a wild green salad.

Pignuts always lose some flavour in cooking. The cutlet style keeps their taste better than the alternatives of boiling or baking them. Early sources recommended adding them to meat stews, but when I tried them with rabbit I found them bland. In cutlet form they at least have a pleasingly soft and stodgy consistency, which is a rare thing in the fibrous world of English nature. T. Cameron suggests roasting them.

By the end of June many of the birds on the farm are sitting on their second clutch of eggs, so I am having no difficulty in my virtual swapping of wild birds' eggs for duck ones. Or, on most of the farm I am not. Walking along the Grove hedge with Edith in a vapid morning shower, we find that the homes of the blue tit and dunnock have been pillaged, the eggs cracked and eaten. Then, from the top of the hedge, where it joins House Meadow, there is the sound of avian mayhem. A female blackbird squawks and flutters around. Out from the hawthorn pops a spivvy magpie with an egg in its beak. I shout at the magpie (something inane, such as 'Stop that!') and run towards it. Edith, who is better built for speed, dashes forward, at which the magpie drops the egg on the grass and flaps insolently off. The little blue egg is unbroken. After some ferreting about in the hedge I locate the nest and, picking up the egg with my shirt cuffs, return it to its rightful place, where two other eggs nestle in the ring of soft dry grass. The blackbirds, naturally, have no notion that I am the Good Samaritan and keep up a constant discontented clucking from a telegraph wire.

When I pass by on the morrow I find that the nest has been abandoned. All around it in the hedge little green crab apples, hazelnuts and sloes are forming and growing but the blackbirds' eggs are dead for ever.

A Calendar of Wild Food at Trelandon

June

Pignut, pigeon, rabbit, sorrel, dandelion, corn salad,
ground elder, elderflowers, sow thistle, dock, ground
ivy, nettles, Jack-by-the-hedge, chickweed, fat hen,
cow parsley, comfrey, burdock, honeysuckle, wild
rose, bush vetch, red clover, yarrow, wild thyme

ONE ADVANTAGE OF a view is that you can see the weather coming.

A cloud of gothic black swarms over the mountain and Edith and I sprint for shelter under an ash, where we sit on our haunches and watch the raindrops ping rings on the river. Edith and I are feeling rather pleased with ourselves; if I had a tail I'd wag it. Tired of family derision regarding our inability to form a convincing man and gundog act, we have been practising in secret; specifically we have been studying Chapter 18 of Keith Erlandson's *Gundog Training*, 'Handling to Direction'. Erlandson writes: 'It follows that there are many occasions . . . both in the shooting and Trial field, when a dog is not in a position to mark . . . a bird . . . To make good the retrieve he must be capable of accepting directions to place him within scenting distance of the bird.'

For weeks we have been practising blind retrieves with a dummy festooned with pigeon feathers, sailing this over Edith's covered eyes, ordering her to 'get out', stopping her on the whistle and directing her with hand signals to where the dummy has fallen unseen by her. Edith has just performed five perfect blind retrieves in a row. I give Edith a Bonio from my coat pocket. She gives me a slobbery lick on the hand.

Time to move on to the real thing, the retrieve of an actual pigeon. This we will do just as soon as we have caught a trout, which is uppermost on my food wish list, because I am becoming ever so slightly tired of eating pigeon each and every day.

As foreplay to the catching of a trout, I decide to read Isaak Walton's *The Compleat Angler*, but on a preliminary flick through the pages it is not Walton's classic instructions on trout-fishing that catch my attention but his remarks on the minnow or 'penk':

> The MINNOW hath, when he is in perfect season, and not sick, which is only presently after spawning, a kind of dappled or waved colour, like to a panther, on its sides, inclining to a greenish or sky-colour; his belly being milk white; and his back almost black or blackish. He is a sharp biter at a small worm, and in hot weather makes excellent sport for young anglers, or boys, or women that love that recreation. And in the spring they make of them excellent Minnow-tansies; for being washed well in salt, and their heads and tails cut off, and their guts taken out, and not washed after, they prove excellent for that use; that is, being fried with yolk of eggs, the flowers of cowslips and of primroses, and a little tansy; thus used they make a dainty dish of meat.

Walton also recommends two other small fish, for sport and eating, the bullhead and the loach ('a most dainty fish' of which 'both the palate and stomach of sick persons' would be grateful), but these swim in too few a number in the Escley to be worth the bother.

But minnows exist in plenty. Could the minnow be the white-bait of fresh water?

For a frustrating week, while the Escley lowers and clears from a summer deluge, I have to wait to find the answer, but then on a day when the sun heats the damp ground so vigorously that tropical steam rises from it, I sit in the alder-strewn shade of what we have named Periscope Pool, after the branch that sticks vertically from its submarine depths. My intention, I admit, had been to catch minnows in the time-honoured childish method: with a net. Alas, the fishing byelaws of Environment Agency Wales, which covers the Monnow and tributaries, are unambiguous: all coarse fish must be caught with a rod and line. And, in the case of the minnow, a tiny No. 30 hook, which is the smallest the Abergavenny angling shop can supply me with.

Walton was almost as good as his word. Attracted by crumbs of bread cast on the water, a shoal of minnow slip into the daub of shallow sunlit water where my hook and its thrashing brandling worm wait suspended over the dusty amber bedrock. A minnow darts at the worm – and seizes the hook with a disconcertingly piranha-ish ferocity for so companionable a little fish. I jerk up the rod and the thrashing silver-bellied minnow is lifted into the killing air. There is no sport, the minnow at three inches is too small a fry for that. Since I am using a mini-telescopic rod with the reel locked, I feel uncomfortably like a garden gnome fisherman with his stick. The minnow goes into the watery cage of the keep net.

The remainder of the shoal do not flee, as I thought they would; they only drift back before coming to make shy enquiries of another worm. One minnow, emboldened or ravenous, makes its attack, and it too is lifted from the pool. Over the next half-hour, four more minnow are caught, until the school floats away, whether from boredom or perturbation I cannot say. A jealous kingfisher rockets past on its way to its hole in the bank, a turquoise flare on the retina.

After dispatching my catch – a club to the head seems like overkill, so I decapitate them with my knife on a flat slate stone – I walk upstream through Bank Field, past the sheep hunkered under the hedge away from the sun, sending up clouds of brown butterflies as I brush through the thistles, until I reach the northern boundary, where the Escley flows through a series of long flat pools between an honour guard of oaks and elders.

The minnows here are no more discerning than their cousins down the bright stream, and in the space of a lazy hour I catch six more. To make a main meal I need more minnows, but I am impatient to try the little fishes on a dishy, so settle for minnow *hors d'oeuvre* instead.

Although tempted by Walton's recipe for minnow tansies, I cannot implement it in full because the cowslips and primroses are past and the yellow aromatic herb tansy does not grow on the farm. (I am not sure that this is a great loss: although tansy, *Tanacetum vulgare*, was given in classical legend to Ganymede to make him immortal, and in medieval times used to make a custard pudding at Easter, modern botany catalogues tansy as potentially toxic. It apparently gives a flavour somewhere in the region of rosemary.) In the kitchen, with all sense of experimentation driven out by eagerness to eat, I go for Walton's recipe in minimum: I gut and de-tail the minnows – one needs a knife as sharp as a scalpel to prevent the flesh of these small fish from tearing – salt them, dip them in egg yolk and quick-fry them in the pan.

There is always apprehension before trying a food not standard, and it comes now, despite how dainty indeed the minnows look curled and crisp on the white dinner plate. With my fingers I gently pick up a fried minnow and cautiously bite at one end. Wow. Fantastic. My paroxysm of pleasure is still coursing when Penny comes into the kitchen and asks, 'Well?'

'Really good,' I reply, 'like subtle trout. Much nicer than whitebait. You should try one.'

Penny, who is one of those vegetarians who eat fish, looks at the proffered plate, looks at me and recalls culinary disasters past. 'Maybe tomorrow,' she says.

Tris comes in behind her, makes a puking face and says, 'What *is* that?'

'Minnow.'

'Suitable only for gnomes, Father.'

'What?'

'In BB's *Little Grey Men* or *Down the Bright Stream* or whichever. The gnomes eat minnows.'

Yes, of course they do. All day an idea of kippered minnows has travelled with me. And now I remember. The last gnomes in England, Cloudberry, Sneezewort, Baldmoney and Dodder, smoked minnows over oak.

I must try that too.

According to Jason Hill's Second World War austerity classic, *The Wild Foods of Britain*, ash keys 'make a good pickle, which tastes rather like pickled walnuts, if they are gathered before they begin to get hard'. Presumably the fruits of the ash are called keys because they hang in bunches like the keys of a medieval gaoler. Singly, the fruit looks like the wing of a locust. The seed, which is the size of a pine nut, is ensconced at the stem end. Raw, it tastes of wormwood.

Dutifully I follow Hill's instructions to pour a boiling mixture of equal parts vinegar and cider, plus a dash of salt, over the keys. The whole is put into the oven for an hour to infuse, then sealed in a Parfait or Kilner jar. After three weeks I try a pickled key.

It tastes of wormwood.

> The breeze is stopt the lazy bough
> Hath not a leaf that dances now
> The totter grass upon the hill
> And spiders threads is hanging still
> The feathers dropt from morehens wing
> Which to the waters surface clings
> As steadfast and as heavy seem
> As stones beneath them in the stream
> Hawkweed and groundsels fairey downs
> Unruffld keep their seeding crowns.
>
> John Clare, *The Shepherd's Calendar*

High summer and the land is bereaved of its floral colour. Only foxgloves stand bright against the dusty hedges, which are becoming quiet, as brood after brood of chicks fly away. Nature has an aura of calm relaxation about her, and so do I. The hours of daylight are still long and I sit outside on the yard on a luminescent evening, when the earth seems lighted from within, with a glass of nettle beer, and do nothing. Thoughts drift over me. I make no attempt to catch them, but one distils: my story of alienation from the land is merely emblematic; it is the tale of the English as a whole. Uprooted by the industrial revolution, the English moved from country to town, where they promptly sought to overcome their severance from their natural habitat by re-creating the countryside in the back garden. After all, what is a lawn but a little meadow? Napoleon was wrong: the English are not a nation of shopkeepers, they are a nation of gardeners.

When the darkness finally closes the curtain on the scene of my indolence, I can feel the displaced air from the beat of bats' wings as they flit around the house. As a child I used to be scared of bats, fearing that they might fly into my hair and become tangled. But as my father pointed out to me, any creature that can fly between electricity wires can certainly avoid crashing into the human head.

—

I go to see my father at the nursing home, partly for his company, partly to ask his advice. He was a great trout fisherman in his youth, and I am tired of catching nothing on my expeditions to the Escley. He is out of bed, and is sitting in what we ironically call his 'electric chair', but which is actually a powered wheelchair. Although paralysed down the right side of his body, my father has become adept at manoeuvring the machine. 'It can turn on a six-pence,' he says, performing a wheelchair pirouette in his bedroom. He is keen to tell me about his adventure in the chair that morning; while taking a spin around the grounds he came across a grass snake sunning itself. 'You should have seen me skedaddle,' he says, laughing. 'It was at least six foot long,' he goes on, his blue eyes shining with a fragmentary glint of youth and happiness. I raise my right eyebrow, à la Roger Moore. 'Oh, all right, about four foot then,' says Dad. His tendency to fishermanly exaggeration reminds me of the other reason I am here. I explain my various fishing predicaments, to which my father replies, 'Try dapping.'

Dapping, apparently, is where the fisherman hides behind a bush (or something similar) on the bank, pushes the rod through and dances the fly on the water by raising and lowering the rod. 'Use a big fly,' my father says, 'something the fish can be bothered with.' With his eyes narrowing conspiratorially, he adds, 'I should put a small worm on the hook as well.'

To double the chance of a catch by pinning a struggling (thus attention-catching) and meaty (thus attractive to the trout's sense of smell) worm on the fly's hook is highly unsporting, if not down-right cheating. Suddenly I feel very in touch with my inner poacher.

That afternoon I perch up high behind a smooth-barked hazel with my feet dug into the black leaf mould of the bank, stick the rod past the hazel and dip a fluorescent green fly on to the slow, trout-ringed pool below. On the fly wriggles a red brandling worm. As I jig up the fly for the third time a wild-eyed, open-jawed monster rises vertically from the primeval nothingness of the pool and clamps its mouth on to the double bait. Shock blocks any mental processes; instinctively I carry on winding the reel handle. I know this, because the next thing I see clearly is a fish flapping at my feet on the precipitous bank, me dropping the rod, me trying to pin the fish down with one hand while scrabbling for a stone with the other. My fingers feel a sandstone lump in the mould and I wriggle it out and hit, hit, hit, hit, hit the trout on the head. The dead fish stares at me. My heart is pounding wildly. The speckle-skinned, snare-mouthed trout is so gorgeously beautiful, so basely ugly that I am simultaneously ashamed and proud – as though I have performed some public duty – to have killed it.

No, on balance I am relieved to have caught my first trout. One, two, three, four, five, once I caught a fish alive! With a piece of baler twine poked through the fish's lip, I carry home my catch feeling every inch the successful man (primitive model) and desperate to wave it in front of my doubting family.

Unfortunately, my grand entrance is rather ruined by finding everyone to be out. Only Edith is there to greet me. She sniffs at the fish, then wags her tail excitedly. 'No, you idiotic dog,' I say to her, 'this is for me.' She is clearly unconvinced and follows me to the kitchen, where I slap my fish on the scales. The red needle hovers at twelve ounces.

So enthused am I by my first trout that I rush back to the river to fish some more. But before I leave the house, I do something I have always wanted to do. I stick a note on the front door which says *GONE FISHING*.

Pickled trout

Adapted from Herefordshire Food *by Karen Wallace, 1982. Her version of the dish serves 6.*

6 medium trout
1 pint/600ml water
1pint/600ml cider vinegar
2 bulbs wild garlic
salt
pinch dried chervil

Cut the heads and tails off the fish. Clean but do not scale. Split the fish and press them flat, skin side down, and cut

away any bony bits with a very sharp knife. Rinse and pat dry.
Slice the garlic and lay it down the length of each fillet. Roll
up the fillets and fit them tightly into a small earthenware or
china terrine. Pour over the water and vinegar, add two
pinches of salt and the chervil. Leave the fish in the pickle for
at least 24 hours. Cover with foil. Cook in the oven at 275°F/
140°C/Gas Mark 1 for 45 minutes.

Do not discard the heads and cut-off tails but boil them up
for stock.

I have the pickled trout, cold, for breakfast. At some undefined, unnoticed point in time, but around the beginning of spring, my palate became retrained and I lost the nagging desire for sweet-tasting breakfasts of the croissant-stuffed-with-apricot-preserve sort. Cold meat is my staple, which, of course, is what the English always used to break the fast of the night with, before the coming of Rice Krispies, even before the so-called 'full English' (of bacon, sausages, eggs, tomatoes, baked beans, mushrooms and fried bread), which is an invention of the 1920s. In *The English Breakfast: The Biography of a National Meal*, Kaori O'Connor notes that the 1901 edition of *Mrs Beeton's Book of Household Management* suggested game pie for the first meal of the day, while on 11 February 1904 the breakfast at Windsor Castle featured *Bécassines* [snipe] *sur canapés*.

——

Over the next days I catch four more trout, varying in size from ten to fifteen ounces. One I stuff with chervil, one I poach in water with wild thyme, but the two which taste the best are the two which are grilled, on a spit made of branches, over a smoky wood fire on the riverbank, the fat red sun lying on the water, and shared with Penny, Tristram and Freda. But, then, perhaps food always tastes better when shared. The smoke of the fire, I note, keeps the biting midges at bay, which is always the bothersome aspect of picnics by rivers in the evening.

My run of fishing luck does not continue. When I reach the brook later in the week the water is running hopelessly low, and a pallid wind is deterring the flies from their dancing. I creep along the bank until I reach a pollarded alder, from behind which I can dap my green bomber faux fly with its real worm accessory into a pool. A trout comes out from under the tree's roots, approaches the worm, retires and comes again. I hook the fish but as I lift the rod he leaps, flashes and falls free. He will not come again today. On the way home I detour via the kingfisher's nest in the bank; the slut of British birds, the kingfisher cannot be bothered to do more with the babies' crap than push it out of the door, to drip festering down the red sandstone bank. As I tut-tut at the kingfisher's house-cleaning methods, my attention is taken by a small black wasp-like fly on the shingle, which I think is a rare yellow-tipped soldier fly. Since I am standing stone motionless, a bird fails to see me and alights on a rock in mid-river: a dipper.

The dipper has many local names which hint at its colour and size, such as water ouzel and water blackbird, but none truly captures the bird's appearance. On the Escley the birds tend to deep chestnut on the back, rather than coal black, and the dipper is three or so inches shorter than the common blackbird.

From its boulder perch, its white bib obscured now and then by its constant bobbing, the dipper looks into the shallow broken water. I think to myself that I have never seen a dipper do its fabled underwater perambulation – at which the bird, as though wishing to oblige me, hops into the glass-clear river, bows its head and walks, literally walks, along the stone bottom, using the flow of the running water over its back to push down its natural buoyancy. I hold my breath, as the bird must be holding its. After some seconds, the bird resurfaces with a manic black larva in its beak, on which it immediately gorges. Some faint movement by me alerts the bird, which flutters off warily but not panic-stricken, calling *zit, zit, zit,* having given its virtuoso performance in the art of underwater hunting.

Originally *Armoracia rusticana* was used as a medicinal herb, but in the fifteenth century the Germans and Danes began using it in the kitchen to flavour fish. The culinary usage of horseradish spread to Britain, where it became forever associated with roast beef.

To gather the plant I have to walk a bare twenty yards from the house, because it grows on the ground disturbed by the builders, a medium it enjoys, along with the field edge and the road verge. From June the long, crinkly leaves of horseradish are plain to see. Young horseradish leaves *can* be chopped into salads but they are testing of the jaw muscles. Much preferred is the pungent, zesty root, although its digging up may well exercise the biceps because it is so extensive. When paring the skin from the excavated root, do so with the windows open because the volatile oils released are more tear-inducing than peeling onions.

The prefix 'horse', incidentally, has no equine connection; it means 'coarse'.

Horseradish sauce

Hill's recipe is simple and effective: 'Work up the hard-boiled yolk of an egg with 2 parts of oil and 1 of vinegar to a thick cream, add salt, a few drops of onion juice or chips of garlic and a heaped tablespoonful of fine grated horseradish (more or less according to taste). The chopped white of an egg may be added, if the sauce is to be used with fish.'

To preserve horseradish roots, store in sand or immerse in cider vinegar.

—

The 'fat' in fat hen acknowledges the greasy nature of the herb's seeds, which were ground by the Anglo-Saxons into flour. So profusely did the plant grow in early England that villages were named after it. (The Old English for fat hen is 'melde' – as in Melbourn in Cambridgeshire.) More recently the plant was gathered as a green vegetable, until it was usurped by its close but cultivated relative spinach. Fat hen's fall from fashion notwithstanding, it is one of the most nutritious 'weeds' of England, rich in iron, calcium, protein and vitamins B1 and B2. A common place to find fat hen is the farmyard, which is why it is known colloquially as 'muckweed'.

On the tongue, fat hen flour is pleasurably reminiscent of buckwheat. But the labour required to make the flour is fabulous. On a sultry late July afternoon I squelch over the pigs' old manure heap (about ten yards by ten yards in size), slapping at horseflies, separating the mealy fat hen plants from the nettles, the sow thistles and the similar-looking Good King Henry. Fearing pathogenic contamination from the pig crap, I snip off every fat hen plant with Penny's dress-making scissors (an unpopular borrowing) rather than pulling it up. Then I strip the seeds into a wicker basket, but many resist my efforts because they are not fully, rusty-pink ripe; the seeds which do oblige me are then spread on a tarpaulin in the sun, fenced off with sheep hurdles to stop the Labradors eating them, because Labradors will eat anything.

On the next day I carry on drying the seeds, turning them occasionally, but then it threatens to rain, so I finish them off in the oven. After this I rub, winnow and grind them. And lo! two days have passed and I have . . . one whole pound of flour. I would probably not have persisted in making it if I had not needed to, but I long ago ran out of chestnut flour. Also, my attempt to make flour from the heads of the grasses in the hayfields at the end of June was an utter, unmitigated disaster. The M. Hulot comic potential of bashing grass-seed heads into a basket with a tennis racquet was always great, and I did not disappoint, mashing my basket hand with an ill-timed swipe from the racquet. I failed to dry the meagre seeds properly and so they succumbed to a fungal growth with frightening speed. When I went back to the hayfields to bash again, rain terminated the harvest. When the rain stopped, the grass heads were empty pale-yellow shells whispering in the breeze. The seeds had flown.

It only occurs to me, as the grinder is whizzing, that the Saxons did not gather *Chenopodium album* from the wild. They farmed fat hen in neat, dense patches. They did something similar with grass, after domesticating it.

Fat hen pancakes with horseradish
In the perfect fat hen pancake the plant's leaves are used as filler and the seeds as the flour for the batter. But see above.

1 large bunch fat hen
½ pint/300ml water
2 duck eggs
¼ tsp salt
4oz/110g fat hen flour/chestnut flour
about 4 tbsp hazelnut oil
grated horseradish

Liquidize the eggs and salt with the water. Add the flour and 1 tablespoon of the hazelnut oil. Liquidize again.
While the batter is chilling, steam the fat hen until tender.
Make pancakes in the normal way, frying them in the remainder of the hazelnut oil. In the centre of each pancake

place 2 tablespoons of steamed fat hen, sprinkle on a
teaspoon of grated horseradish and roll the pancake up. Place
in an oiled dish and bake at 375°F/190°C/Gas Mark 5 for
10 minutes.

Summertime and the living wild is relatively easy. In the heat my appetite shrinks, and slices of cold pigeon, cold poached (cooked in water rather than illegally gained) trout, or rabbit with green salad or vegetables see me through days in a row. There are still enough bird's eggs in the hedge nests for me to substitute duck eggs and make *omelette aux fines herbes sauvages* or 'minnow thymes' – my version of Walton's tansies – but squirrel has become pie in the sky, because I cannot see him in the heavy foliage to shoot him. On a panting July midday, when someone seems to have left an oven on outside, I take Edith for a jolly around the shimmering fields for no particular reason other than to enjoy ourselves and see what is what. The thump of a hay-baler sounds from down in the village, which prompts me to walk up and check that the curlew chicks have gone from Road Field. Edith and I meander through the lengthy golden grass, disturbing clicking grasshoppers but no curlews. The field can now be safely cut. By farming rights Road Field should have been cut in June, when the seed heads of the grass were full and I was Monsieur Hulot incarnate, but eight-foot offset mowers towed behind giant tractors do not mix with fledgling curlews.

Edith and I carry on with our walk, tongues hanging out, noting how plant life on the farm is divided by what side of the hedge it lives on, as surely as people are separated by the tracks in the town. On the east, sunnier side of the hedges the hawthorn berries are premature autumn red, while on the west side there are still some slow-maturing elderflower heads to pick.

High noon in high summer. The sheep are shorn, but even so

they hide in the wells of shade behind the trunks of trees. Hedge brown and comma butterflies flutter desultorily along the field edges, a bumble bee haphazardly scouts the perfumed clover, and a cock yellowhammer perched on the track stock fence is the only bird in all Herefordshire that can be bothered to sing in the heat and the dust. The Englishman and his dog continue their midday walk. Despite all appearances to the contrary, they are not mad (not even the man, with his sunburnt nose, shorts and wellingtons) because they end up at the grass verge on the track, where the perfect fruit for summer waits to be picked.

Wild strawberry.

That evening Edith and I go to work. We have killed time. Now we will kill a pigeon and Edith will bring it in. I am tooled up with the Baikal shotgun, cleaned and oiled, and a cap pulled down well over my eyes, my face smeared with mud. Despite the sapping humidity I am wearing my Barbour, made into the perfect country camouflage by eons of mud, blood and grass stains. Edith's collar, with its tinkling name tag, has been removed. Dogs imbibe their master's mood. She is quivering with excitement. But focused. Very focused. Reservoir dog? Retriever dog, certainly.

In long shadows, we walk down Bank Field towards the river, sidestepping the thistles and passing the sheep as they meander uphill to bed. When we reach the great ash tree, we stand underneath its umbrella and begin our vigil. Midges bite, my forehead under my cap prickles with sweat, a vole scurries about our feet but we do not move. The only sound on the evening air is Edith's panting, the slosh of the Escley over the waterfall and the distant chatter of house martins as they hunt flies high in the firmament. To take my mind off my discomfort I rehearse the kill: the ash is about twenty-five yards from the flight line of juvenile wood pigeons roosting in Quarry Wood and my intention is to broadside one as it passes in front of me, so that it falls to the ground in the riverbank trees. Then Edith can perform a blind retrieve.

I hear the beat of their wings before I see them. Three wood pigeons coming from downstream, flying low and fast. Very fast. Rays from the sun, which is conveniently buoyed above the western horizon, catch and illuminate the birds. I take the shot later than intended, when the birds are past me, and for a moment I believe that I have missed. The left-hand bird flies on and on. Then it stutters and falls out of the sky.

The retrieve Edith has now to perform is much further than planned, and will take her across the river and into the wood beyond. I send her off; she stops at the river fence and turns to me. I signal her right and she leaps the fence, to be swallowed by the gloom. Although I can no longer see Edith the black Labrador in the church dark of the river thicket, I can hear her. She is splashing through the river, she is pounding through the trees of the wood on the other bank. She is too far to the right. I walk forward and beep on the Acme Thunderer whistle to stop her. This is the crucial moment: will she turn and look at me? Since I am silhouetted by the sinking sun she should, with canine eyes, be able to see me through the trees. I signal her left. Off she goes. Left. There is not much more I can do, because I am far from sure when the bird hit the ground. Now it is up to Edith and her nose.

Minutes pass. A tawny owl toowitts in the upstream oak. Bats flicker about the river. A cow, one of ours, lows. There is not one breath of air in the night. I take off my coat and hat and lie on the earth, still warm with the stored heat of the day, and watch for the first star to switch on in the ink-blue dome. Across in the wood I can still hear Edith snuffling. Another minute or two slips by.

When I'm about to give up hope and whistle Edith back, I detect the sound of a dog leaping into water. Edith on the return. Despite the heat of the night, I shiver once, involuntarily, in nervous anxiety: has Edith got the pigeon?

Over the fence comes Edith, a running shadow in the dusk. She is almost here.

And pressed into my hand is a fat bundle of feathers and a wet nose.

———

This July day of wild strawberries and retrieved pigeon was summer's zenith. Thereafter, the summer fell apart. A portent came on the last day of the month.

———

A dank morning more suited to winter than July. I am woken at 6am by the sound of ducks quacking. A bolt of horror forks through my head: I must have forgotten to shut the ducks in their wooden house last night. Do we still have four? Panic propels me outside where, to my relief, I see four bright white ducks waddling through the wet, black grass, looking for slugs. Walking back I almost step in a thin white steaming turd on top of a molehill. The turd of a fox.

Fox excrement is invariably white, coloured by the bones they eat. Leaving excrement somewhere prominent is a way of marking territory, of announcing presence. Domestic dogs achieve the same effect by kicking up dirt and grass after they have crapped to make an accompanying feature, a motion humans mistake as a tidy-minded dog seeking to cover its waste.

Why the fox did not seize its chance to take the ducks I cannot fathom, for the wire stock fence of the duck pen would not have stopped it. The dogs, which might have deterred it, were slumbering safely inside. Foxes hunt hardest, take more risks, in the summer, when they have cubs to feed; I have known them take a violent, hissing gander in broad daylight then.

That night, when the rain clouds have occluded the moon and the dark is bottomless, I quietly walk down to the duck pen and suddenly switch on the mega-torch. Swinging the beam towards the neighbouring Bank Field I pick out two pairs of amber eyes staring back at me. Going up on to the yard, I shine the torch into House Meadow and up into Little Field. Another pair of devil-eyes. I repeat the exercise until midnight, and every time I find three foxes circling around in a canine version of the Indians in John Ford's Western movie *Fort Apache*. In the morning I see fox spoors in the mud around the duck pond and the duck hut. The musty stink of fox offends my nose. They have also raided one of the metal dustbins on the yard.

If the foxes are willing to risk death to scavenge a bin they must be finding game very scarce. Presumably, then, so are the other predators of the valley, who too have voracious infant mouths to satisfy.

So where does this leave me?

A CALENDAR OF WILD FOOD AT TRELANDON
July

Trout, fat hen, horseradish, pigeon, rabbit, squirrel, sorrel, dandelion, ground elder, sow thistle, nettles, chickweed, comfrey, burdock, bush vetch, yarrow, wild thyme, ash, salad burnet, timothy, fescue, coltsfoot, wild strawberry

WHEN IT FIRST RAINS, I am almost glad. Everything I gather is juicier, crunchier, and I have tired of a run of listless misty days, which are neither good nor bad. Besides, I like sitting under the oaks' canopy and watching the raindrops plip on the Escley, and the dry land will willingly absorb the precipitation. There is no immediate danger of the Escley running too high to fish. On the contrary, I catch one small trout and a handful of minnow below the waterfall (a grandiose term for where the Escley pours over stone springboards and falls eighteen inches) but when, after two days, I do not get as much as a bite I move my pitch upstream.

There is an immediate compensation in my decision. As I walk along the bank a wood pigeon bashes out of a hazel bush just above my head. It would not have left its departure so late unless it was sitting on a nest, so I clamber up and, sure enough, between an ivy-clad fork sits an untidy bundle of twigs. In an ungainly monkey-swing I manage to pull myself up and peep over the edge of the nest. Two exquisite china-white eggs lie there. Of course there are two, for as the folk rhyme goes:

> Coo-coo-coo
> It's as much as a pigeon can do,
> To bring up two;
> But the little wren can maintain ten
> And keep them all like gentlemen.

I mark the tree by green-fracturing two of its bottom branches, leaving them hanging down on the field side. Every day, with metronomic regularity, I check the eggs, which turn into downy micro-pterodactyls, which turn into fat fledglings. Soon the fledglings will be fat squabs, will be my dinner. A picture of them plump, naked and side by side on a willow-pattern plate becomes permanently overlaid in my mind's eye. My mouth spontaneously and uncontrollably salivates at the thought of them.

One should not count one's squabs before they are dispatched, however. Early on a soft-lit August morning I wake up with a terrible intuition, pull on my wellingtons and run down, pyjamas flapping, to their nest. I know before I pull myself up that they have been stolen from me.

Sure enough, the pathetic bowl of sticks is bare. At two weeks old they were too young to fly away. Something has taken them.

Or perhaps not. For one happy, irrational moment I scrabble around the base of the tree, then further, into the dank shingle of the brook, believing that they might have fallen out and I could turn back time, and replace them.

No such thing has occurred, of course. They're dead meat in another predator's stomach.

Welcome to hard times, welcome to Nature red in tooth and claw, welcome to dog eat dog.

At the age of six or so, my grandmother took me for a walk along the lane towards Westhide. As we poked in the hop-yard hedges, peered into ditches, tested the blackberries for ripeness, she suddenly said, 'Can you smell the rain, John?' I could not smell any rain. Neither could I see any rain clouds in the Indian summer sky. I looked up at my grandmother's brown, weather-stained face and was astonished: she seemed to be both dreaming and concentrating, both receiving and sending signals. In another age, one would have said she was tuned in. In an earlier age still, one would have said she was in communion with nature. When I copied my grandmother, nothing happened; I was trying too hard. Since she was still standing with her head half cocked, eyes alert, nose tilted to the air, I tried again. Maybe I pretended I was a wild animal. A fox, probably.

The intensity of what happened next on the lane to Westhide lives with me still. The doors of perception opened. I could hear things I had not noticed before (the stag beetle crawling over dried blackberry leaves in the hedge bottom), I could see the unseen (the blackbird sitting on her nest hoping we would pass) and I could smell an olfactory kaleidoscope of scents, odours and fragrances. And yes, I could detect the rain on the air.

Unremarked by the Met Office forecasters, unknown to the barometer hanging in my grandparents' long hall, the rain came four hours later.

Of course, what my grandmother was doing – and what she was trying to teach me – was to use senses, not intellect, to interpret the subliminal signals of Nature. (In retrospect, my guess is that my grandmother was alerted to the incipient rain by the plants of the hedgerow, such as herb-robert, changing their posture.) The use of 'animal instinct' is less fanciful than it seems; women constantly use non-rational skills to understand people – particularly other women. The hunter-cum-forager only has to adjust the same skills for a different quarry.

Under the pigeon's abandoned nest, I adopt the pose of my grandmother forty years before, and close my mind but open my senses. As with the manual tuning of a radio there is a moment's wait before the correct frequency is found. But then I see, as though magnified, the clues to whodunit: the faint scratch marks by the nest; the green nuts pulled off the hazel bushes further along the bank; the few grey hairs caught in the stock fence.

A grey squirrel has been here, and probably chanced on the squabs on a nutting expedition.

There is more news from Nature for those who care to hear it. Actually, it is what I cannot hear that troubles me. I slip along the bank and listen to the trees. I pad to the top of Bank Field and listen to the blackthorn hedge. Nowhere can I hear the clamour of baby birds. Even though it is late in the breeding season some birds should still be in the nest waiting impatiently to be fed by their parents. But the hedges are silent.

Working along the hedge, carefully pulling its spiny branches apart, I find two abandoned nests, one a robin's, one a blue tit's. Both contain naked and dead chicks. This time the squirrel is guiltless; the culprit is altogether more ancient and mighty. The weather has not only been wet; it has been cold. Consequently there has not been enough grub life to grow little birds.

As I tread back to the house, I muse on how few are the sloe berries in the hedge.

Like Nature, the vet has news I do not want to hear. It is news I expected but shut my mind to. Jenny James phones to report that a blood test on Freda's white fairy-tale pony, Poppy, shows her to be riven with cancer. There is no cure. She has to be put down. Jenny suggests we do this immediately, to spare Poppy pain. I want Freda, who is at school, to have a last evening with her so-so-loved pony. Jenny and I compromise on the next morning, after I assure her that I will call her if Poppy starts showing signs of distress.

When Freda comes home, she runs into the sitting room. 'Dad! What did the vet say?'

Freda is expecting good tidings, that Poppy's mystifying illness has finally been diagnosed and treatment is forthcoming.

I don't really need to say anything. She has seen this look on my face before, when I had to tell her that Sniffy, her first Jack Russell, had died of a crush injury. But I say it anyway. 'Freda, I am so sorry but Poppy has to be put down. She has cancer.'

Her face flushes red and she howls. I wrap her tight in my arms and wish I could draw all the hurt into me. Penny and Tris come in. 'How bad?' says Penny.

'The worst,' I reply. Soon Penny is crying too. Tris remains dry-eyed because at thirteen you don't cry, do you, it's embarrassing.

That night Freda, even though we put her into bed with us, hardly sleeps. At two in the morning, she wants me to take her out to Poppy. In the light cast from the sitting-room window, I watch Freda hang on to Poppy's neck and tell her that she will always remember her. Then she wails again, 'Daddy, why, why does Poppy have to die? I prayed so hard!'

Eventually, Freda exhausts herself so that I am able to lead her limply away. As we walk back across the yard, she suddenly turns her head to look at the stable, where Poppy appears at the door. She looks at Freda and whinnies, before retiring again to the dark recess.

I know that, for as long as I live, I will see that moment. A moment where a pony told a girl that she loved her too.

The next morning we bundle Freda off to school, so that she does not have to see the end. At ten on the dot, Jenny's red Skoda arrives on the yard, to be greeted by the dogs, who love the archive of interesting smells that clings to it. We hardly talk as we walk down to the stable. Terminations are not great fun for vets either.

At the stable, I say to Jenny plaintively, 'I've promised Freda that Poppy won't fall and hurt herself when the injection is given.'

'Usually, when I've done these, the pony lies down as though it was going to sleep.'

And that is what happens. I hold Poppy's blue head collar, the one she was wearing when she came to us three years ago, as Jenny injects a sedative, then an OD of anaesthetic.

Poppy swoons and, by guiding her with the head collar, I

make sure she goes down on her knees and then on to her side in the centre of the stable. She doesn't bang into the wall.

All the while I whisper in her ear that Freda loves her.

'Has she gone?' I ask Jenny, who takes out a stethoscope and listens for a heartbeat.

A moment's pause. 'She's gone.'

Around me the world voids into an echoing glass chamber of loss.

When Jenny drives away it starts raining again. It rains too when I dig a grave for Poppy, in House Meadow, where Freda used to ride her, with a hired mini-digger. We bury her in a shroud of sheep's fleece so she will be comfortable, with a red rose and purple sweet peas adorning her head collar. Penny, her head bowed in grief, puts in a note. As I turn on the digger to bulldoze in the covering earth, my tears are falling faster than the rain.

———

The rains take their toll on the warren by the house. Lying below the level of the old, filled-in farmyard pond, the warren floods, the water driving out or drowning the inhabitants in the lower burrows. For the first time since myxomatosis three years ago, there are no rabbits scampering around the yard in the bookends of the day and only the occasional pile of pellets lets me know that there are any survivors.

There are still plenty of rabbits under the hedge in Road Field. I drive up in the jeep in the late afternoon, with the four-wheel drive engaged, because the surface of the grass is slick with wet. I park and wait. At last light, a rabbit comes out. This is Colonel Bigwig, as it always is, to test the air. He gives the jeep a hard stare, as if to suggest that he does not entirely approve of my choice of 4×4. Rabbit, I say, you are lucky, I could be driving something seriously infra dig, such as a BMW X5. Persuaded by my argument, Colonel Bigwig gives an invisible all-clear signal and a herd of rabbits creep out on to the grass where it is short and sweet, where they have nibbled it before. The passenger window is already down, the barrel of the Weihrauch resting on the ledge. I ignore Colonel Bigwig and shoot one of the does.

A torrent of scuttling, flashing white bobs. The doe, shot behind the head, is quite still. I get out of the jeep, pick up rabbit, push the urine out of her bladder and put her in the boot, then drive off.

Not exactly a drive-by shooting but somehow very Chicago South Side, I think.

Every day, in every way, my food options lessen. Perhaps August, that awkward month at the end of summer, is always like this. It is the month when the majority of plants are past their youthful green best, while the tantalizing fruits of autumn are not yet mature. It is the month when all the farm's easy kills have been taken by the family-minded fox, weasel, stoat, buzzard, kestrel, tawny owl, little owl, sparrowhawk, hobby and red kite (to name the predators I have noted at Trelandon so far this year) and what is left for the gun is sprightly and clever and taxing of one's time and skill. It is the last month of the closed season on wild duck, a legality that seems to drag unbearably over the four weeks. It is the month when the curtain comes down on the long nesting season of birds, and the supply of eggs dwindles to nothing.

Such are the expected problems of August. A late summer of rain has piled a novelty on top of these: the Escley is too furious to fish; in fact, it is too furious to get close to. Each day it barges along its course, knocking down unsteady hazel bushes.

Once again I become very dependent for my meals on the humble rabbit, though I fancy that experience has emboldened me to prepare it in new and exotic ways.

Garlic mustard rabbit

This is a wild version of the Mustard Rabbit in Leith's
Cookery Bible *by Prue Leith and Caroline Waldegrave, 1991.*
Serves 4

1 rabbit, skinned and cleaned
1 tsp fat hen flour
2 tbsp garlic mustard seeds crushed in 1 tbsp cider vinegar
1½oz/40g goose fat
2 bulbs wild garlic, crushed
1 pint/600ml mushroom stock (made from Jew's ear, shaggy
ink caps, chicken of the woods or another seasonal fungus)
1 tbsp chopped yarrow leaves to garnish

Sever the rabbit's head, then joint the animal into 6 pieces.
Soak the rabbit in salted water for 4 hours (to whiten it).
Remove, drain and pat dry. Spread the garlic mustard
and cider mixture over the rabbit pieces and leave
overnight.

The next day preheat the oven to 350°F/170°C/Gas Mark 4.
Heat the goose fat in a frying pan, add the garlic and brown
the rabbit pieces all over. Remove them with a spatula and
place in a casserole.

While the pan is still on the heat, stir in the flour and cook
for 1 minute.

Take the pan off the heat and stir in the stock. Return to the
heat and bring to the boil, stirring all the while.

Pour this sauce over the rabbit. Cook in the oven for about
1½ hours, or until the rabbit is tender.

Lift the rabbit on to a warmed serving dish. If the sauce is
too thin, boil rapidly until it thickens and shines. Pour the
sauce gently over the rabbit pieces. Garnish with chopped
yarrow leaves.

Serve with a full red country wine, such as elderberry or blackberry.

In his *Shepherd's Calendar* John Clare declared August to be the month when

> Harvest approaches with its bustling day
> The wheat tans brown and barley bleaches grey
> In yellow garb the oat land intervenes
> And tawny glooms the valley thronged with beans.

But this year, wheat rots where it stands and Penny's runner beans, enervated and lank, struggle to climb their poles. Herb-robert, that faithful forecaster of the hedgerow, hangs its flowers in sadness. Only when the sun is out will it raise up its head and allow its hairy stalk to turn red. A member of the geranium family, herb-robert, *Geranium robertianum*, is edible, but only at a pinch. I am taking that pinch.

Currently I spend most of my days with my nose to the sodden land seeking plants with the single-mindedness of an orchid-hunter. There is a pay-off: as well as herb-robert, I discover another plant on the farm whose existence I have hitherto overlooked. Silverweed.

I can find no explanation for why I have failed to spot silverweed's silken-topped, downy-bottomed leaves before. But there they are, sprawling six inches high at the back of the Copse Field ditch. Doubtless I would be more overjoyed to find a pot of gold, but finding silverweed is not a bad second prize. *Potentilla anserine* is the tuber the British ate until the arrival of the potato. Like burdock, silverweed tubers are exceptionally high in starch, about 30 per cent per volume. The root is also exceptionally versatile: it can be eaten raw, it can be roasted, baked, boiled, steamed, dried and ground into flour for bread and gruel.

Silverweed would be a great accompaniment to meat. Unfortunately, for three raining days in a row I fail to shoot a single rabbit or pigeon. My stomach gnaws with hunger. Every daylight minute I am out looking for food, yet sometimes only return with bitter handfuls of stringy plantain, nettle and goose grass. The world and I are out of kilter; extreme hunger evidently buggers my connection to Nature. Oh, if only the sweet black-berries were ripe! But they, like the other fruits of the hedge, are retarded by the unseasonal rains.

There's less of me than there used to be. Quite a lot less. I get off the bathroom scales, step on again and watch the electronic digits increase – except they don't. The mirror doesn't lie either; the bones under my eyes stick out. I look like a portrait by Lucien Freud.

Perhaps I can sell *The Wild Life* as a diet method. Lose a stone in a week! Guaranteed! Low carb, low sugar, low everything. The Sweet FA diet.

I crave meat and its stomach-filling ways. And so comes the day when I decide that snails must go on the menu. As a child I ate snails often – such is the peril and the privilege of having a French teacher for a stepmother – at the upscale Greyfriars restaurant in Hereford, taking home the mollusc's banded shell as a sort of medal. Yet *escargot*-eating is neither exclusively French nor reserved for exclusive restaurants; in his *Wild Foods of Britain*, Jason Hill records that ready-cooked snails were still sold in Bristol, where they were scoffed by the workers in the tobacco factories.

According to Hill, the Bristol proletariat ate the common or garden snail (*Helix aspera*) gathered by the ton from the

Cotswolds, the West Country version of the Cockney's jellied eels. The true edible snail (*Helix pomatia*) is also to be found in Britain, mainly in the south; it was likely introduced, along with dessert apples, plums and central heating, by the Romans, who farmed them on bran and wine.

Collecting snails from the garden, especially if one has an old stone wall, is child's play and is therefore a job I give to the children. (An alternative method is to lay out some rhubarb leaves in the evening, and next morning pick the snails from under them.) After half an hour, Tris and Freda return with twenty-two snails, all of the common or garden type, in a plastic bucket. Snails are in no sense a fast food, because before eating they need to be purged of toxins, in case they live in close proximity to deadly nightshade (and ours do) or on plants sprayed with herbicides.

So the snails stay in the pink plastic bucket, with a saucer of water and a handful of dandelion and wild garlic leaves, and a swathe of muslin tied over the top. The herbage feeds and flavours the molluscs. For a week I fodder and muck out; finally, I starve the snails for twenty-four hours.

Escargot are protein-rich and make a sophisticated *hors d'oeuvre*. I still do not want to consume them. It does not help that Freda has given them names and turned them into pets. Eventually, on an afternoon when the children are staying with friends, I boil up a cauldron of water and drop the snails in.

I think I can hear them screaming.

Snails

Snails are at their best from spring to autumn, unless they are vine-fed (farmed), when they are at their prime in winter. They can be eaten whole like oysters, a method to be applauded if one finds them gristly. The venerable Great War forager T. Cameron advised:

'Throw the snails into a pot of boiling water in which has

been placed a handful of ashes, and let them boil for 20 to 25 minutes. Remove them from their shells, and let the latter boil another 15 minutes in a stock made of water, salt, onions, and carrots cut up, with parsley, thyme, and a clove of garlic. Keep stirring all the time in order to cleanse the shells. Make a paste of butter mixed with parsley and garlic chopped very fine, pepper and salt. Put a little of this into each shell, replace the snail, its operculum having been cut off, and stop it in with a little more of the paste. Place the snails thus treated on a plate and bake in the oven until thoroughly hot.'

For a 100 per cent forager's recipe, one should boil the snails in slightly salted water for 25 minutes; remove from shells, rinse in water, place in a small oven dish with a little goose or duck fat, chervil and chopped wild garlic and salt. Cover and cook at medium heat for 10 minutes.

Snails are as low down the food chain as I go. There are other edible animals which creep and crawl around the farm, but I cannot bring myself to consume them. Save size, there is little to distinguish the grasshopper from the locust, although size is, despite what everyone says, important. Since the common field grasshopper is a paltry 2cm long, and given that only the hind legs are eaten, I would need to catch hundreds in the hayfields to make a mouthful. The grasshopper's hind legs are a singing supper, for they are also what it uses to 'stridulate'. According to T. Cameron, a much greater insect treat than the grasshopper is the caterpillar, although only if it is the offspring of the large white (*Pieris brassicae*), the small white (*Pieris rapae*) or the green-veined white (*Pieris napi*). No other butterfly larvae will do. Given that Penny's purple sprouting broccoli swarm with the green larvae of the large white butterfly, a meal of them would be easy pickings.

On a mid-morning of rare August sun, I stand in the vegetable patch and stare at the caterpillars as they robotically swing their heads from side to side, eating, eating, eating. With a stick I scrape tens of them into a seed tray, take the wriggling mass into the kitchen and get as far as putting some fat in the frying pan to quick-fry them. But that is as far as I get. Caterpillars might be organic and protein-packed, but their consumption would do nothing for one's self-respect.

I'm not that desperate. Because this I know: it is the nature of England to provide. I am only required to hold on. However, I am seriously worried about Ray.

Ray Pritchard is the affable agricultural contractor who lives on the Bryn pitch, the steep lane on Merlin's Hill. Ray has remained affable even though Hattie, our grandma yellow Labrador, once bit him on the elbow. 'She had a bit of a nibble,' as Ray put it. At the end of July I phoned Ray and asked him to cut and bale the grass in Road Field, now that the curlew chicks had flown their scrape-in-the-earth nest. Ray had suggested cutting the roadside hedge at the same time. 'You've got the show coming up,' he pointed out.

Ah, the Longtown Show. Trelandon was once the venue for the village show – which is formidable enough to be sponsored by Waitrose – but some years ago, before we moved here, it relocated to Llanwonog, the farm on the other side of the lane. All the same there are standards to be kept up; once on show day I caught two village elders tutting over my sky-high thistles in Road Field. Village pride, they clearly considered, was singularly lacking in the owners. With this humiliation in mind I told Ray, 'Better put our best face on then. Cut away.' Ray, as good as his word, promptly short-cut-and-sided the road hedge with the flail cutter on his Ford tractor.

Rain, however, has prevented Ray from doing the grass. You need dry weather to mow and bale grass, even grass which, like ours, will be ensiled in plastic-covered round bales. We are now in the third week of August and it is still raining. Every time we drive down the long rutted track to the farm past Road Field, where the pale empty-headed grass hangs down, one of the children says, 'When is Ray coming to cut the grass?'

Every day, I give the same answer. 'Whenever the ground dries out.'

Whenever. So sodden are the fields that I am beginning to wonder if they will ever dry out. I am seriously worried whether Ray is going to find a window of opportunity. In the jeep, Tris and Freda continue their routine and sing the Hoosiers' *Worried About Ray*. I'm so painfully worried about Ray.

The weather finally breaks. One day without rain. Two days. On the evening of the third day, I hear the sound of machinery in Road Field. The mowing goes on until well into the night, the field illuminated by the tractor's spotlights. Feeding the dogs on the yard before I go to bed, I can tell by the sounds of revving that the tractor is not finding it easy to haul the mower around the field.

Sure enough, when I go to look at the mown grass next morning I can see a small island of uncut grass ringed by tractor ruts a foot deep in the squelching red earth. But six acres of grass lies in neat rows in Road Field, and two acres in Little Field. Not bad, I think, not bad at all.

Forty-eight hours later, all the grass is baled, in sixty-six green-wrapped rolls lying dotted around the fields. 'Pardon my French, but that was a bit fucking tight,' says Ray, coming by to tell me the job is done. It was. The rains have begun again.

Or perhaps, 'il pleut de nouveau'.

———

There are still two acres of long grass standing in House Meadow. These I have saved from Ray's mower because, below the yellow mist of the grass heads, the meadow is thick with a crop of young sorrel leaves. Sorrel is a plant that lusts for the acid soils of west

Herefordshire. On a Sunday afternoon, when the sun deigns to appear again, I give Penny and the children carrier bags and lead them into the field to help me with the harvest. Penny conscientiously picks the young tender leaves, which have all the appearance of baby spinach. At first the children find it hard to spot the sorrel leaves in the bottom of the sward, but suddenly Tris shouts, 'I've got a sorrel mine!' Soon after, Freda discovers a green bonanza. 'I'm in sorrel heaven!' she exclaims.

When eight bags are full, the children start crawling like Indians through the grass, whooping with joy when they spot the other one. Penny carries on picking, singing to herself. I catch a green grasshopper in my hand, then open my fist and let it go. With one bionic leap it is free. The peal of Clodock's church bells wafts up the clement valley as they announce evensong.

Sorrel soup
Serves 6

2 pints/1l pigeon stock
about 25 young sorrel leaves
2 silverweed roots
1oz/30g goose fat
salt

Wash the sorrel leaves and slice the silverweed roots. Melt the goose fat in a saucepan, add the silverweed and cook for a couple of minutes. Add the sorrel leaves and continue cooking until these wither. Finally, pour in the pigeon stock, plus a pinch of salt. Cook gently until the silverweed is soft. Put the soup into a blender and process until smooth. Serve immediately.

Sorrel soup is the forager's friend because, unlike many soups, it abhors milk or cream. These sorrel curdles.

In fruitless times sorrel makes an acceptable substitute for apple. Jason Hill in *Wild Foods of Britain* recommends folding raw sorrel leaves and sugar 'into pastry as though for an apple turnover'.

Hill has a useful list of other alternatives, which include:

Almond essence – laurel leaf
Apple sauce – sorrel sauce
Capers – pickled elder buds, pickled nasturtium seeds
Caraway seed – sweet cecily
Cloves – herb bennet
Cucumber – salad burnet
Gelatine – carrageen
Ginger – tansy
Lemonade – crab-apple tea
Mustard – horseradish sauce, 'sauce-all-alone' [garlic mustard]
Onions – chives, 'sauce-all-alone'
Pepper – lady's smock
Pickles – ash keys, samphire
Spices, savoury – juniper berries, wild marjoram
Spices, sweet – herb bennet, tansy, elderflowers
Sugar – honey
Tea – lime flowers (dried), elderflowers (dried), woodruff (dried)
Vinegar – sorrel (in salads, etc.)
Worcester sauce – elderberry ketchup

We have postponed this day three times because of the rain. For my mother's eightieth birthday we are taking her on a day trip to Borth, on Cardigan Bay, because she likes it, because its rock pools and endless beach are postcard perfect, because it is where Herefordians go to be beside the sea.

Today the weather forecast in *The Times* has a sun logo with one drop of rain – signifying sun and mere showers – over West Wales, so we rush to pick up my mother from her home in north Hereford, telling her that she is going on a 'mystery tour', but my mother is no fool. Only five miles down the road towards Kington she says, 'I hope you've all got your swimming costumes and buckets and spades.' We have. We also have a packed picnic lunch, one which has caused me anxiety, because it is the sort of hamper one traditionally takes to the beach: cheese sandwiches, ham sandwiches, cucumber batons, tomato quarters, hummus, cold potatoes, crisps, apples, cake, coffee in tartan thermos flasks. And I am going to partake, because to take my own (rather meagre) wild food picnic would spoil my mother's day. She would fret, I would feel self-conscious. I could, of course, forage on the beach, but that would be a distraction at a birthday party. Worse, as Penny points out, my mother might then feel as if her birthday trip was an excuse for me to feed myself.

I drive by inner sat-nav over the mountains of Wales to Borth, so familiar is the journey. Old Radnor, Penybont, Rhayader, Llangurig, Capel Bangor, Bow Street (improbably) – the names of the villages and towns on the route reel off in my head. I try to calculate how many times I have travelled this way. Well, at least once a year – more likely twice – until I was eighteen, so say thirty times; then when Tristram was born fourteen years ago, the habit of visiting restarted, and we have taken him and Freda to Borth about ten times. I, then, have been to Borth some forty times.

Familiarity gives me a distinct advantage in the game of 'The First to Spot the Sea'. When I was a boy the prize was a shilling; inflation has pushed the pot to £1. As the provider of the prize, I am reasonably certain to keep my money. Although in the back of the car Tristram and Freda are straining at their seatbelts for a better view, I know to the yard the right-hand corner by the renovated cottage, where, as the road descends from the hills, one can glimpse the grey sea on the horizon.

And so, I win again.

Borth is a one-street town, all length and no depth, trapped as it is between the Irish sea and a black marsh. Technically, it is still the holiday season, but few have been brave or foolhardy enough to attempt the Welsh coast this summer, and we park in a prime spot, next to the RNLI station and the rock pools. The weather forecast did not lie. There is sun, but it is strained, thin sun. We do not complain, any of us, because we have seen much, much worse weather in Borth.

Out of the stuffy Audi, I am hit by the nakedness of the sea air. The air at Trelandon is unusually pure – the lichens which coat the apple trees are the proof of that – but the smells borne by it are so much more intense and polysemic. Probably a seadog can find complexity on the ocean breeze, but all I can nose is oxygen and salt. I sound as though I am complaining again; actually I love to be beside the seaside, beside the sea, with its widescreen views and dreamy atmosphere.

The glassy water laps hypnotically at the stones, as it begins its retreat to low tide. Black-backed seagulls squawk fishwifely overhead. The kids play a carefree game of advancing out along the groynes and running back before a wave comes. Somebody else's children are playing catch with a yellow tennis ball. My mother, every inch the archetypal seaside grandma in her head-scarf, anorak and striped deckchair, is nattering happily with Penny.

So why can't *I* relax? The question is rhetorical. I know why. I am so conditioned to vulpine opportunistic scavenging that I cannot stop assessing the environment for food sources. Behind my smile and occasional conversational pleasantry, I am doing it now. On the tidemarks, between the detritus of wood and lost fishing nets, I can see at least four types of edible seaweed, pulled out of their beds and dumped by a recent storm. There is long-bladed kelp, bright green sea lettuce, bubble-popping bladderwrack and fanned-out carrageen. In the rock pools below the cliffs I can see mussels on the boulders as they emerge from the waves.

Serendipity strikes. My mother suddenly breaks off from talking to point at the stranded discordant ribbon of seaweed on the shingle. 'It's good for the garden, that, Penny. You should get John to put some in a bag for you.'

I do. I go to the Spar shop on the corner and buy a roll of bin sacks and fill two.

The wind sharpens its edge. We talked of swimming but one by one we chicken out, with the exception of Freda who sails down the boat ramp in her costume and cap, splashes water up her bare arms and then dolphins into the sea. She surfaces to announce, 'It's lovely.' I hover protectively on the top of the runway in case of sharks, giant waves, cramps and all the other terrors of the parental imagination. A family nearby, seeing Freda frolicking, think that the water must be fine and enthusiastically change into their costumes. One by one they venture down the concrete ramp, dip their white toes into the water, shriek and run back. Freda learned to swim in the mountain river that is the Escley. She is inured to cold. She is the only person in the sea for a mile or more of beach.

Only the picnic tempts her out. There have been countless testing times over the last eleven months when I have fantasized, salivated about exactly the sort of carbohydrate-loaded food spread out on the picnic rug (held down with stones at the corners because the wind is rising. Soon we will have to build windbreaks). Here's the laugh: now I am sanctioned to eat such foods I have no appetite for them. Uncertainly, I peck at a cheese sandwich; even though it is an organic mature cheese I once adored, in my mouth it separates nauseatingly into salt and fat. As for the bread, I almost gag on its chewiness. My encounter with a ham sandwich is no better; I can taste the pig's fear as it went to its drawn-out death at an abattoir. Neither does the meat have the firm, muscly texture of game, game which has run and flapped free, game which has eaten this and that and not just that, game whose fibres have been enlivened by existence in a varied and natural world. The biscuits are bland. The cake ditto. Of all the treats on the rug only the purest, the closest to the natural – the apple, the coffee – give me pleasure.

Here a bigger laugh still: I sit surrounded by my one-time fantasy picnic and all I want to eat now are mussels clinging to the rocks under the cliffs. But serendipity, unlike lightning, strikes twice. Tris and Freda want to go rock-pooling, so does Penny. I should, and do, stay with my mother. We retire to the car to talk. I tell Mum that we had a Plan B for her mystery tour, which was to drive around the Woolhope area of Herefordshire, where Poppop had a farm, the Probyns, when she was a girl. She tells me that the spring at the Probyns periodically ran dry, at which she and her second sister, Margaret, would have to fetch water from a public standpipe, carrying it in buckets back to the farm. The stock, though, got the first water. Only when they were watered could humans quench their thirst.

The car door opens. We have talked so much that the windscreen has misted over. Penny, the breeze blowing her black hair across her face, is standing there with two sandcastle buckets full of midnight-blue mussels. 'For you,' she says.

In the afternoon we drive to the northern end of Borth, to Ynyslas and its giant sand dunes bordering the Dovey estuary. Looking across the estuary to the painted Georgian houses of Aberdovey I see, way off in the middle of the flats, what appears to be a little lawn. Without investigating I know what it must be: a bed of marsh samphire (*Salicornia europaea*).

Rich in soda, marsh samphire was formerly utilized in the making of glass, so bestowing on it the colloquial name of 'glasswort'. What a difference a couple of centuries make. Lightly steamed marsh samphire is the dish *de nos jours* in posh restaurants. I have heard, too, that it is a succulent, salty nibble when raw.

Just as I am worrying how I might surreptitiously collect the samphire, my mother announces she needs the loo in the visitors' centre. Since women are pack animals at loo time, Penny and Freda announce that they will accompany her. No sooner have they begun walking along the wooden boards towards the hut than I tip the picnic remnants out of a carrier bag into a bin and start trotting over the flats towards the samphire. Tris, who likes any opportunity to race the old man, is immediately beside me, jeering me on. 'Is that as fast as we can manage these days, Father?' he taunts. As I have spent a year on a paleolithic, flab-reducing, muscle-toning diet I increase my speed. He runs faster still. I also have a slight vestige of pride in my sprinting skills – I held the school record for the 200m – so turn up the pace some more.

We are nip and tuck to the marsh samphire – where we literally run ourselves into the ground, because what appeared to be sturdy mudflat is actually shin-deep brown ooze. I do not care: close up, the samphire are emerald-green, succulent and branched cacti, living not in anything as humdrum as a lawn but in an enchanted bonsai forest.

I tell Tris to hold the bag open and I start picking. No wild plant, unless abundant and on permitted land, should be uprooted so, stooping, I cut the samphires off at mud level with the fruit knife from the picnic. So plentiful are the six-inch-high samphires that the bag is full within a minute. I cut one last one and bite into it. The samphire justifies its gastronomic reputation, being sensuously salty, fleshy and juicy. The attached grains of sand only add authenticity, because what snack at the seaside does not contain sand?

Slipping and laughing, Tris and I grope our way back to terra firma, the bag between us, then trot to the Audi. At the very moment we slam the boot down on the samphire hoard my mother and her escort return. My mother looks at Tris's mud-splattered trainers and jeans, then at my equally besmirched canvas beach shoes and jeans. 'What have you two been doing?' she asks.

'Having a race along the sand,' I reply.

'Oh John! At your age. Oh, isn't it nice to be out though,' she adds.

Yes, it is. Yet as we drive back over the night mountains, I realize that as an adult I've always viewed the seaside as an escape from unsatisfactory aspects of my life – work, a house in a location I disliked, work again, the renovation of Trelandon going stratospherically wrong, whatever. But now I don't feel the need to escape. I like where I am, I like what I'm doing.

For once, I'm looking forward to getting home.

Pickled samphire

Samphire starts to 'melt' almost as soon as it is picked and will not keep for more than a day without preservation. Boiled and submerged in vinegar, however, it will outlast the winter.

Wash the samphire in fresh, not salt, water. Place in a large saucepan, add three tablespoons of cider vinegar and cover with water. Bring the water to the boil and continue boiling for ten minutes. Drain, then insert lengthways into preserving jars. Fill with cider vinegar to just under the rim. Seal tightly. A pinch of dry chervil or juniper can be added for spice.

Moules marinières sauvages

Supposedly mussels (Mytilus edulis) should be resisted unless there is an 'r' in the month, but at the beginning of May and the back end of August they are also tastily full of roe (eggs)

and milt (sperm). In the middle of summer they can be grittily difficult to masticate. Mussels take three years to mature; the biggest mussels are those which live permanently underwater and can permanently eat. For those you have to dive. When foraging for mussels, whether under the sea or on the fore-shore, one needs to be absolutely certain that there are no human contaminants nearby. Likewise mussels should not be gathered when there have been incidents of red-tide algal bloom. Mussels are filter-feeders and concentrate toxins in their flesh. Mussels infected with the algal toxin Paralytic Shellfish Poison can cause paralysis, even death, in man.
Serves 4

4 pints/2.25l mussels
4oz/110g butter
3 bulbs wild garlic, chopped
¼ pint/150ml water
¼ pint/150ml dry white wine (dandelion is good) or cider vine-gar
pinch wild thyme
salt
watercress, brooklime, hairy bittercress or wintercress

Scrape the beards from the mussel shells and wash under a running tap, discarding any mussels that remain open when tapped with a knife. Place in a saucepan with the water, wine, thyme, salt and garlic. Put the cover on the saucepan and cook on a low heat until the mussels have opened (about 5 minutes). Tip the mussels into a colander over another saucepan, removing any mussels that are still closed. Boil and reduce the mussel stock. Season with salt.

Transfer the mussels into a wide bowl and pour the stock over the top. Garnish with the cress.

———

A few days after the trip to Borth I wake at 5am feeling unfaithful. An odd, worrying thought runs around my head: perhaps, because of my dalliance with the sea and its foods, the farm will no longer yield to me its wild larder? In the jargon of counsellors, are we still in relationship? I try to find sleep again, but the need to seek the answer becomes uncontainable.

Through the wet black grass I walk directly to the copse, scattering the jackdaws picking at the warm depressions in the meadow where the sheep have slept. If the copse provides for me, all is well. If the copse has nothing for me, then I am in trouble.

What I find there makes me laugh aloud with joy. Along the edge of the copse is a little troop of aniseed agaric mushrooms standing to attention amid the ground ivy. Aniseed agaric is the most beautiful of British fungi, with a vivid blue cap and body. It is also edible.

———

Bluebell, Penny's Labrador, is on heat and confined to quarters. To give her some exercise and the opportunity to crap before bed, I walk her up the stony track, which crunches awkwardly underfoot, and makes me worry that we will wake John and Claire. Iridescence in the cloud cover marks where the moon is struggling to break through; the moon has not quite won, but it has not lost either. Beside the track the seedy white heads of hogweed catch the strained gleam and act as guiding lights. There is warmth enough for the insects of the dark to be a-wing, and fleets of little moths drift about the hedge while crane flies (daddy longlegs) hang grotesquely in our way. In the slumbering August silence I can just detect the high-pitched chirp of bush-crickets. There is something else on the midnight air. I can smell the first motes of decay, the first motes of ripening fruit.

Summer is over.

A CALENDAR OF WILD FOOD AT TRELANDON

August

Jew's ear, pigeon, rabbit, snails, dandelion, silverweed, plantain, sorrel, nettles, aniseed agaric

AUTUMN

THE MORNING MIST lies in a wedding ribbon along the valley bottom. A wood pigeon sits on the dead elm, as though it is the lookout on the mast of a schooner easing through fog, but today I am not ready with a gun. I am sitting in the paddock, my back leaning against the gatepost, my bottom on a damp-defying plastic feed sack, thinking.

The condition has a name – Seasonal Affective Disorder – and is usually applied to depression caused by the dark of winter. For me, the crunch time, the time when I am doubled over with seasonal sadness, is the end of summer, when the sharp, musty smells of autumn come, the day shortens and the cold is a different sort of cold, a thinner, keener, bone-touching cold. The End-of-Summertime Blues. This year? Barely a passing grey cloud through my consciousness.

But then I am less prey to inner blackness anyway. Contradictorily I don't really want to be thinking about this, because I suspect that part of my problem in life has been that I think too much, but out of respect for what Nature has done for me I feel honour-bound at least to acknowledge its balms.

The mundane: being productively busy, all day, every day, prevents navel-gazing. Conversely, idle hands make for mental mischief.

Less mundane: a wild food diet obviously improves mental well-being because its lower levels of sugar and carbohydrate prevent the fuzziness that comes with the sugar rush. Then, the constant exercise needed to pluck and kill that diet releases endorphins, Nature's happy pill. More, as science increasingly reports, exposure to Nature is good per se, even at low levels; famously, the psychologist R. S. Ulrich found that hospital patients who had a view of trees recovered more quickly than those whose rooms looked on to a brick wall. Contact with Nature increases alpha wave activity in the brain. Alpha waves, which are in the range of 7–12 HZ, are the waves that the brain creates when it is relaxed. Ipso facto, mental and physical health is improved. Interestingly, the resonant frequency of the earth's electromagnetic field (Schumann's Resonance) is in the same HZ range as alpha waves; consequently when people are outside they may literally be in sync with Nature. The corollary of all this is that being trapped inside the house or office or school is not good for one. In his book *Last Child in the Woods* the American author Richard Louv details how children – families as a whole, actually – are increasingly prone to stress and mental disorders (and obesity) as a result of being 'shut in'. A century ago, Henry David Thoreau made the same observation: 'Staying in the house breeds a sort of insanity always.'

Being outside, though, is not enough, because one has to be with Nature, not against it. One of the problems with farming is that one is always fighting against it, trying to control it. And modern farming is worse because it no longer operates on a natural clock. Lambs at Christmas are a prime example. Ewes naturally come into heat in October and have a five-month gestation period; their lambs are then born in March, when the grass is beginning its spring flush. Consequently the lambs have food galore. Christmas lambs, on the other hand, need massive amounts of manufactured food known as concentrates. Effectively Christmas lambs are a defiance of Nature. Small wonder that farmers are prone to depression.

Some months ago, I cannot pin down the date, I surrendered to Nature. Although I had entered into the landscape as a hunter and gatherer, and was even using its own means – instinct, for instance – to find food, I was still protesting internally about the weather, about the speed of the seasons, about the lack of foods at certain times. When I surrendered to Nature – by placing my trust in it to provide – I found that the rhythm of the wild life is a propulsive force, moving me from one day to the next, from one season to the next. Today it might be raining, tomorrow there will be sun. This season is dead and cold, but spring will come again, because it always does. The wild life goes around in circles and cycles.

Thoreau again. There is a line from *Walden* that has stayed with me since I read it all those months ago: 'I went to the woods because I wished to live deliberately, to front only the essential facts of life, and see if I could not learn what it had to teach, and not, when I came to die, discover that I had not lived.'

I too went to the land to find a simpler life. Instead, I found myself. The failure to complete the rebuilding of Trelandon had fractured my vision of myself. My self-confidence was in ruins and needed to be rebuilt. The most fundamental aspect of being a human is the securing of food and liquid from Nature. If you can do that, you can do anything. I needed to know that I could do that. When I did it I had self-worth. Thereafter, the only way was up.

What I had never understood before immersing myself in Nature was how alienated I was from my own history. When I got closer to Nature, I became closer to my family and its centuries of living on the land in Herefordshire. And then I got closer to my real self.

While I have been registering these thoughts, another part of my brain has registered that I can see 102 fields from my vantage point in this paddock, on this farm, in this God-loved corner of England.

The ragged noisy boy intrudes
To gather nuts that ripe and brown
As soon as shook will patter down
Thus harvest ends its busy reign
And leaves the fields their peaces again
Where autumns shadows idly muse
And tinge the trees with many hues
      John Clare, *The Shepherd's Calendar*

September is the time of berries – elder, blackberry, hawthorn, rosehips, to name just four – as well as dying leaves. But this wet, sunless year, the berry harvest is late, later than I've ever known it. In the first week of September I stand under the cascades of brambles in the hedges, and where there should be red and black, there is red and green. In fifty yards of hedge in Bog Field I find a meagre handful of ripe blackberries. The elderberries and the hawthorns are doing better, so I will not want for drink or jelly to accompany meat, or for work to do in preserving sources of vitamins and minerals for winter, but there is nothing quite like a big sweet blackberry in the mouth.

Two blackbirds come to the hedge. These are the true experts of blackberry picking. They find one, two, three, four, five blackberries – and then they give up too.

Do not despair, blackbirds. Our berry-picking time will come. If we have faith, we will be rewarded. Not yet, though, because it is raining again.

Once, when I was very young and the autumn frost was deep, I went with my grandmother to the hop yards on Dent's farm where my grandfather was the acting bailiff. She and other women from the village, all headscarves, macs and wellingtons, spent the morning stripping the dead bines off the wires, piling them on to an enormous bonfire. At 'dinnertime' they gathered round the fire, poking out from the ashes potatoes that had been put in at the start of work. Two 'potatoes' were bigger than the rest, covered in mud, and to much laughter were prodded and pulled apart with the knives used to cut the bines. Inside the mud coverings were two perfectly cooked rooks, the feathers coming off in the mud to reveal flesh as clean and smooth as linen. With good-natured teasing ('Jahn'll try it! G'ahn, Jahn!') I was given first taste – and I could only manage a shuddering titbit on the tongue.

Forty years later I've developed quite a taste for rook. The rooks are here at the moment in Bog Field, where the cattle's hooves are digging up the wet ground, bringing worms and other invertebrates to the surface. The rooks follow the cows, like gulls follow the trawler.

Stewed rook

Rook was a staple of the rural poor until the end of the Second World War. The bird has a strong taste, similar to pigeon, and the best birds are 'branchers' (fledgling birds) shot in May. Older birds lose flavour.

This recipe for stewed rook is adapted from an eighteenth-century recipe for rook pie (as in 'four and twenty blackbirds baked in a pie') by Elizabeth Foley, a Herefordshire gentlewoman.

Serves 4

4–6 fledgling rooks
½ pint/300ml elderberry wine
½ pint/300ml water
1 tbsp hawthorn jelly
4oz/110g wild duck fat
3 bulbs wild garlic, crushed

First catch your rook; a .22 air rifle is best, and be careful to pick off the rooks at the back of the crowd, which are the youngest. Don't bother to pluck; skin off, decapitate and degut. The feet are fragile enough to simply break off. Then cut each rook in half along the breastbone and trim to leave just the breast and thick part of the leg.

Heat some wild duck fat in a heavy pan, and lightly brown the rook pieces with the garlic. Transfer to a large casserole dish. Pour the elderberry wine into the pan, together with a large tablespoon of hawthorn jelly and the water. Bring to the boil, stirring all the while. Simmer for 2 minutes, then pour over the rooks. Cover and cook in an oven preheated to 400°F/200°C/Gas Mark 6 for about 2 hours. While the rooks are stewing, it's quite a good idea to get stewed yourself on elderberry wine.

The traditional ingredients for rook pie are as follows:

4–6 fledgling rooks
1lb/450g beef chopped into 1in/2cm pieces
6oz/170g butter
salt
pepper
puff pastry

Substituting rabbit for beef and duck/goose fat for butter works deliciously well. The pastry for the pie top can be made from burdock, fat hen or silverweed flour. Chestnut flour is too sweet.

The rain gets heavier. On Saturday morning I set out to drive Tris to the school bus stop in the jeep but we get no further than Clodock, because there is a wall of stone and tarmacadam across the valley road; an adjoining lane has been washed on to it. Beyond the wall the road is deep in water, too deep even for the jeep. We return home. No school today. Since it is only seven thirty Tris goes back to bed.

I stare out of the window, sipping yarrow tea, and cannot see the mountain through the torrents. No shooting today either. It's going to be a day of culinary make-do.

There is no let-up in the rain. Tired of sitting indoors, in the afternoon I take a spade and head down to the bottom of Bank Field, intending belatedly to dig up more burdock roots for winter. No way. The Escley has burst its banks, and is currently flowing over that burdock. During the night the Escley knocks down the stock fence along the river, and invades far into Bank Field and Copse Field. Even through stone walls three feet thick we can hear it roar. When the waters finally retreat, leaving the grass combed beautifully smooth, I find flotsam in the riverbank trees. On the river bend before Copse Field, where the water backed up, it reached twelve feet above its normal level.

What is the difference between a rook and a jackdaw? About five inches, the rook being eighteen inches and its ash-headed cousin measuring thirteen. Their favourite place to dine in the country is the open field, though both will scavenge. They are similarly gregarious; indeed, they frequently flock and feed together. The rook is maybe not as saucy as the jackdaw, whose impertinent stealing is immortalized in Richard Harris Barham's poem 'The Jackdaw of Rheims' (in which the jackdaw is canonized as 'Jem Crow') but otherwise what *is* the difference?

Over the last week I have shot three rooks in the absence of anything else to put in the game bag. But now the rooks have stopped visiting. Either they have wised up or they have found an easier food source. My guess is they are in thrall to a late cereal harvest in the bottom of the valley, now that the sun has begun to dry the land. The jackdaws, however, are still here, because they live here, in the disused chimneys at the end of our house, in the tall Victorian stacks of our neighbours and, especially, at Little Trelandon two fields away, which, being stone ruins, is quintessential jackdaw accommodation. Every day the jackdaws – about thirty of them – flock down to feed in Bog Field, argue raucously, then flap up into the sky, tumble around and flock down to feed again. Before starting up the whole Attention-Deficit-Disorder cycle again.

One dewy morning, as the jackdaws wait vulture-patient on the electricity wires in House Meadow, I feed the ducks by their pond. As soon as I have gone, I know that the jackdaws will glide down and freeload on GM-free layers' pellets as they always do. I feel like shooting them. Which brings up the question again: what is the difference between jackdaws and rooks? Because if one can eat rook, surely one can eat jackdaw? Killing a jackdaw would then be killing one bird for two reasons, food and pest control.

In the upstairs office I switch on the laptop and google 'jackdaw eating'. My only hit is an injunction against such a thing from the Old Testament; Leviticus II lists the jackdaw, along with the white owl and the carrion vulture, as a culinary 'abomination'. Not the rook, only the pale-eyed jackdaw. Even the word of God fails to convince me; in the back of my mind is an infidel memory that one of the Turkish sultans considered the jackdaw a delicacy.

Kyak. Kyak. Kya. Kya. As I google I can hear the jackdaws at the pig trough. One flies up on to the roof of the house, before skidding down, its talons scraping the slates all the way to the gutter. Like rooks, jackdaws are classified as pests. Creatures that used to be called 'vermin' in less sensitive times. Shooting jackdaws is perfectly legal should there be sufficient reason: such as that they are eating highly expensive pig feed. Besides, the corvids are too populous on the farm, to the detriment of songbirds, whose eggs and chicks they snack off. My mind made up, I go downstairs and get the Weihrauch from the gun cupboard, sneak out of the front of the house and down the yard, the rifle at attention. The noisy safety catch is already off. At the bottom of the cow byre I peek cautiously round the corner. Three jackdaws are about ten yards away, next to the duck pond, strutting and pecking. Crouching down I feed the gun around the corner, following with my head, until an immature jackdaw appears in the telescopic sight. Compared to the distinct grey hoods of the adults, the juvenile's hood is of less colour and sharpness. A gentle squeeze of the trigger. A dead bird.

Kyak. Kyak. The adults flee, leaving the lifeless juvenile on the grass. Picking the jackdaw up I am surprised – perturbed – by its lightness. I roast the jackdaw because I do not want its death to be in vain. I shot it for food, and food it shall be. That is the contract I have with the land. There are no *actes gratuits*. I shoot for food, I shoot to maintain an order that benefits the whole of the wildlife on the farm. But I never again shoot a jackdaw for food.

They are five inches too small to be worth bothering with.

September permits me to shoot a much bigger species of bird than the jackdaw; the inland duck season opened at the beginning of the month. So far, though, no mallard have come to Trelandon.

Edith and I daily fight our way through Victorian mist and Passchendaele mud down to the river, to check, to make sure. I see duck shit on the stones, I see the dropped feathers from preening but these are the detritus from mandarin ducks. A tell-tale feather is red. Edith and I continue our patrol through the ghost fields until a poor rabbit makes the mistake of its life. Out it launches from its grass den and heads for the Bank Field hedge but inexplicably stops instead of going underground. Perhaps it cannot see me in the mist and thinks I cannot see it.

The rabbit is shot cleanly through the head. I am pleased by this. I am pleased that the rabbit did not suffer, I am pleased by my skill.

The dead rabbit is all of twenty-five yards away and I could collect it myself, but I send Edith. Practice in retrieving, like practice in killing, makes perfect. Besides, our relationship is based on the fact that I scratch and fill her tummy, she retrieves for me. This she does out of love.

Edith's mouth is soft and the beautiful fur of the rabbit barely dented or wet. I take a moment to appreciate this creature of Creation, on whose kith and kin I – and many of us – depend. That afternoon, at last, the sun returns. And it is true September sunshine, mellow and beneficent. In the sky the swallows and house martins, with a brood still to get away, swoop for joy. In the hedges the gossamer traps of the money spider, slung between twigs and blades, sparkle. Now the fruits of the hedges will begin to ripen, with the exception of the poor sloes, meagre in number and fleshlessly tiny. But that is the way of Nature, win some, lose some. There may be few sloes this year, but the weather has brought a branch-breaking crop of crab apples.

One afternoon there's a knock at the door. Looking out of the sitting-room window on to the yard, Freda sees a car she recognizes. 'It's the green man,' she calls out.

The green man is George Woodward from the Monnow Fisheries Association, who are restoring our riverbank by thinning the darkening trees later in the year, which will improve the river as a habitat for wild trout and other aquatic life. George wears a fetching uniform of a hue that Robin Hood would have died for. It suits him, but then there's something of the ex-army NCO about George: the straight-back, hale-fellow-well-metness, the kitbag of polished anecdotes.

When I open the door, George greets me with 'Ah, Mr Lewis-Stempel, how are you today?'

'I'm very well, George. And you?'

'Mustn't grumble, mustn't grumble.'

But we do grumble; we grumble about the recent torrential rain. George has returned from Northumbria, where he was acting as a loader on a shoot. 'The rain, well ... it was like that scene in *The Last of the Mohicans*, where they're standing behind that waterfall. It was coming down like that waterfall.' George would have been marooned, except for the fact that one of the guns had a private helicopter.

After swopping watery horror stories (mine was 'the Escley was twelve feet above the usual level'), George comes to the point of his visit. 'We're doing an audit of fish on various stretches of the Escley and wondered if we could do one here? It wouldn't take long and the lads wouldn't get in your way.'

'George, help yourself. It's no problem at all.' A thought occurs to me as we stand on the doorstep. 'As a matter of interest, how do you do the audit?'

'Ah, by stunning the fish with an electrical charge. The lads put two terminals in, send the current between them, and the fish come belly up.'

'Now that,' I say to George, 'sounds like my type of fishing.'

The audit has a scientific purpose, which is to establish what the fish density is now so that the effectiveness of the restoration can be gauged. As it happens, a medical emergency with my father means that I miss the audit arranged for the next day. When I finally arrive home at noon, to a convention of pick-ups on the yard, the electro-fishermen are packing to leave.

Seeing me, Robert Denny, the project leader, comes over. His priority is game fish, so he's keen to tell me about the brown trout found in the forty-three-metre stretch of water they electrified. 'One of twelve inches,' he says, holding his hands suitably far apart, 'lurking under the tree roots. Then there were some three-inch juveniles . . . obviously more trout will come up soon to spawn. And, ah, then there was a bullhead, stone loaches, minnows. Oh, and a crayfish.'

A crayfish. This is a revelation. I did not know there were any in the brook.

The white-clawed crayfish (*Astacus pallipes*) is a miniature brown lobster, which grows up to 10cm long. Britain's only native freshwater crayfish, it has some unpleasant habits, such as devouring compatriots unlucky enough to have recently moulted their shells, but it makes pleasant eating.

My failure to notice crayfish in the brook is almost excusable. The crayfish is largely nocturnal, spending its days under a stone or in a hole in the bank.

As soon as is decent, I terminate the conversation with Robert Denny and trot indoors to look up the ways and means of catching crayfish. Reaching down the ever-reliable *Wild Foods of Great Britain* I find T. Cameron advises:

> I have caught them singly upon hooks baited with worms; but the best way to capture a number at a time is to put a bit of 'high' liver in a basket, with a stone in the bottom, and lower it by means of a cord into a likely haunt. The crayfish will swarm into the basket, which must be smartly lifted or they will escape over the edge. The fish should be dropped into boiling water for a few minutes, when they turn pink; and they are eaten cold with mayonnaise sauce or with a salad-dressing as for lobster.

I'm about to start hunting for a basket and length of rope, when it occurs to me that crayfish are now probably a protected species. And they are: white-clawed crayfish are listed on Schedule 5 of the Wildlife and Countryside Act 1981, which makes it illegal either to take them from the wild or to sell them without a licence from the appropriate nature conservation agency. The white-clawed crayfish is also included in the IUCN Red Data List.

Our native crayfish is under attack from the signal crayfish, a cheap, brash American escapee from farms founded in the late 1970s to supply the restaurant trade. Oversized and over here, the 30cm signal crayfish, with its bright red claws, out-eats its British cousin in fish eggs, insect larvae and invertebrates. The signal crayfish is also an accomplished walker, who can cross the fields to colonize new waters. Worse, the signal crayfish carries the plague, a fungal disease (*Aphanomyces astaci*) to which the indigenous crustacean has no resistance. Since the 1970s, the population of the white-clawed crayfish has declined by half; the high streams of the Welsh borders are some of the last places in which it holds out.

Late that evening on the Escley I use Cameron's method of high meat (a rabbit thigh left out in the sun) to try to catch a crayfish, not for the eating but for the interest. There is something deeply shivery about sitting in the near dark, waiting for a crustacean to scuttle into a metal bucket laid on its side, in water, with flesh inside. To make the experience worse, it takes almost two hours before the switch-on of the torch confirms that a crayfish has entered the trap. Quickly hauling the bucket upright, I wade in and pull it out to the bank. Sure enough, the torch shows a bewildered crayfish in the bottom of the bucket, with its science-fiction antennae scoping the water. No, I do not eat it. I treasure it. I feel privileged that the crustacean lives in the Escley, and that I have met it.

What did I see in the field today? I saw a brambling.

'Is that a brambling?' I say to Penny, as we near the house after a stroll down to the river, the kids at school, a chance to talk like adults. 'Do you know, I'm sure it is.' Clinging to a strand of barbed wire, ruffled and exhausted, the bird flits off into a hawthorn. I follow on, trying to get a definitive look, but every time I get close the bird hops teasingly to the next bush. Still, when I compare the picture of the bird in my mind's eye with that of a brambling in R. S. R. Fitter and R. A. Richardson's *Collins Pocket Guide to British Birds*, awarded a lifetime ago as a form prize, a brambling it is.

I have never seen a brambling, an uncommon winter visitor, before. Too much in touch with my inner twitcher, I add it to the list of birds seen at Trelandon in the last twelve months, which now totals sixty-one species: jackdaw, blackbird, house sparrow, chaffinch, wood pigeon, blue tit, carrion crow, buzzard, robin, wren, magpie, woodcock, goldfinch, tawny owl, pheasant, mallard, raven, collared dove, meadow pipit, pied wagtail, little owl, great tit, long-tailed tit, grey wagtail, rook, song thrush, jay, heron, dunnock, kestrel, starling, tree creeper, fieldfare, redwing, kingfisher, red kite, nuthatch, greenfinch, lapwing, greater spotted woodpecker, sparrowhawk, bullfinch, green woodpecker, wheatear, herring gull, Canada goose, mandarin duck, curlew, skylark, house martin, chiffchaff (or it may have been a willow warbler: I can't tell them apart), blackcap, swallow, swift, feral pigeon, pied flycatcher, dipper, linnet, spotted flycatcher, redstart, brambling.

There are two species on the list that I could have shot for food but did not do so. Sentiment was not the reason, for both are plague birds. These were the Canada goose and the herring gull. They flew too high.

A wild mallard did not, falling to my shotgun in the third week of September.

The hot end of September is deceptive. The sap of plants is falling towards winter stasis, yet I am scurrying around at silent film speed trying to gather in hazelnuts before the squirrels (tricky because they will eat the cobs while they are still green), and elderberries and blackberries before the thrush family. My internal pager – which runs on experience, seasonal rhythm, temperature – is going off almost every hour to announce that some fruit, on some side of a hedge, somewhere on the farm, is coming ripe. Since there are only days to go before Michaelmas, 29 September, on which date folklore insists blackberry picking should stop, I recruit Penny and the kids to help me. Actually, they come out of their own volition; everyone enjoys blackberry picking. After school, for hazy, languid afternoons in a row, we work along the hedges picking blackberries into bowls, talking, observing, hunting for the biggest, juiciest berry of them all. Sometimes Tris wanders off to get his air rifle in the hopes of potting a rat or a rabbit, but we do not mind as long as he is outside. And a gun is a great way of getting a fourteen-year-old boy into the outdoors.

Of course, it has not been a bad way of getting a fortysomething boy outside either.

Blackberry kissel

The blackberry (Rubus fruticosus) or bramble has been eaten by humans since Neolithic times. It is one of Nature's super-foods, rich not only in vitamin C but also in antioxidants. Blackberry bushes vary tremendously – the botanist W. C. R. Watson lists 286 species in his Handbook of the Rubi of Great Britain and Ireland – although in all forms the ripest berries grow at the tip of the stalks; the other berries mature more slowly, often in October. Since this is after the taboo date of 29 September, you may wish to know that you can justifiably pick blackberries until 10 October; in 1752 the English

*calendar was adjusted by eleven days. The old Michaelmas of
29 September is consequently today's 10 October.*

*Kissel is a Russian pudding made of the juice of stewed
fruit, sweetened and slightly thickened with flour.
Traditionally, cranberries are the fruit used, but blackberries
are better.*

*2lb/900g blackberries
2 tbsp silverweed or chestnut flour
1 tbsp honey
2 pints/1l water*

*Rinse the blackberries and simmer them in water for
10 minutes. Strain and force through a sieve. Retain the liquid
and reheat while mixing in the honey.*

*Mix the flour with cold water and slowly stir it into the juice
until the liquid is thick and syrupy.*

*Pour the hot kissel into a serving dish, cover and cool for at
least two hours.*

*The dish can be made with the pulp included, though some
dislike the pips.*

*The culinary possibilities of blackberries are almost endless;
they can be turned into sauce for game, beer, a vinegar,
bramble jelly (of course), cordial, wine, syrup, pie and
sorbet.*

From the brook, on an afternoon of low sun, with hazel leaves
falling on the water, I catch two medium (7oz, 8oz) trout in the
furthest upstream pool on our stretch of river. These are the last
trout to be hooked by me before the end of the season on 30
September, and their catching is prudential because we have a

friend, Tracy, coming to dinner and I have declared that I can cook wild food for all. Including fish-eating vegetarians, such as Tracy and my wife.

And I do.

I also think that I achieve a reasonable approximation of the fateful meal at Rules that began this journey a year ago, complete with white linen and silver cutlery.

Dinner Menu

Hors d'oeuvres
Mushroom soup
or
Cobnut pâté on fat hen toast

Mains
Wild duck with blackberry sauce
or
Trout with aniseed agaric mushroom stuffing
served with roast silverweed chips, steamed sorrel
and mashed burdock

Pudding
Blackberry kissel

Elderflower cordial, sloe wine, dandelion wine or
blackberry wine

Dandelion coffee

I put hops around the table in honour of my grandfather.

As September turns to its end, I get a long-awaited treat. The oaks, utterly barren last year, are now dripping with acorns. Standing underneath the giants on the riverbank, in a late afternoon of exhilarating wind and a quarter moon over Merlin's Hill, pink cloudlets fleeing west, the acorns bomb down through the canopy. Even though the traditional time for the acorn harvest is a month away, there are already acorns enough for me on the floor, ripe and brown and separated from their cups which, as everyone who has read BB's *The Little Grey Men* and *Down the Bright Stream* know, make excellent pipes for gnomes.

So plentiful are the acorns that I pick some for the pigs too, a carrier bag's worth, because with wheat at £180 a ton why the hell not? My predecessors here at Trelandon would have done the same, or even folded the pigs around the base of the trees. Acorns are a pig's natural food; in some forested places residents used to have the right of 'pannage', that is letting their pigs loose upon fallen oak fruits. This not only fed the pigs, it removed a source of poison for cattle and horses, since acorns contain tannins which convert to tannic acid and dissolve the guts of these animals.

The same tannins make acorns too bitter for human taste, although I find this difficult to believe when the pigs grunt their happy thank you in the paddock. Peeling off the shell, I pop a pale wholesome-looking acorn kernel into my mouth. Then spit the bits out. Now I know why American Indians buried acorns in the ground for a winter or more in order to leach the bitterness. They made flour from the acorns; my aim is ersatz coffee of Third Reich vintage.

Acorn coffee

The recipe is simple enough: peel the acorns, boil for 10 minutes, leave to dry for a day. Then roast on the middle shelf of the oven at 250°F/120°C/Gas Mark ½ for about 15 minutes, before grinding in a coffee grinder. Put the ground acorn powder into a cafetière or percolator, at the rate of 2 teaspoons per cup, and add boiling water. Drink.

The resultant acorn beverage tastes nothing like coffee. For a split second I am disappointed but when I recover I realize that the drink is extremely pleasant, reminiscent of the barley cup that was once a staple of health food cafés.

Dawn on the last day of my wild food year. Frost grips the ground. On the oak beam in the outhouse, fledgling swallows sit testing their wings. Today, tomorrow at the latest, they will be off.

Walking down through the paddock, Edith so close to my leg that she bumps her head when I change direction to keep next to the hedge, the *cok-cok* cry of a male pheasant comes from the copse.

This is where we came in. The swallows are going, the pheasant is to be shot. Nothing in cyclical, seasonal Nature has changed, but I have. I'm walking in the footsteps of my ancestors. (I even have Joe Amos's limp.) I am walking closer to the land.

I am walking closer to me.

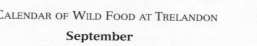
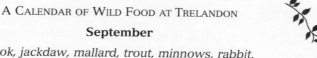

A CALENDAR OF WILD FOOD AT TRELANDON

September

Rook, jackdaw, mallard, trout, minnows, rabbit, dandelion, silverweed, sorrel, aniseed agaric, blackberries, elderberries, hazelnuts, acorns, shaggy ink caps, haws

INDEX